Also by Elizabeth Minchilli

Eating Rome

Italian Rustic

Restoring a Home in Italy

Private Tuscany

Villas on the Italian Lakes

Private Rome

Deruta

Eating My Way Through Italy

Eating My Way Through Italy

Heading Off the Main Roads to Discover the Hidden Treasures of the Italian Table

ELIZABETH MINCHILLI

St. Martin's Griffin ☙ New York

www.stmartins.com

Text photographs courtesy of the author

Library of Congress Cataloging-in-Publication Data

Names: Helman-Minchilli, Elizabeth, author.
Title: Eating my way through Italy : heading off the main roads to discover the hidden treasures
    of the Italian table / Elizabeth Minchilli.
Description: First edition. | New York : St. Martin's Griffin, 2018. | Includes index.
Identifiers: LCCN 2017060762| ISBN 9781250133045 (trade paperback) |
    ISBN 9781250133052 (ebook)
Subjects: LCSH: Cooking, Italian. | Food—Italy. | Helman-Minchilli, Elizabeth—Travel—Italy. |
    Italy—Description and travel. | LCGFT: Cookbooks.
Classification: LCC TX723 .H4528 2018 | DDC 641.5945—dc23
LC record available at https://lccn.loc.gov/2017060762

Our books may be purchased in bulk for promotional, educational, or business use. Please
contact your local bookseller or the Macmillan Corporate and Premium Sales Department
at 1-800-221-7945, extension 5442, or by email at MacmillanSpecialMarkets@macmillan.com.

First Edition: May 2018

10 9 8 7 6 5 4 3 2 1

This book is for Jane,

who was the best travel mate and friend

I could ever hope for

Contents

Acknowledgments

How do I begin to thank everyone who has helped me in the course of traveling up and down this country over the last twenty years or so? The biggest thanks of all goes to the men, women, and families that are featured in this book as well as those whose work and lives I have written about on my blog and on my apps. This book could not have happened without you. I would specifically like to thank the following people and businesses who shared their recipes, knowledge, and enthusiasm: Matteo and Gianluca Bisol at Venissa; Mauro Stoppa; Ilaria Miani; Bonifacio Brass at Locanda Cipriani; the Tintori family of Vecchia Dispensa; Isabella Giliberti and Marisa Vandeli at Zoello Je Suis; Silvana Ghillani; The Tasca D'Almerita family; Lucia di Mauro and her family at IASA; Alberto Zampino and his family at Pastificio Gentile; Sergio Cinque at Pastificio Faella; Fabrizia Lanza and everyone at the Anna Tasca Lanza Cooking School; Emanuele La Barbera and Alessandra Rabitti of Fattoria Il Secondo Altopiano; caper producers La Nicchia and Bonomo & Giglio on Pantelleria; Michele Fuso from Cutrofiano; Paola Abraini and Sebastiano Secchi and his family at Agriturismo Testone; honey master Luigi Manias; Corrado Assenza at Caffè Sicilia; Pierpaolo Ruta at Antica Dolceria Bonajuto; and Marisa Baglioni.

While I manage to do a lot of research on my own, I also depend upon colleagues (who are also some of my greatest friends) to share their discoveries and knowledge with me, which they do with great generosity. Thank you Rolando Beramendi of Manicaretti; Carrie Blakeman of Rogers Collection; Ishan Gurdal of Formaggio Kitchen; Ari Weinzweig and the "Parm Squad" from Zingerman's; Alessandro Grassi of Grassi + Partners; Beatrice Ughi of Gustiamo; Sara Baer Sinott of Oldways Preservation and Trust; Maria Chiara Passani and Simone Ficarelli of the Consorzio del Parmigiano Reggiano.

And then there are the friends that are always there, either physically with me at the table eating, or else in my mind and in my life, lending support, friendship, recipes, and advice. Thank you for sharing your knowledge, your experiences, and your friendship: Evan Kleiman, Anya Von

Bremzen, Alice Feiring, Melissa Clark, Gillian McGuire, Eugenia Radunsky, Judy Witts Francini, Andrea Francini, Vincenzo Lodato, Pamela Sheldon Johns, Jennifer McIvaine, Salvatore Denaro, Laura Evans, Scott Gudgeon, Sam Youkilis, Edward Youkilis, Sienna Reid, Douglas Andrews, Elisabetta Povoledo, Marietta Cambareri, Martha Richardson, Lawrence Jenkens.

Thank you to my agent, Elizabeth Kaplan, who makes juggling contracts look effortless while sending the email equivalent of warm hugs from across the ocean whenever I need them.

My most ardent fan, and the one that made sure this book happened, is my editor, Michael Flamini. Thank you for your unbridled enthusiasm for all I do and your open-armed embrace of all I write. It is a complete joy to work with you.

I am extremely lucky to be working with the extraordinarily talented and generous team at St. Martin's. Thank you, Gwen Hawkes, for shifting through my messy manuscript and making it whole. And to Young Lim: I love my cover! And additional thanks to the rest of the St. Martin's family.

It is difficult to call what I do work, because I love it so much. Most of that is because I get such huge support and encouragement from the readers of my blog, apps, and books and those of you who tag along, joining the fun on social media. Thank you from the bottom of my heart for your love and support for everything I do.

As always, my biggest thanks go to my family. To my parents, Joseph Helman and Barbara Wood, my first, and most important, travel companions up and down Italy. And to my sisters, Robin Helman Whitney and Jodi Helman Multer, for sharing the backseat of that Fiat 124 with me and for being part of this delicious adventure from the beginning and continuing to share your support and love. And thank you to my other parents: Roger Wood for your support of all I do, and to Ursula Fey Helman, who has taught me almost all I know about grace and style in an Italian setting. And I can't forget my brothers-in-law, Phillip Whitney (always willing to taste anything I cook) and Kevin Multer (my grilling guru).

This book owes much to my Italian family, the Minchillis. Thank you, Rosa, for sharing your kitchen, your life, and especially your son with me. Thank you, Stella, for sharing recipe tips and family advice over the balcony. And to Maurizio Minchilli and Loredana for opening your home in Sardinia to us and for sharing essential Sardinian tips, and my nieces, Fabia and Claudia, for your love and support.

Finally, to Domenico, Sophie, and Emma. You, more than anyone, know how much time I spent on this food-filled road I've been traveling. Thank you for putting up with my trips away, my time spent writing, but mostly thank you for being the best companions I could hope for on all of our travels together.

Eating My Way Through Italy

CHAPTER ONE

Food in Mind ...

've always traveled with food in mind. This is the way I was brought up. When people ask me what religion I am, I have to say I have a hard time figuring that one out. Yes, I'm culturally Jewish, and we celebrated the high holidays, but we also put up a Christmas tree and certainly looked forward to our Easter basket.

If I have to cite a book that was our family bible growing up, that would be easier: the *Michelin Red Guide*. I'm writing "we," but I'm not sure my sisters held this tome in as high regard as I did. And by growing up, I mean the formative years after I turned twelve, and life as I knew it changed drastically.

After growing up in the suburbs of St. Louis my father decided it would be a good idea to pick up and move to Rome for an indefinite period of time. While I'm sure that I was as upset as any other twelve-year-old at being ripped from everything I knew, the experience has obviously had a profound and lasting effect on me. I mean, here I am, forty years later, still in Rome. My life, my career, my family, my friends: it all has to do with my father's fateful decision.

But getting back to the *Michelin Red Guide*, when we moved to Rome we definitely settled in. We had an attic apartment in a Roman palazzo, I went to school, my parents shopped at the daily market in Campo dei Fiori, but we also had a car (a Fiat 124 if you're curious). We used that car to head out of Rome almost every weekend and most of the summer.

My memories of bumping around in the backseat with my sisters (there were no seat belts of course) alternate between fights of who had to sit in the middle and me ignoring the scenery to get through yet another volume of Agatha Christie (the only English language books readily available).

While I may have been a typical twelve-year-old in terms of ignoring the Alps as they passed by outside our window, the inklings of my future career of me telling other people what and where to eat were already beginning to show. Before we got anywhere near our destination, I would lay down my "mystery-du-jour" and grab the copy of the current *Guide Michelin* that was sliding around on the back windowsill to decide where we would be dining.

I was a master of deciphering the arcane little symbols that were printed on the little bookmark that came with the guide. Forks and Knives? At least two. And if they were red? Even better. And the little flowers that were, in fact, stars? We actually did make it to a few of those as well.

But it wasn't just the red guide that I was using to navigate. I was also cross-referencing with the paperback *Michelin Green Guides* of historical sites. Because for me (and this is key) food has never been an end in and of itself. Yes, we had to eat well. But the entire experience—getting there, ordering, talking to the people who prepare the food, walking around the place—was always just as important. Somehow I understood, from an early age, the cultural import of each bite we were taking.

In other words, food may have been the map we used to get to a specific place, but it was also the key that opened up an entire world.

And that is what this book is about.

Today, after a lifetime living and eating in Rome, a lot of people consider me to be an "expert" on Italian food. While I am proud to share everything I've learned, cooked, and devoured in this ancient city, I'm quick to correct them. Yes, I know the byways of *cacio e pepe*, *pizza bianca*, and other Roman specialties. But these are Roman specialties. So when you ask me to hold forth on Italian food, you're going to have to be a bit more specific.

Did you mean the type of dried fava beans that only really show up in a certain region of Puglia? Or maybe the deep-fried chickpea fritters that you can buy from street vendors in Palermo? Risotto you say? You better get on a train headed north.

What most people don't realize is that the entire concept of Italy is more a state of mind than a geopolitical—much less a gastronomic—reality. Italy has only been a country for the last 150 years. While that might seem quite a while to American ears, it's just a baby in terms of the millennial-long reality that is the Italian peninsula.

So when I tell you that there is almost nothing left that can surprise me about Roman cuisine, just the opposite is true for the rest of Italy. Luckily for me, I've had the great opportunity to travel—for work and for pleasure—from the tip of the heel in Puglia to the shores of Lake Como in the north. I've traveled to the islands of Sicily and Sardinia and to the hills of Umbria, Abruzzo, and Tuscany. I've walked the beaches on each of the long coasts, and visited almost all of the major cities in between.

Eating My Way Through Italy takes up where my previous book, *Eating Rome,* left off. If all roads lead to Rome, they also lead out of it. I have taken to those roads, and I am excited to share the dishes, customs, and recipes that I've discovered over the course of my career.

When I first thought of this book, my main aim was not to provide an encyclopedic or comprehensive guide to Italy by way of food. Instead, I wanted to tell you stories of my own experiences. Experiences—and meals—that led me off the beaten track to discover places, people, and food that may be outside your comfort zone.

To me, the most luxurious aspect of travel these days is to end up in a place

where there are few tourists. I know this is almost impossible. And I'm not telling you to completely ignore cities like Rome, Florence, and Venice. But I am suggesting that, with food as your guiding star, you might wander off those overtreaded paths and discover places you never knew existed.

In *Eating My Way Through Italy*, I share my stories of travels through Italy in search of food. Through the exploration of specific meals or ingredients, I hope to inspire you to do the same.

Each chapter takes one type of food as its theme (sorry, but that's just the way I roll). So while I might appear to be talking only about Parmigiano Reggiano, for instance, what I'm really getting at is something that reveals a past and current history that exists only in one very specific place. It is that sense of place that I hope will inspire you, whether you travel there, or simply use that ingredient in the comfort of your own kitchen.

These are simply the tales of where my own stomach has led me, more often than not, down new paths. You can use it as a blueprint, following my trail of bread crumbs, or—as I hope you do—follow your own appetite to meals yet unknown.

CHAPTER TWO

Capesante, Scampi, and Vongole in the Suburbs of Venice

When I first started thinking of this book, I envisioned itineraries that would take you out into the wilds of lesser-known regions like Puglia, Friuli, and Umbria. Florence, Venice, and Rome? Been there, done that, right? Wrong. Especially when it comes to Venice.

These days when most people think of Venice, it's the crowded, almost Disneyland-like area around Saint Mark's Square (Piazza San Marco). Hordes of tourists make this part of Venice a kind of nightmare to navigate—especially in high season. The tiny alleys get jammed with day trippers, off big cruise ships, ticking off as many of the major sights as possible, and every year it seems to get worse.

But I love Venice. And often I am there, for better or worse, at high season. Usually visiting during the *Biennale* (what my friend Gillian refers to as the "Death March of Art"), which takes place every two years in the summer, I find myself struggling to get through the throngs on my way to the exhibition grounds and the various shows scattered throughout the city.

So I've developed a plan for the times when the city seems just too full. I head to the suburbs. And, no, I don't mean the ugly industrial area of Mestre, which is filled with squalid 1- and 2-star hotels and hostels. I'm talking about the original suburbs of Venice: the islands of the lagoon.

My relationship with the lagoon dates back to a time before I ever set foot in Venice. My father, coming back from his first fateful trip to Venice (we were to move to Italy within the year) brought me back a small gift, as he usually did. A hand-blown family of glass crabs, the largest no bigger than a walnut. I was fascinated by them, arranging them and rearranging them on a shelf in my bedroom. How did their fragile legs make it back intact in my father's suitcase? And what was this place where—or so he said—there were shops full of these creations.

That is when he told me about Venice. Not only was there an entire island dedicated solely to the production of my little crabs and other manner of glass creations but also a string of islands where people lived, worked, ate, and played.

And this is where I go to beat the crowds:

the islands. As it turns out, these days Murano (the island closest to the center of Venice, and where my glass crabs were crafted), is almost as crowded as the Piazza San Marco. I am not the only person to fall for the charms of hand-blown glass. But over the years I've ventured farther, taking all manner of boats to reach my goal of finding tranquility.

San Pietro di Castello

One of my favorite oft-ignored jewels in the lagoon is actually one that is closest and easiest to get to from the main city. San Pietro di Castello is located way at the eastern end of Venice, tucked into the area between the Giardini della Biennale and the Arsenale. Although I had walked up and down Via Garibaldi in Castello many times, I'd never continued beyond where the street splits and then becomes the narrow Fondamenta Sant'Anna before turning into a wooden bridge, spanning the water, to end up on the island of San Pietro di Castello until recently.

My aim was to visit a building a friend had recently restored, which was the ex-house of the bishop of the church, which gives the island its name. And, in fact, that church, with a classical facade by Palladio, is reason enough to head there. The wide lawn in front of the church is scattered with benches, beneath shady trees, and is almost always empty save for the few elderly locals letting their dogs off the leash for a run.

But that is by far the fanciest part of this island. There is practically nothing else on it. Not even a bar or store. Which is in itself pretty miraculous in overly touristy, hyper-commercialized Venice.

So what do you do on San Pietro? Not much. Just walk around empty alleys. If you find the gate to the right of the church open, pop into the church's courtyard. And when you're hungry head back over the bridge to Via Garibaldi, which is where you'll find one of my favorite restaurants in Venice.

The holy grail in Venice—at least for foodies is finding that little hidden-away place where locals go. In a city like Venice, which makes its living from the tourists who come here each year, these simple places are a dying breed.

Trattoria alla Rampa is the exception. This small restaurant, with a hand-painted sign outside, is located in an area of Venice where few tourists venture. Just north of the Biennale gardens, the small streets leading off of the wide Via Garibaldi are hung with laundry belonging to the mostly working-class families that live here. La Rampa opens its doors at 5 a.m. Yes. You read that right. They open that early because that is when the men who live in this neighborhood—policemen, firemen, garbage men, and other workers—head off for the day. They stop by La Rampa for a quick breakfast, and the place remains open for the rest of the day until just after lunch.

Since the trattoria is slightly below the level of the sidewalk, a ramp (where the place gets its name) leads into the restaurant. There's usually a few men lined up at the *bancone*, enjoying a coffee or a glass of wine and maybe a sandwich. A low doorway at the back leads to the dining room, where a dozen tables are set for lunch.

The menu changes daily. If they have it, I always order *spaghetti al' nero di seppie*, thick strands of spaghetti coated in inky sauce. But this is also the kind of place that will have nearly forgotten recipes that never appear on menus throughout the rest of the city because they don't appeal to tourists. And, in fact, this is where I discovered *La Castradina*.

I had actually seen these haunches of cured meat hanging in all the butcher shops near the Rialto earlier in the day. I'd never noticed them before, in all the times I'd been to Venice, but all of a sudden they were everywhere.

The butcher told me that they were *castradina*, a Venetian specialty. Since it was a Saturday, he was sort of rushed, and maybe even a bit bothered by my questions. He hurriedly explained that castradina was a leg of lamb that had been soaked in salt water for a few weeks, and then smoked.

Sounded good to me.

The butcher whacked one in half, wrapped it, and sent us on our way along with a xeroxed recipe.

It wasn't until the next day, at lunch at La Rampa, that I got the full castradina story. As it turns out, the reason I'd never seen castradina before was because it's only eaten one day a year: on November 21, the day of the *Madonna della Salute*. And since I'd never been in Venice in November before, it was completely off my radar.

Pilgrims would come from all over, including from Eastern Europe, to pay homage to the Madonna della Salute on this festival day. After traveling all that way, they would be offered a warming bowl of soup, which included castradina.

It's definitely hearty peasant food, made to warm you after a wet November day on your way to pay homage to a saint. But it's not nearly as heavy as it sounds, since the bulk of the soup is actually meat broth and cabbage. But if you're hoping to find it on your next trip to Venice, make sure your vacation coincides with the Saint's day, and pay a visit to La Rampa as well.

Mazzorbo

If you've never heard of Mazzorbo, don't worry. Not many people have. It's a tiny island in the lagoon, connected to Burano by a bridge. On the surface, there really is not much reason to go there; just the feeling of having stepped back in time and into a rural agricultural landscape that happens to be in the middle of the lagoon. In other words, the complete flip side of the Venice you know.

About eight years ago though, Mazzorbo came onto the international radar (including mine) when one of Italy's biggest wine producers, Bisol, took over and restored one of the original vineyards on the island. They now run the estate, Venissa, and have turned it into something truly magical. Working together with local agronomists, they have managed to revive one of the oldest vineyards in the entire Veneto as well as the walled vegetable gardens. Today in addition to the hotel and restaurant, there is also a center for agricultural research, vocational training, and an education center.

Whenever I visit Venice, I try to stay at Venissa at least one or two nights. While I love the drama and beauty of Venice, my time on Mazzorbo makes me want to buy a house and spend the rest of my life on the lagoon. The combination of being on a farm but also on the sea, is so magical that it's hard to describe.

Burano

My aim in exploring the islands in the Venetian lagoon is usually to get away from the massive amount of tourists that clog the alleyways of the main part of the city. Heading out to Mazzorbo, Burano, Torcello, and beyond is my game plan. This

usually works very well. But like anything, timing is essential.

While an island like Mazzorbo remains pretty much empty all day long, Burano, only a walk away across a wooden bridge, is another story. The island used to be home to famous lace-makers, and up until recently most tourists came here to visit workshops and bring home a doily or two. These days I have a feeling that most of the lace is probably coming from Asia. But the island continues to draw its share of tourists because of its unique kaleidoscopic technicolor buildings. The two- and three-story homes are each painted a distinct and bright color. My understanding is that the locals, who were fishermen, painted their buildings so distinctively so that they could spy their homes from far out at sea. The tradition still continues (as does the fishing) but in these days of social media sharing, they also provide the perfect backdrop for one-of-a-kind selfies.

Avoiding the tourists is pretty easy. Either head to Burano after 4 p.m. (for some reason all the tourists head home in the evening), or else duck into one of the oldest restaurants on the island like Da Romano or Gatto Nero.

Torcello

In my mission to get out of the center of Venice and onto the lesser trafficked islands, there is one place I always revisit: Torcello.

Torcello is located in the upper reaches of the lagoon, just north of Mazzorbo and Burano. When the *vaporetto* lets you off, there is no choice: take the little canal-side path through fields to finally arrive at the most perfect Romanesque church imaginable. There are a few houses and a couple of restaurants along the way, but for the most part it's a natural paradise.

My memories of Torcello go all the way back to my days as a graduate student. Being the good art historians that we were, my friend Marietta and I decided to take the vaporetto to Torcello to see the Cathedral of Santa Maria Assunta. While the church, and the floors especially, were breathtaking, it is (of course) the lunch, that I remember. It was a Sunday, and being a Sunday, Marietta and I had a tradition of treating ourselves to a long lazy lunch. After doing our art history thing at the church, we headed back down the rustic path to one of the *trattorie* that we had seen on our way in. It was a sunny summer day, and our outside table, beneath a vine-laden pergola, looked out over fields as well as the canal. I'm sure the liter of white wine may have had something to do with it, but the intense sense of being in a place so perfectly attuned to both the man-made and nature was perfect. It's the memory I've kept from that first visit and one I experience every time I go back to this island.

Although the Cathedral is the most famous monument on the island, many people have heard about Torcello through its almost equally famous restaurant: Locanda Cipriani. Although it was far above my graduate school budget all those years ago, I have since dined here in style many times.

Yet dining at Locanda Cipriani is not necessarily all about the food. It's got no hot young chef, nor does it do much on the creative side. But having a meal here can be one of the most magical Venetian experiences (even if it is a bit on the touristy side).

The Locanda Cipriani was opened by Giuseppe Cipriani in 1934. That would be the same guy who brought you Harry's Bar and the Hotel Cipriani. Legend has it that he fell in love with the island of Torcello (who doesn't?) and decided to open a small restaurant and hotel. The place is today owned by Giuseppe's grandson.

Locanda Cipriani shot to fame through the patronage of one very special guest: Ernest Hemingway, who wrote one of his novels while staying in one of their six rooms. After the war, partly due to his influence, it started to become a hot stop for stars* and card-carrying members of la dolce vita.

While stars still may come here, you're more likely to find high-end tourists from America, Russia, and Germany. And the food? Really very, very good. Not cheap, but not silly expensive either. The service is impeccable, and the entire experience of a trip out to Torcello to see the Romanesque church, have a walk along the pathways that bisect the fields, and finally lunch in the Cipriani's garden is unique.

Eolo: On the Water

As much as I love escaping to distant islands, there is another even more luxurious way to escape the crowds: stay on the water.

During a recent trip to Venice I stayed at Venissa on Mazzorbo for two nights. And while it was tempting to just while away my time on this agricultural oasis, I was lured farther out onto the lagoon one evening by my friend Mauro Stoppa.

Mauro sailed over to pick me up, along with some friends, for dinner on the Eolo, his traditional Venetian *bragozzo*. This flat-bottomed 1930s fishing boat, with bright orange sails, has been lovingly restored, and Mauro has been taking guests out on it for the last fifteen years or so, exploring the lagoon, and the surrounding areas. The flat bottom allows it to travel across shallow waters, escaping the more trafficked canals.

We left Mazzorbo and headed off past Burano and Torcello and into the wild northern part of the lagoon that most people never see. Fishermen were bringing in their nets, birds were coming home to roost and we finally anchored far from almost any sign of civilization. As we sipped prosecco, Mauro got to work in the galley preparing our dinner. Because, besides owning this fabulous boat, Mauro is also a fabulous chef, using the wooden galley below decks to transform the bounty of the lagoon into stellar meals.

As the sun set, and the moon rose, we sipped our way through many bottles of prosecco while nibbling on delightful appetizers. Eventually a pristine table was set up mid-deck, complete with crystal, silver, and twinkling candles. The main course was an incredibly fresh *spigola* that Mauro bought from a fisherman who pulled up alongside our boat. The rest of the dinner combined fish as well as fresh herbs from the surrounding islands and produce.

Where to Eat on the Lagoon

Venissa

Fondamenta di Santa Caterina
Isola di Mazzorbo, Venice
+39.041.527.2281

➤ If you don't stay overnight at Venissa, on Mazzorbo, but want to experience it anyway, it's very easy to get to Mazzorbo from Venice. You can come for lunch or dinner, or just stop by for a drink on your way to Burano. A glass of Bisol prosecco, some crostini from the kitchen, as you watch the sun set over the field of cabbages and artichokes. What's not to like about that?

The resort has two distinct restaurants. The Osteria Contemporanea offers local seasonal dishes with a modern spin, while the Ristorante takes things up a notch, offering fine dining and highly creative food. With a changing rotation of chefs, the menu is firmly rooted in the seasonal and local products of the lagoon. Much of the produce comes straight from the municipal vegetable garden located right outside the door of the restaurant, or else from nearby San Erasmo to the south. The food though, is high-end and creative..

Gatto Nero

Trattoria al Gatto Nero
Fondamenta Giudecca 88, Burano, Venice
+39.041.730.120

➤ Gatto Nero was opened in 1965, when Ruggero Bovo took over one of the oldest osterias on the island and turned it into a more formal restaurant. A few of the tables hug the canal outside, but the interiors are just as charming, with the walls covered in framed paintings and prints, the tables topped with starched white cloths and the food served on colorful custom-made plates.

But the food is what you go for, obviously. The seafood-centric menu focuses on specialties of the lagoon. *Capesante* (sea scallops) barely grilled and served in their shell; tiny shrimp nestled in a bed of soft white polenta; *cannolicchi* (razor clams) and *granseola* (crab) drizzled with a bit of olive oil.

And this is the place to have *risotto di gò*. The broth, carefully made from tiny little local fish, is extremely delicate, yet flavor-packed. If you still have room, the *fritto misto di pesce* is pitch-perfect.

Do try to save room for dessert. They serve one of the best tiramisu I've ever had: classic, rich, and dusted with bitter cacao. And, of course, the classic *esse*, S-shaped cookies that are dipped in a glass of sweet wine to end the meal.

Da Romano

Via Galuppi 221
Burano, Venice
+39.041.730.030

➤ In this century-old restaurant it's pretty easy to escape the crowds even in the middle of the day, in the middle of the summer. Despite 100-degree heat outside, most tourists opt to sit on the blazing outdoor terrace. Instead, head in to the main dining room. Not only is it blissfully cool, but it still preserves the ambiance of the original osteria.

The crazed marble terrazzo floors and central columns date to the last century, and the walls are filled with the artwork of the artists who used to exchange their work for meals. While there are sure to be tables filled with tourists (this is Venice after all), the bar located at the back is always populated by locals stopping by for a pre-lunch *ombra* (glass of wine).

The kitchen is still very much overseen by a nonna, and the dishes haven't changed for decades. Their most famous dish is one that comes from the fishing tradition of the island: *risotto di pesce*. Made from a local, boney fish called *gò*, the broth is delicate and takes a special skill to result in a clear, strong base for the risotto. Don't be deceived by the blah-looking plate of white rice: it is packed with a delicate fishy flavor unlike any other risotto I've had.

For my main course I usually choose the *frittura di nonna gigia*: a mix of calamari, shrimp, and a few little sardines. The lovely idea that makes it different is the addition of strips of fried pepper and carrots.

Pasticceria Garbo

Via S. Mauro 336
Burano, Venice

➤ My favorite bakery not only in Burano, but in Venice. A bag of their simple cookies are always in my suitcase when I head back home to Rome

Locanda Cipriani

Piazza Santa Fosca 29
Torcello, Venice
+39.041.730.150

➤ This is one of the most famous restaurants in Venice, and the time to go is when the weather allows for sitting in their shaded private garden overlooking the Romanesque church's bell tower.

What to order? Start off with a Bellini. Please. Giuseppe Cipriani invented this

heavenly concoction of peach puree and prosecco. While every bar and restaurant serves them now in Venice, rarely do you get one so good.

This is the place to stick to Venetian classics. *Moeche* (soft-shelled crabs) if they are in season. Small, baby artichokes grown on the nearby island of San Erasmo are gently sautéed with wild mint. All of their seafood pastas and risottos are pitch-perfect. And I have to say that the *canocchie* (a type of local crayfish) were the best I've had in Venice: fresh, plump, and drizzled with fruity olive oil.

Eolo

Mauro Stoppa
info@cruisingvenice.com
+39.349.743.1552

➢ One of the most charming and watery experiences you can have in Venice is aboard Mauro Stoppa's Eolo, an antique fishing boat. Mauro is not only the skipper but the chef as well, and he prepares meals based on the fruit of the lagoon.

Where to Stay

Venissa

Fondamenta Santa Caterina 3
30170 Isola di Mazzorbo
Venezia, Italy
info@venissa.it
+39.041.527.2281
Fax +39.041.527.2323
GPS: 45.439639, 12.322887

➢ I would certainly suggest staying at Venissa. The handful of rooms are modern and beautifully designed, but are not super fancy (and so pretty affordable) and give you an opportunity to get to know Mazzorbo. Burano is only a short walk away, across the charming wooden bridge, and Torcello is easily reached by boat.

If you do stay overnight, the breakfast is one of the best I've ever had anywhere, ever: freshly made pastries and vegetable/fruit juices, heavenly yoghurt and jams made from local berries and fruit.

Casa Burano

www.casaburano.it/
info@casaburano.it
+39.041.527.2281

➢ Venissa has recently restored a series of houses on the island of Burano. Each one is unique and beautifully furnished with contemporary Italian furniture.

Locanda Cipriani

Piazza Santa Fosca 29

Torcello, Venice

+39.041.730.150

➤ Locanda Cipriani has only five rooms, but staying here is following in the footsteps of Hemingway. The rooms are very traditional and cozy and some overlook the garden.

When in Venice . . .

- Go off-season. Although the "season" seems to be getting longer each year, you can be assured of finding less crowds from November up until *Carnevale* (sometime in February). However, Christmas and New Year's tend to be crowded as well.

- Pick a hotel away from the center. Don't be scared of staying on an island. Taking a boat back and forth is part of the fun of living the watery life.

- Timing is everything: If you do want to wander around St. Mark's Square, do it after the sun goes down. Any day trippers that may have been there are long since gone.

Esse

Makes 24 cookies

One of my favorite bakeries in Venice is on the island of Burano. Although the island has its fair share of touristy stores, it also has a sizable population that actually lives there. This bakery caters to locals as well as tourists, and so you can count on the quality. Pasticceria Garbo's shelves are mostly filled with the various cookies that Venetians do so well. So good are the baker's cookie-making skills that local women bring in their own ingredients for him to turn into cookies. "The ladies bring in their ingredients," Giorgio, the baker, explained to me with a smile. "Butter, eggs, flour, and sugar. And I make their cookies for them while they watch. And do they watch! They want to make sure that their ingredients go into their cookies. Sometimes it gets pretty crazy back there, with just me baking and all those ladies talking away!" While there are a few different types of cookies, including *bussolai* from Burano, the perennial favorite are esse, the *S*-shaped cookies that are perfect for dipping into sweet wine.

Although some recipes call for squeezing the dough out through a pastry sack fitted with a fluted tip, which results in a ridged cookie, it's much more common to see this flat version. It is formed by rolling the stiff dough into tubes, and forming the snake-shaped cookie. If, instead, you feel like making the other cookie from Burano, the *bussola,* it's easy: just form them into rounds instead of *S*'s.

> 2 pounds (1 kilo) all-purpose flour
> 14 ounces (400 grams) unsalted butter, cut into small cubes, at room temperature
> 1⅓ pounds (600 grams) granulated sugar
> ¼ teaspoon salt
> 11 egg yolks
> 1 large egg
> 1 teaspoon finely grated lemon zest
> 1½ teaspoons pure vanilla extract

Place the flour in a mound on a pastry board. Make a well, and place the softened butter in the center. Add the sugar and salt and, using your hand, mix to combine.

Crack the eggs into a bowl, add the lemon zest and vanilla, and stir with a fork to break up the eggs and combine with the other ingredients. Add this mixture to the well, and blend with the butter-sugar mixture. Pull in the flour and mix until all the ingredients are blended. Don't overmix. Seal the dough in plastic wrap, and place in refrigerator for at least 1 hour.

When ready to bake the cookies preheat the oven to 400°F (200°C). Line two baking sheets with parchment paper.

Break off pieces of dough, about 3 ounces (100 grams) each, and form them into ropes about 19 inches (15 centimeters) long. Place each one on the lined baking sheet in the form of an *S*. Repeat for all the dough.

Bake for 15 minutes, reduce the oven temperature to 320°F (150°C) and leave in the oven for another 10 minutes.

The cookies will still be soft when you take them out of the oven. Let them cool on the sheet, and then remove them once they have hardened.

Bellini

The Bellini was invented in the 1930s by Giuseppe Cipriani, and was originally served at his place in Venice, Harry's Bar. Made of white peach puree and prosecco, the original drink was tinged pink by the addition of a bit of raspberry or cherry juice. The name, Bellini, is said to have been inspired by a particular shade of pink on the robe of a saint in a painting by fifteenth-century artist Giovanni Bellini.

What most people don't realize is that while seemingly simple (peaches + prosecco) a good Bellini is all about the quality of ingredients. I found out all about it when I stopped by the Locanda on Torcello for a drink. (Walking that path can make you thirsty!)

Bonifacio, Giuseppe's grandson, who now owns the Locanda, explained that only white peaches will do, and since they are so delicate and have such a short season, they prepare the puree and then preserve it, to use that throughout the year when fresh white peaches are only a distant memory.

And the prosecco has to be the highest quality as well "Or else it will give you an immediate headache," warned Bonifacio as he opened up a bottle. "Even better? Champagne!" Well, of course. Champagne is always better.

So once you've got these two things down, the rest is easy.

White peach puree
Prosecco

To make the white peach puree, pick perfectly ripe white peaches that are at the height of the season. Wash and remove the pit. Place the pieces in a blender and blend until smooth.

Pass through a sieve, pushing the puree through to get all of the juice.

To assemble the Bellini, in a glass pitcher, combine 1 part peach puree, with 2 parts prosecco. Stir well.

Strain into a glass to avoid getting foam into the glass.

CHAPTER THREE

Barrels of Balsamico in Emilia-Romagna

have issues with balsamic vinegar, I admit it. It has to do with change, and the fact that I don't like change. Especially when change is, in my opinion, bad.

One of the things I love most about dining at authentic old-fashioned restaurants throughout Italy is the ritual of ordering a salad. If you ask for an *insalata*, the waiter will respond with a question: *mista* (with some carrots and tomatoes) or *verde* (green)? Then a no nonsense glass bowl with your salad of choice is brought to the table, undressed. There is no discussion of French versus blue cheese. And if you think there is really such a thing as "Italian Dressing," think again.

Don't worry though, you will not be expected to eat those leaves naked. You will, however, play an important role in dressing them. At this point the little cruet caddy makes its way to the table. I absolutely LOVE these. I remember the first time I saw one in Rome, when we moved here. The metal caddy landed on the table and the two bottles containing green olive oil and pale yellow white wine vinegar had pride of place. On one side would be a stubby set of salt and pepper shakers. And on the other, a glass cup full of toothpicks. I thought this was fabulous, that you got to dress your own salad right there at the table. And it makes sense, because in theory everyone likes their salad dressed just a bit differently.

But these days, when the caddy makes its way to the table there is one huge difference that drives me completely mad. The white wine vinegar has been replaced by a dark brown, sickly sweet, version of balsamic.

Why???!!!

It's not that I don't like aceto balsamico. I do. But what comes to the table is most definitely not true aceto balsamico, and secondly, even if it were, I wouldn't want to be putting it on my green leafy salad.

OK . . . rant over.

And now we can get back to the main focus of this chapter, which will help to explain, a bit, the above rant.

Aceto balsamico currently has an identity crisis. The identity of "Balsamic Vinegar" has become so separated from its place of origin that it is almost unrecognizable. And going to see true *Aceto Balsamico Tradizionale* being made, as it has been (and still is) for the last six hundred years, restores your faith in humanity. The story of Aceto Balsamico Tradizionale takes

place in a very small area of central Italy in Emilia-Romagna.

My introduction to true aceto balsamico happened about twenty years ago in the small town of Modena. After a visit to the fabulous market, I made my way to one of the oldest food stores in town, Osteria Giusti. After nosing around, I decided that I should probably buy a small bottle of what I had heard was one of the specialties: Aceto Balsamico Tradizionale. I should have known something was up when the bottle had to be taken down from a shelf behind a locked glass cabinet. And then I heard the price. Could all those zeros (OK, I was paying in old-fashioned lire) really be attaching themselves to the price tag of a 100-milliliter bottle of blackish ooze?

The packaging itself should also have been an indicator that this was something special. The orange box was hinged, and opened more like a jewelry case than food packaging. Nestled inside, cushioned against any abrupt movements, was a hand-blown, crystal-clear, glass bottle, its sturdy cork coated in thick red wax. The contents was black, thick, and utterly mysterious. Not like any vinegar I had ever known. And that is when I realized that the stuff that had begun to show up on restaurant tables and across grocery store shelves had next to nothing to do with what was in this exquisite bottle.

My in-depth education in all things balsamic began in the small town of Castelvetro, just south of Modena. It is there that

the Tintori and Pelloni family age balsamico just as it has been done for hundreds of years. My first visit was over fifteen years ago, and in the ensuing years Roberta Pelloni and Marino Tintori have been joined by their son, Simone. Although in this part of the world it seems that almost everyone and his aunt produce balsamico in their attic, I put my trust into this family for several reasons. First of all, their dedication to this elixir comes through a thorough appreciation of its use in bringing out the best in food. Until recently, the

family restaurant, Il Castello, was a testing ground for new and exciting recipes And then there is the fact that Roberta is known for her exquisite preserves. Pickled onions in balsamic vinegar, local duroni cherries in laurel liqueur, and whole preserved candied chestnuts are just some of the ancient recipes that Roberta has revived, preserving, literally, a forgotten way of life.

It was Marino who first explained the complicated and time honored way of producing balsamico, and it was Simone, who recently took me through the entire process again. Because I'll warn you right now: the process for aging true balsamico is not only an art, it is a complicated one.

And here I have to be clear about something that needs to be said within the context of this book. When it comes to products like Aceto Balsamico Tradizionale—or olive oil, or pasta, or just about anything that is made by hand in a specific way in a specific place—the learning never stops. I never think "Oh, I've 'done' balsamico, now I know everything and I can move on." Each time I visit, each time I taste, I am experiencing something new. Whether it is historical, technical, or even personal, the learning (thank god) never ever stops.

So during my most recent visit, while Marino was in the back office, Simone gave me a balsamico refresher course.

Aceto Balsamico Tradizionale has been made in the region of Modena and Reggio Emilia for over five centuries, in exactly the same way they are still making it today. In fact, it is difficult to say exactly when it was invented since the technique has, traditionally, been jealously shrouded in secrecy. Every family made their own, but there are no ancient treatises or recipes to be found.

Although we think of balsamico as a "food" it wasn't always so. It was only during the last two hundred years that balsamico has been considered a gourmet

delicacy. Originally it was considered to have medicinal properties, and there are many references to its use as a curative. For instance, Lucrezia Borgia sipped balsamico in 1508 while giving birth, and in the seventeenth century it was thought to ward off the plague.

By the eighteenth century the stuff was considered so precious that aristocratic families used it as valuable gifts to heads of states and visiting dignitaries. And, of course, each family's balsamic heritage became part of its inheritance. And although each time I visited Vecchia Dispensa, it was the men of the family—Marino or Simone—who showed me around, the precious wooden casks used to age the balsamico are actually passed down through the women of the family.

One of the most important things to understand about balsamico is that it is not a vinegar. Unlike wine vinegars, balsamico tradizionale does not begin life as an alcoholic beverage. Local grapes—Trebbiano, Spergola, Occhio di Gatto, and even Lambrusco—are used, with each producer adopting his own special recipe, mixing different varieties. The fruit is left on the vine for as long as possible, with the harvest coming around the end of September when the natural sugars in the grapes are at their highest.

The grapes are then pressed, much like in wine making. Yet here the process differs. The *mosto*, or grape juice, is brought into the *acetaia* and poured into large shiny copper kettles. A low flame is lit and the mixture is left to simmer for up to 30 hours. The resulting brew, which has thickened to an almost syrupy stage, is then ready to begin its long transformation into liquid gold.

In addition to the original sets of barrels that were handed down through Roberta's family, they also continue to add *batterie*—sets of barrels—to their collection. A variety of woods are used, which lend the essential aromatic flavors to the vinegar. The sets are made up of up to twelve barrels of descending size, yet increasing aromatics: oak, mulberry, chestnut, cherry, and juniper.

When I first visited Vecchia Dispensa their barrels were located beneath the rafters of their attic. Recently the family gained access to the historic tower in the village and so the barrels are kept on the top two floors of this dramatic space.

The smell, of about fifty barrels full of fermenting grape juice, can be overwhelming. Yet it is precisely this closed environment that allows the natural yeasts to circulate, multiply, and transform. During the summer months, the vinegars are allowed to evaporate and oxidation and fermentation begin to work their magic. Equally important are the freezing winter months, when the vinegar lies dormant. This time-consuming process cannot be rushed.

To qualify as "Aceto Balsamico Tradizionale" the mosto must be aged from fifteen to twenty-five years. Each year, in the autumn, the vinegars are carefully decanted, from one barrel to another. Part of the contents of the smallest, juniper wood barrel is decanted, to be sold or else to ferment further in ever-smaller barrels. The resulting headroom in that barrel is then topped up with balsamico from the previous barrel, and so forth, so that the largest barrel is emptied to be filled with the new mosto. But there is no precise formula or treatise. The timing and choice of woods is all-important and determines the quality and uniqueness of each bottle of balsamico. It is an art form that has been jealously guarded by individual families for centuries.

To reach the thick syrupy stage of the Balsamico Tradizionale Extra Vecchio takes a minimum of twenty-five years. Each set of barrels is dated though, and some date back to the seventeenth century. So if you come across a bottle dated 1650, you know that the final product contains some traces of the liquid first put in that barrel that many years ago.

How Balsamic Exploded onto Tables All Over the World

During the 1960s a group of Balsamico Tradizionale producers decided to raise awareness of their product by marketing it as an elite condiment. So far so good. But in seeking to turn it into a financially successful business, they made the fateful decision to change the time-honored method, thereby increasing production. One of the first things they did was to change the ingredients. Up until then there was only one thing used in the making of Balsamico Tradizionale: mosto, the cooked down grape juice. Instead they decided to create a new type of balsamico, that allowed for the addition of wine vinegar. This addition of vinegar (already fermented) speeded up the entire process dramatically.

The problem was in the naming and branding, or lack thereof. While there were vastly different methods of production, for the next thirty years it was all generically labeled as Aceto Balsamico, or Balsamic Vinegar. Finally, in 2009, the "new" product was officially recognized and received the IGP denomination of Aceto Balsamico di Modena. At the same time, the old-fashioned method was also recognized as Aceto Balsamico Tradizionale. These new denominations were developed with the aim to differentiate the cheaper Aceto Balsamico di Modena from the true authentic Aceto Balsamico Tradizionale.

The need for this differentiation was necessary because the decision to market to a worldwide audience with a newly developed product succeeded. But succeeded almost too well. When the market for balsamic vinegar exploded in the '60s and '70s, the product that flooded the market was the newly invented *Aceto Balsamico* (the one with the added vinegar) and not the *Tradizionale* (the one aged in barrels for years). So the name, *balsamico*, or *balsamic* became literally and figuratively diluted. It became known as an aceto, or "vinegar," which the Tradizionale never was.

If you're confused, don't worry. That was part of the marketing ploy. From this point on it became almost impossible to explain the difference to consumers. The horse had left the barn, and the world became enamored of this new, sweet vinegar, never realizing or knowing about the original use, taste, or history of true Aceto Balsamico Tradizionale.

By the 1980s, the makers of Aceto Balsamico Tradizionale realized what was happening and decided to self-impose strict regulations to protect and preserve this unique product. Yet because that process had never been written down, and was, in fact, still guarded jealously by families, it was not easy to formulate the rules. Yet the threat to their way of life, and the methods, was so great that they collaborated and developed a strict process and labeling system to distinguish it. At the same time they had learned the power of marketing, and so as an additional way to distance themselves from mere vinegar, they also designed the special glass bottle and box, that so entranced me back in Modena.

The Rules of True Aceto Balsamico Tradizionale di Modena

- Aceto Balsamico Tradizionale di Modena has to be made from 100 percent *mosto cotto* (cooked grape must).

- The grapes must come from the region of Modena.

- The process must be aged in a *batteria*, a set of wooden barrels.

How Aceto Balsamico Tradizionale Is Made

- The grapes are harvested at the end of September and mosto is made.

- The mosto is put in the largest barrel, called the *Badessa*. It stays there 5 to 6 months. The barrel is open, and the sugars transform into alcohol, and then into vinegar. The alcohol evaporates. The Badessa always has a bit of the mother left in it to help the mosto transform into vinegar. (Since the word *Badessa* means "Mother Superior," this makes sense!)

- The liquid is transferred from one barrel to the next. *Rincalzare* means "to top up" and *travaso* means "to transfer" from one barrel to the next.

- Starting with the smallest barrel, the balsamico is taken out, ready to be consumed. But a little is left at the bottom.

- Then some balsamico from the next size up is transferred to the smaller one. And so on, up until you get to the Badessa, which is practically emptied.

Yet even if these are the outlines of how to get from grape to bottle, it is not at all straightforward. Making Aceto Balsamico Tradizionale is a craft, and a very personal approach that considers taste at each step of the way, and qualities that are affected by humidity, sugar, and acidity. The most difficult part is to achieve what is referred to as "perfect balsamic qualities." The maestro works with the tools of time and wood, and is able to balance the use of both to create the perfect balsamico as his goal.

Many people think of Aceto Balsamico as something sweet and, in fact, the lesser-quality stuff you find in supermarkets can be very sweet. But in the production of Aceto Balsamico Tradizionale, sugar is just a consequence of this complicated process, and must be balanced carefully. And older balsamic doesn't always mean better. It's the perfume and aroma that are the goals.

After being aged for a minimum of twenty-five years, the balsamico is ready to be judged. It is sent to the *Consorzio* (the Consortium of Balsamic Tradizionale producers) and tasted by a panel of judges. If it meets their standards, then the producer can package it in the special bottles and apply the label "Aceto Balsamico Tradizionale Extravecchio 25 Years." It if doesn't quite meet the standards, then it is called twelve years old (even when, in fact, it is twenty-five years old).

If it is refused? Then it goes into a kind of limbo. It can't be called Aceto Balsamico Tradizionale, but it is still a much better product than the IGP Aceto Balsamico di Modena. Most producers then sell it as a *"Condimento."* These condimenti are often quite good and a very good value. But since the label Condimento has no regulation, you really have to know who you are buying from.

Aceto Balsamico di Modena IGP

Back to the stuff that you are used to buying and/or being served at your local trattoria.

There are rules for that, too.

- The mix of Aceto Balsamico di Modena is 30 percent wine vinegar and 70 percent mosto.

- The mix must be aged a minimum of 60 days in wood.

This sounds good, *but* there is no regulation regarding the mosto (the grapes can come from anywhere) and most of the big producers use industrially made mosto with up to 2 percent added caramel for sweetening and for coloring (this is allowed). And while 60 days in wood sounds like a long time, it's actually not enough time to lend it any balsamic flavor at all.

BUT (you knew there was a *but* coming): Not all Aceto Balsamico di Modena is not created equal. The rules only describe the minimum requirements to define this product. There are actually many producers who make Aceto Balsamico di Modena from local grapes, age it for at least a year, and do not add caramel to the mix. And this high-quality version is actually very good and very useful for many dishes.

How to tell which is which? Price is a good indicator. If a bottle costs a few dollars or euros, then chances are it hasn't been aged for a year. Also, the organic label is useful since to use an organic label you actually have to say where your ingredients come from.

OK. Are you confused enough? We haven't even gotten to the tasting part yet, which is, of course, the main thing.

True Aceto Balsamico Tradizionale is something to be savored, meditated over, and appreciated. The best of them, the oldest, are simply enjoyed as is, on a spoon. Don't expect the mouth-puckering taste of vinegar. Instead the taste sensation is a layered, complicated experience reflecting perfectly a complex aging process that can take twenty-five years, or sometimes much more. As you put it on your tongue the taste hovers between sweet and sour, and your taste buds explode with pure intensity. Yet once you swallow, the sensations keep coming. Slowly the different woods, the sugars, and grapes, everything that has gone into making the balsamic, float into your mouth.

While it might seem strange to buy a bottle of something like this to sip from a spoon, remember that in the sixteenth century kings and queens were doing just that. Whether or not there is true medicinal benefits involved, having a spoonful of a truly great Aceto Tradizionale Balsamico can be an absolutely addictive, and haunting, experience. Once you've tasted it, the experience will remain with you forever.

Not to end on a sour note, but to return to the beginning of the chapter and my rant about using balsamic vinegar on your salad. By this point I hope you're learned a bit about not only Aceto Balsamico Tradizionale but also its lesser cousin, Aceto Balsamico di Modena. It's that lesser cousin, which is basically vinegar with sugar and coloring that you are putting on your salad. If you like sweet vinegar, then fine, that's up to you. While I'm not opposed to using sweet vinegars on some kinds of salads (beets come to mind for instance), I personally think the pairing of leafy greens with sickly sweet dressing to be disappointing.

And while we are on the subject: Balsamic vinegar is not for dipping.

There. I've said it.

When you sit down in a restaurant and are faced with a bread basket, that bread is supposed to be eaten with your meal. It is not meant as an antipasto. In Italy, Italians do not make a soup of olive oil and balsamic dressing on a plate before their meal, to sop up with bread. Why? Here are a few reasons:

- Eating all that bread will fill you up before your meal even gets to the table.

- The olive oil that shows up on the table of most restaurants is not going to be that great anyway, so do you want to fill up on that?

- And finally, having vinegar-soaked pieces of bread before any meal will not only spoil your palette for the rest of the meal, but will make any wine you drink taste completely horrible.

To sum up: At the end of your meal, when you have a bit of dressing left at the bottom of your bowl, and you would like to sop it up with bread, that is fine. Specifically making a bowl full of salad dressing to eat before your meal? Absolutely ridiculous.

Some Uses for Aceto Balsamico Tradizionale

Once you get your hands on a precious bottle of the real stuff, you want to make the best of it. While the Modenesi are known to drink it straight up after dinner, as a kind of *digestivo*, you may want to try the following:

- **Roasted Asparagus:** Carefully wash, trim, and dry the freshest asparagus. Lay them flat on a roasting tray, and drizzle with olive oil and sprinkle with sea salt. Roast in the oven on high heat until tender and browned at the edges. Let cool and serve drizzled with balsamico.

- **Strawberries:** Wash and cut strawberries and toss with a bit of sugar. Drizzle balsamico over each serving.

- **Vanilla Ice Cream:** Yes, balsamico drizzled over fine vanilla ice cream is a pleasure that can only be experienced.

- **Parmigiano Reggiano:** As a prelude to a meal, or just to go with drinks, serve chunks of Parmigiano Reggiano, drizzled with balsamico.

Following are some recipes that I took away with me from my most recent visit to the kitchen of Roberta Pelloni in Castelvetro.

Ricotta, Cherry Jam, and Balsamic Tart

Makes one 10-inch tart; serves 8

The area around Modena is well-known for its sour cherries and Roberta uses them to make jams, which find their way into this tart

For the crust

2½ cups (300 grams) all-purpose flour

⅔ cup (150 grams) unsalted butter, at room temperature

½ cup (100 grams) granulated sugar

1 teaspoon finely grated lemon zest

1 egg yolk, beaten

For the filling

1 cup (250 grams) cow's milk ricotta

½ cup (100 grams) granulated sugar

1 cup (200 grams) sour cherry jam

1 tablespoon Aceto Balsamico di Modena

Aceto Balsamico Tradizionale, for drizzling

Make the crust: Combine all of the ingredients in a bowl and mix, using your

hands, until it comes together. Seal the dough in plastic wrap and chill in the refrigerator for 30 minutes.

Preheat the oven to 350°F (180°C).

Make the filling: Beat the sugar and ricotta until very smooth. Set aside.

Stir the Aceto Balsamico di Modena into the jam. Set aside.

Line a 10-inch tart pan with a removable bottom with parchment paper. Roll out ⅔ of the dough on a floured surface. Transfer to the tart pan. Don't worry if it breaks, the dough is very forgiving. Just patch it together. Trim the edge along the rim.

Spoon the jam filling onto the crust. Then carefully spread out the ricotta on top of the jam, using the back of a spoon to smooth it out.

Roll out the remaining dough, and cut into ½-inch-wide strips. Top the tart with the strips, weaving them in a lattice pattern. Brush the dough with the beaten egg yolk.

Bake the tart in the preheated oven for about 40 minutes. Let cool before serving.

When ready to serve, place the slices on individual dessert plates and drizzle with Aceto Balsamico Tradizionale.

Risotto di Zucca

Serves 4 to 5

For this recipe you want a winter squash with a lot of flavor, but little water. In this part of Italy they use one that comes from Mantova. But if you have butternut squash, that will do fine.

> 1½ pounds (800 grams) winter squash (*zucca*)
> 1 pound (500 grams) riso canaroli or vialone
> 2 tablespoons finely chopped onion
> 4 tablespoons unsalted butter plus 1 tablespoon to finish the risotto when serving
> 6 cups (about 1½ liters) light vegetable broth
> 2 sprigs fresh rosemary
> ¾ cup cubed pancetta
> 2 tablespoons Aceto Balsamico di Modena
> 1 cup grated Parmigiano Reggiano
> Aceto Balsamico Tradizionale, for drizzling

Preheat the oven to 320°F (140°C).

Prepare the squash: Peel the squash and cut it into 1½-inch cubes. Spread the squash out on a baking sheet.

Roast in the preheated oven for 1½ to 2 hours, until very tender. (At this point it makes a very good side dish drizzled with Aceto Balsamico Tradizionale.)

Melt 4 tablespoons of butter in a saucepan, add the onions, and cook over medium-low heat until soft.

Add the rice to the butter and onions and stir it until it is evenly coated with butter and lightly toasted.

Increase the heat to medium-high, add the broth gradually, breaking up the squash with a spoon. Continue to cook, stirring and adding more broth.

In the meantime, cook the pancetta in a frying pan over medium heat until it renders its fat and is browned. Add the Aceto Balsamico di Modena, and let evaporate.

When the risotto is almost done, add a few sprigs of fresh rosemary and 1 tablespoon of butter. Turn off the heat and stir in the cheese.

Serve on the risotto on individual plates, topped with a tablespoon of the pancetta. Drizzle with Aceto Balsamico Tradizionale.

Visiting an Acetaia

It is well worth visiting an acetaia, and there are many that are within easy reach of Modena.

Vecchia Dispensa

Piazza Roma 3
Castelvetro, Modena
+39.059.790.401
www.lavecchiadispensa.it
info@lavecchiadispensa.it
➤ Located about a half hour south of Modena, in a small village, a visit here makes for a nice day trip from Modena. Easy if you have a car; there is also a bus that goes there.

Acetaia Malpighi

Via Vignolese 1487
Zona San Donnino, Modena
+39.059.467.725
www.acetaiamalpighi.it
➤ One of the biggest acetaia in the area, they receive over 25,000 guests a year. Their tours are highly organized, followed by a tasting. Also located about a half hour out of town.

Acetaia di Giorgio

Via Sandro Cabassi 67
Modena
+39.059.333.015
www.acetaiadigiorgio.it
➤ A small family-run acetaia, it is located only 2 kilometers from the center of Modena, so easy to get to by public transport or taxi.

Acetaia Giusti

Strada Quattro Ville 155
Modena
+39.059.840.135
www.giusti.it
➤ Located just outside of town, this is the oldest producer of aceto balsamico in Modena, dating back four centuries.

Restaurants

Danilo

Via Coltellini 31, Modena
+39.059.225.498
Open daily; lunch and dinner.
➤ Very old-school, this forty-year-old restaurant serves all the classics. They have a huge cart of *bollito* (boiled meats) with all the trimmings, and their *tortelloni in brodo* is not to be missed. Even though I usually fill up on their somewhat heavy fare, I usually find room for one of their old-fashioned desserts: cooked pears or apples.

Hosteria Giusti

Via Luigi Carlo Farini 75, Moderna
+39.059.222.533
➤ With only four tables in the backroom of this salumeria, Hosteria Giusti is one of the most difficult tables to book in Modena (Osteria Francescana is harder, of course).

Because of its almost hidden nature, it's become a cult destination. When I first went there fifteen years ago, the backroom was just that: a few wooden tables in a small room. The room is still the same size, but these days the tables are topped with starched white cloth and the silver is shining. The food is traditional, but topped up a few notches.

Osteria da Ermes

Via Canaceto 89, Moderna
+39.059.238.065

➤ I couldn't nab a last-minute table at Giusti, so I headed to Osteria da Ermes, where reservations are nonexistent. Show up ahead of the 12:00 opening time, and stand in the line that has probably already formed. About noon Ermes will come outside, have a look at the crowd, asking who is with whom and then start ushering you inside. He is basically out to fill up every seat possible. Since I was alone, I was seated at a table with three other local men.

There is no menu. Instead a waitress comes by and offers a choice of 2 primi and 5 secondi. It is all hearty, workingmen kind of food. And so to start off, a plate full of headcheese and salami, which I shared with my new friends.

My *pasta al forno* came to the table rich with béchamel and meat and piping hot. I ordered zampone with beans, for my main course, which was way more than I could handle after the hearty first course. Luckily one of my table mates was utterly

disappointed with his *pollo fritto*, which was more bones than pollo and more sautéed than fritto. He gladly took most of my zampone off my plate, which is lucky since Ermes refuses to clear away any plate that still has food on it.

To finish we all shared a big plate full of *bersone*, a dry sugary cake that makes sense once I followed my table mates' lead by dipping it into what was left of my glass of fizzy, slightly sweet, Lambrusco.

Fifteen euros each, for all that food, and wine and bread, and I was back on the sidewalk, having made room for all those other people waiting.

CHAPTER FOUR

Stuffing Myself with Stuffed Pasta

had always read about how passionate people were about food in Emilia-Romagna. Specifically, while on the train to Modena, I had just finished reading yet another article about one of the most famous chefs in the world, Massimo Bottura, whose Michelin-starred restaurant, Osteria Francescana, is located there. The main theme of the article? About how protective the Modenese are of their nonna's cooking. Bottura made it sound like this was the most important thing in the world to them. I, of course, thought he was probably exaggerating to add a bit of drama to a magazine article.

Until, that is, I got in a taxi at the Modena train station and with absolutely no prompting on my part at all the driver began to talk about his nonna's cooking. It was lunchtime, and maybe he was hungry. But he got real specific, real fast. Not only were his nonna's tortellini the best there were, one of the reasons they were so good was because she didn't use just any Parmigiano, but 30-month-old Parmigiano Reggiano. Not 18-month-old. Not 36-month-old. But specifically 30-month-old Parmigiano. "The kind from the red cows," he specified.

All this and I hadn't even picked up my rent-a-car yet.

When I told people that I was going to Modena, a smallish town in central Italy, everyone assumed that I was going to Bottura's restaurant. Since I am a food writer and Francescana has been declared the Best Restaurant in the World, that might be a natural assumption. Massimo Bottura has been on the cover of every possible publication, been the subject of documentaries, and his restaurant, Francescana, is one of the most difficult reservations to get in the world.

But my answer was no. I'm not going to Francescana. (I've actually never been there and am not 100 percent sure if I ever will.) I'm not even really staying in Modena itself. I'm getting in a car and heading 15 kilometers south, to a nothing town (it's basically an intersection) in the middle of nowhere to stay in a hotel (well, motel really) with a view out over the fire escape because someone told me that is where the best tortellini are.

Like many Italians, I have a soft spot in my heart for tortellini. Even if tortellini are specifically from Emilia-Romagna many Italians eat them at special occasions or in restaurants all over Italy. When I was a child in Rome in the 1970s one of the biggest treats I could imagine was ordering a bowl of tortellini with heavy cream, ham, and peas. And even though my husband, Domenico, is from Bari, about as far south as you can get, he still wants tortellini in brodo for Christmas.

Tortellini Legends

According to legend, the tiny, belly button–shaped, meat-filled pasta sprang to life by someone peeping through a keyhole. It may have been an innkeeper in the fifteenth century in Castelfranco (near Modena) who spied Lucrezia Borgia through the keyhole. The beauty of her navel made him run downstairs and re-create it in pasta form. Or it may have been another innkeeper, a couple of centuries earlier, nearer to Bologna, who was spying on Zeus and Venus (who somehow happened to be staying at his inn). This time it was the beauty of Venus's belly button that lead to tortellini inspiration.

Whatever its origins, as I began to do research on various types of stuffed pasta, tortellini—and finding the best ones—was at the top of my list. I asked a few people from the area, and even though all of them claimed that their mother produced the best ones, many of them also mentioned a small hotel, or restaurant, just south of Modena.

Was it a hotel? Or was it a restaurant? Or was it both? The answers to those

Silvana, making Anolini

questions was all tied up in a mini soap opera involving who exactly made the best tortellini at that specific intersection in the middle of nowhere.

After a simple search, I discovered that there was a hotel, Zoello Je Suis, as well as a restaurant attached, Ristorante Zoello. And so I called up the hotel, made a reservation, explained my tortellini research, and asked if I could talk to them about tortellini, follow them into the kitchen, and learn all about how they made their pasta. Sure, no problem.

When I arrived the first night, after I checked in, the owner of the hotel suggested that I go next door for dinner. I was a bit confused, since I assumed the restaurant was part of the hotel. "No, the restaurant belongs to my cousins," said the owner. "I think you should go next door, eat their tortellini, and then you can judge." Judge what? "How much better ours are."

Five minutes in town and I was already in the middle of a tortellini tug of war.

The history of the duel goes back to 1938, when Paola and Mario opened a small shop that eventually turned into a small osteria. Originally the shop sold a bit of everything including groceries, cigarettes, and dry goods. But Paola began making food as well, *pollo alla cacciatora*, *trippa*, *baccalá*, and, of course, tortellini. Eventually they set up a pergola outside, with a few tables. On the weekends they had live music. Since the small town is just a 20-minute drive south of Modena, it soon became a destination known not only for a good time, but for good tortellini. Zoello was Mario's nickname and so the restaurant, and eventually the hotel that they opened in the 1970s, took his name. The *tortellini di Zoello* became famous and driving there for a plate of *tortellini in brodo* became a food fad before there were food fads.

Families grow, and several years ago the daughters of Paola and Zoello, divided the business in two. The hotel went to Marisa and the restaurant to Antonella. While Antonella continues to make tortellini in the restaurant, Marisa's tortellini, made in the kitchen of the hotel, are sold in the market in Modena.

So which tortellini were better? I found out that that's a silly question to ask and a nearly impossible one to answer. If there is one thing I learned in this land of passionate tortellini making, for an outsider like me just about every plateful of tortellini in brodo I had was not only excellent, but so far superior to any tortellini in brodo I had ever had anywhere else, that it was like it was a different food.

First of all the pasta itself was always thin enough to see the filling but firm enough to have some bite. The filling itself changed slightly from tortellino to tortellino, but that was part of the fun. Always meaty, with an underlying umami that came from aged Parmigiano and just a hint of spicy complexity that came from both the mortadella as well as a touch of nutmeg. The biggest difference from place

to place though, was in the brodo. Always made from *cappone* (capon), in some places it was a bit saltier, some a bit fattier, some a bit richer.

Anolini in Parma

There are a series of towns in Emilia-Romagna that all run in a straight line, more or less, along the Autostrada A1 connecting Bologna, Modena, Reggio Emilia, and Parma, with Bologna being the biggest in the bunch. Although one is not farther than 30 kilometers from the next, I found that when it comes to stuffed pasta, you better know your terms before asking for something.

Maria Chiara Passani, who works at the Consorzio di Parmigiano Reggiano, had organized a few visits for me to local *rezdore*. Loosely translated, *rezdora* means "housewife," but what it really means is queen of the kitchen. It is the word that is used to describe the women, usually older, who are keeping alive the traditions of the recipes of Emilia-Romagna. And so I was thrilled to be able to visit some of them near Maria Chiara's hometown of Calestano, just south of Parma.

When I first walked into Silvana Ghillani's house, everyone was in the kitchen, talking. I spied the pasta she had made earlier that day, laid out carefully on the kitchen table, with a dish towel covering it. I lifted the edge, and said, "Oh! ravioli!" All conversation stopped. Everyone was looking at me. I thought, "Oh no, I should never have touched the towel." But no, it wasn't that. While Silvana gave me a look, Maria Chiara explained what had shocked everyone. "Those aren't ravioli," she said. "They are *anolini*."

Never heard of anolini? Me, neither. Nor even seen them. This is how specific stuffed pasta can be. I doubt there is even a restaurant in Rome that serves anolini. Or possibly even in Bologna. They are very specific to the region around Parma and involve an even more complicated procedure than tortellini.

Like tortellini though, anolini are all about the stuffing and the brodo. And both are all about the meat. And while both anolini and tortellini are pasta stuffed with meat, served in a meat broth, they couldn't be more different. The process for making both the broth and the fillings are so completely different, that I'm including both recipes here. Even if they are a bit daunting, reading both will start to give you a sense, more than anything else, about how seriously people in this part of the world take their food.

Every single ingredient has its reason for being there, and a specific way of preparing it. Not just any bread crumbs, but fresh bread, cut in cubes the day before, then dried out in the oven then turned into crumbs in the food processor, but "Not too fine, not too big, but in the middle." Also? The bread itself was homemade.

One thing that we tend to forget today, is what a special occasion eating any of these stuffed pastas were. While watching Silvana make both the stuffing for the anolini, as well as the broth, I realized just how expensive these ingredients must have been in the past. There was a ton of meat involved, both for the filling and the broth, as well as expensive aged Parmigiano Reggiano. Today, with industrially made, stuffed pasta filling up aisles at the supermarket, it was both impressive, and daunting, to see the skill and time and effort that went into making these miniature works of culinary art.

Although the term anolini refers to stuffed pasta in general, in the Parma area they are always stuffed with a stuffing of pot roast and Parmigiano. And the shape is always round, and always smooth along the edge.

Stuffed Pasta 101

Tortellini: Small, navel-shaped pasta stuffed with a mixture of meat, cured meat, and Parmigiano. Traditionally served in broth, ideally made from capon.

Tortelloni: Shaped like tortellini, but bigger, they are not stuffed with meat, but with either a mixture of ricotta and spinach, or pumpkin.

Cappelletti: Like tortelloni, but the filling is usually just cheese—either Parmigiano Reggiano, Grana , or even robiola.

Tortelli di Erbette: Square-shaped pasta stuffed with a mixture of ricotta, spinach or Swiss chard, and a huge amount of Parmigiano Reggiano. Served with butter, sage, and even more Parmigiano.

Anolini: Round pasta stuffed with pot roast, bread, and Parmigiano, served in broth made from capon, and lots more Parmigiano.

Ravioli: The name given to any square-shaped stuffed pasta throughout the rest of Italy. But god forbid you should call a *tortello* a *raviolo*, because it's just not.

Where to Eat Tortellini in Modena

I Tortellini di Marisa
Mercato Albinelli
Via Albinelli Modena
Stand 29
+39.059702.674
➤ Marisa's tortellini are available at the historic Mercato Albinelli, ready to take home and cook.

Ristorante Zoella
Via Modena 181
Settecani di Castelvetro, Modena
+39.059.702.635
Open for lunch and dinner. Closed Friday.
➤ This is the historic restaurant where you can order a bowl full of Zoella's famous tortellini. You might as well, since that is what absolutely everyone else in the restaurant is doing.

Danilo
Via Coltellini 31
Modena
+39.059.225.498
Open for lunch and dinner. Closed Sunday.
➤ This is as old-school traditional ristorante as you can get. Perfect service, and if you want *bollito* (I always do), they have a steaming cart full of cuts of meat with all the trimmings. But first have pasta. They always have *tortellini in brodo*, as well as tortelli stuffed with zucca.

Festa del San Nicolo—Sagra dei Tortellini

Castelfranco Emilia

First week of September

➤ This is the tortellini party to end all tortellini parties. It takes place in the supposed birthplace of tortellini, Castelfranco, the first week of September. Expert tortellini makers from all over the area descend to help produce a virtual river of *tortellini in brodo*, all carefully prepared by hand.

Where to Eat Anolini

Ristorante Cocchi

Viale Antonio Gramsci 16

Parma

+39.0521.292.606

➤ Definitely order the anolini, which are outstanding, but absolutely don't miss the *torta fritta* with as much of the *salumi* as you think you can eat. It was really some of the most extraordinary cured meats I'd ever had.

Trattoria del Tribunale

Vicolo Politi 5

Parma

+39.0521.285.527

➤ This rustic trattoria is located in the center of town, and is always crowded. I prefer sitting upstairs, since it's a bit less chaotic, or if the weather is nice, at one of the outside tables.

Anolini in Brodo

Serves 8

This recipe is extremely complicated and long, and requires beginning it the day before.

For the stracotto

    1 pound (½ kilo) top round beef
    1 to 2 marrowbones
    1 pound (½ kilo) veal rib
    1 pound (½ kilo) pork loin
    8 whole cloves
    Extra-virgin olive oil
    1 garlic clove
    1 small branch rosemary
    1 celery stalk
    ½ carrot
    1 small onion
    1 shallot
    One 3-inch stick cinnamon
    1 tablespoon tomato paste
    ¼ cup white wine
    1 tablespoon kosher salt

For the stuffing

    12 ounces (330 grams) bread
    1¾ pounds (900 grams) 30-month-old
        Parmigiano Reggiano, grated
    4 large eggs
    Stracotto juices
    Stracotto (see below)
    Salt
    Freshly ground black pepper

Stuffing Myself with Stuffed Pasta 45

For the broth

2 pounds (1 kilo) chuck tender

¼ capon

1 carrot

1 medium onion

2 celery stalks

2 tablespoons kosher salt

For the pasta

1⅓ pounds (630 grams) "0" flour

⅔ pound (300 grams) semola di grano
   duro flour

9 large eggs

3 tablespoons extra-virgin olive oil

Pinch of salt

Extra grated Parmigiano Reggiano,
   for serving

First make the stracotto: At least one day before you are going to make the anolini, make the stracotto (pot roast). Wash and peel or trim the vegetable. Rinse the meat and dry it well. Salt and pepper the meat and, using a thin knife, make small slits in the meat and insert the cloves.

Pour the olive oil into a heavy-bottomed pot large enough to hold the meat and vegetables snuggly. Place over medium heat and add the garlic, rosemary, and vegetables. Add the meat and bones and brown evenly and well, turning it. It should take about 20 minutes.

Once the meat is well browned, add the tomato paste and cook briefly. Add the wine and cook, stirring, until it has evaporated. Then add tepid water, about three-quarters of the way up the meat, along with the cinnamon. Bring to a simmer, reduce to a very low simmer, add the salt, and with the lid askew, cook very slowly for 6 to 7 hours.

Let it cool in the refrigerator. Once chilled, eliminate the fat that will have risen to the surface. Remove the meat and vegetables and set aside. Strain the small bits out of the sauce that has been created and set the sauce aside.

Make the stuffing: Cut the bread into chunks and toast it in a 400°F (200°C) oven for 15 minutes. Let cool, then process to form crumbs (not too fine).

In the bowl of a food processor, finely grind the cooled meat from the stracotto.

Place the crumbs in a bowl. Add enough of the warmed sauce from the stracotto to make it a fairly solid, but moist, mass, mixing it well. Let the stuffing come to room temperature.

Once it has cooled, add the cheese, salt, pepper, eggs, and finely ground meat. Mix well with your hands. Let this mixture rest, in the refrigerator, at least overnight.

Make the broth: Wash and trim the vegetables and put them in a large pot. Add the rinsed pieces of meat. Cover with cold water by a few inches. Bring to a quick boil over medium heat, and, using a slotted spoon, remove the foam that floats to the top. Reduce the heat, and with the lid askew, let the broth simmer for 3 to 4 hours.

Mix the two flours together and add the eggs and olive oil. It will be shaggy at first, but put it on a board and knead until it comes together and forms a dough. Keep kneading until the dough is silky and elastic. If it is too dry, add a bit more water, and if it is too wet, a bit more flour. Cover the dough with plastic wrap and chill in the refrigerator for at least a half hour.

When ready to assemble the anolini, take the dough out of the fridge. Cut off a piece, being careful to keep the rest covered with plastic wrap so it doesn't dry out. Using a pasta machine, make a sheet of pasta measuring about 3 to 4 inches (8 to 10 centimeters) wide and place it on a floured surface. Cut the sheet in half, across the middle, so you have two long sheets.

Using a spoon, drop teaspoon-size amounts of filling along the center, leaving about 1 inch (2 centimeters) of space between each one. Place the other sheet on top of the filling, pressing with your fingers carefully to make sure there are no air pockets. Then, using an anolini cutter, or other round cutter, cut and seal each anolini.

Strain the broth of the meat, and bring it to a boil. Cook the anolini in the simmering broth, for 3 to 4 minutes. Serve in bowls, topped with abundant grated Parmigiano Reggiano. on the side.

Tortellini

Serves 8

The flavor of tortellini comes from a mixture of meats. Everyone has their own secret recipe for both the filling and for the broth. This is the recipe that I learned from Marisa at Zoello Je Suis Hotel. It differs from traditional recipes in a few ways. Rather than use prosciutto, Marisa prefers culatello. And in addition to pork, she also uses a bit of beef as well as some sausage. Although she let me watch her make it, she refused to give me exact quantities. "I have to have some secrets!" she said.

For the filling

2 ounces (50 grams) beef round, cut into cubes

3½ ounces (100 grams) pork loin, cut into cubes

1 Italian (non spicy) sausage

2½ ounces (60 grams) mortadella

2½ ounces (60 grams) culatello

4 ounces (120 grams) 30-month-old, grated Parmigiano Reggiano

Pinch of nutmeg

Salt

Freshly ground black pepper

Marisa, making tortelini

For the broth

2 pounds (1 kilo) chuck roast or brisket

½ capon

2 celery stalks

For the pasta

1½ pounds (800 grams) "00" flour

8 large eggs

First, make the filling: Place the cubed beef, pork, and sausage in a pan and cook until done and well browned. According to Marisa, the meat should "sing" and that's when you know it's done. Set the meat aside to cool off completely, then put it in a food processor and grind with the mortadella and culatello. Process until it is completely blended. Add the cheese, nutmeg, salt, and pepper and mix well. Let cool, then refrigerate overnight.

Next, make the broth: In a large pot, cover the meat and celery with abundant cold water and bring to a boil. Using a slotted spoon, skim off the foam that rises to the surface. Add salt and let simmer for 2 to 3 hours.

Finally, make the pasta and form the tortellini: Mix the eggs and the flour together on a board or in a bowl, and knead until the dough is silky and smooth. Let rest, wrapped in plastic, in the refrigerator for an hour. When ready to form tortellini, roll out the dough with a rolling pin or pasta machine to the finest setting.

Using a knife, cut the dough into 1¼- to 1½-inch (3- to 4-centimeter) squares. Using your fingers, place a tiny bit of filling in the center of a square. Close the square to make a triangle, making sure the edges are well sealed. Then, using your little finger in the center, bring the two lateral corners to meet up, pinching them together, while leaving space in the middle where your finger was, forming a little navel-shaped pasta. Repeat a million times until you've used up all the pasta and filling.

To serve, cook in drained broth, for about 4 minutes. Serve with abundant grated Parmigiano Reggiano.

CHAPTER FIVE

Risotto, Cassoeula, and an Understated Sense of Style in Milan

suspect that one of the reasons I love Milan so much is that it is so decidedly not Rome. Don't get me wrong, I love my city. But a visit to Milan is the well-ordered, manicured, stylish antidote I need when I get "over-Romed."

I just realized that I forgot one adjective above: delicious. Because while Milan is mostly known as the style and financial capital of Italy, I am, of course, interested in neither. Actually, that's not 100 percent true. While I certainly don't go to Milan for "business," and the fashion world has always left me cold, the world of design and the Salone del Mobile that takes place twice a year, is thrilling. But then again, that's where design meets home, which is my sweet spot. So no surprise there.

While I knew I wanted to include Milan in some way in this book, it was difficult to choose a hook for this chapter. One iconic dish or product that sums up the city on a plate for me? Just not there. So rather than try to force the issue using a bowl full of rice or veal or . . . to stand as a metaphor for style or chic, I've decided to share some of my favorites spots.

For me, Milano has always been about the hearty, wintery dishes of this area. As you may have heard, weather in Milan can be a bit gray and wet. It's pretty much true, at least for three-quarters of the year. And so, three-quarters of the time when I visit, a plateful of something completely fatty, creamy, and/or starchy is what I am craving.

But that's not to say I only steer toward the old- and homey-style trattorie that still abound. I'm an equal opportunity eater, and absolutely love the newer spots that have opened up in the last decade that embrace the traditional in a new, and slightly lighter (nah, not really) way. And some of these are located in restaurants that draw me in as much for their unique setting, as for their food.

So I'd like to share five typically Milanese dishes at five of my favorite places. And then I'll share a handful of my favorite settings that also have great food.

Five Favorite Dishes

Riso al Salto at Antica Trattoria della Pesa

One of the very first things I ever ate in Milan—close to two decades ago—was a plate of *riso al salto* at one of the city's most historic trattorias. At the time, I thought it was the best thing I had ever put in my mouth.

Even though much has changed in the last two decades—new openings, creative cuisine, ethnic and foreign influences—the riso al salto at Antica Trattoria della Pesa remains one of my favorite dishes in town.

While 80 percent of my fondness for this dish has to do with the dish itself (and I'll get to that soon enough) I admit that at least 20 percent of my love is due to the setting. It is old-world charm defined. White curtains make the interior mysterious from the outside and diffuse the light inside. Marble floors, well-used antique furniture, starched white tablecloths, and gleaming silver abound. And the waiters: professional, black-aproned waiters that take everything very seriously.

Lunch is my favorite time since I love the filtered light, falling on teapots full of flowers. Even when the sky is gray and dark outside, everything here seems crisply white and bright.

Every time I go, I think I'm going to venture off into other parts of the menu, to try

their *ossobuco* or *costoletta*, or one of the old-timey Milanese classics like *cassoeula* or *foiolo* (tripe). But no. Somehow that riso al salto ends up in front of me every time.

Riso al salto is something that is 100 percent Milanese. It is made with leftover *risotto alla milanese*, made the day before. The rice is then put in a small pan, with plenty of butter and made into a kind of pancake, becoming crispy on the outside. In other words it's the best part of the pot when you make risotto, the crispy, toasted, buttery bits that get stuck to the bottom of the pan.

I've had it at other places, and while it's usually never badly done, at Antica Trattoria della Pesa it is done the best. During a recent visit I got a chance to go in the back and see how it was prepared and learned a few secrets. There is a LOT of butter involved (not really that much of a surprise). Also, the addition of crunchy sea salt adds not only texture but also a saltiness that is essential. And then there are the factors that are hard to re-create: a small pan that has been doing its job forever, as well as a cook with that expert twist of the wrist to flip it over. Yes, it's all in the *salto*, or the "flip."

Antica Trattoria della Pesa
Via Pasubio 10, Milano
+39.02.655.5741
Closed Sunday.

Artichoke Salad at Alla Collina Pistoiese

I am such a sucker for the kind of ritual and old-fashioned elegance that you find in Italian restaurants. This is a very different thing than my fondness for simple trattorias. No. I'm talking about the hushed quiet that you experience when you are ushered into a true ristorante, where the waiters wear pressed white jackets and the tables are formally attired as well. My favorite time to head to these types of places is at lunchtime. This is when the clientele—usually businessmen—are as serious (and timeless) as the food itself.

When I'm in Milan I always try to make time for a visit to Alla Collina Pistoiese. A Milanese bastion of fine food, it's been in business since 1938, and has been serving their version of Tuscan food in the center of town ever since. It is a true ristorante in every sense of the word. And although it is Tuscan, most of my favorite dishes are a sort of geographically ambiguous ristorante fare that only shows up at these types of places.

If it's winter, and particularly cold and miserable outside, I usually order one of the meatier main dishes. One of those old-fashioned "restauranty" kinds of items like veal scaloppina with marsala or lemon or steak tartare. I also have a fondness for those dolce vita–sounding items like *Filetto alla Woronoff* and *Robespierre con patate* (who even knows what they are)?

But mostly I love going in the spring, when the meatier side of the menu is joined by vegetable dishes that are as old-fashioned as they are deliciously filling. Luckily at Alla Collina they treat their vegetables just as seriously as their meat.

For my main course I order one of my favorite springtime dishes: *Asparagus Bismark*. I'm not sure where the name comes from (the same place as Woronoff and Robespierre I'm thinking) but at least I know what it means. A bunch of bright green asparagus, steamed, drained, and topped with perfectly fried eggs. At Alla Collina Pistoiese they are nestled atop a pool of butter and grated parmesan cheese, that—with the broken and runny egg yolk—made the most luscious sauce imaginable.

But before I even get to the asparagus I make a point to order artichokes. I love artichokes prepared any which way, but Alla Collina Pistoiese is one of the rare places that serves them raw, as a salad. This is because it's not an easy thing to prepare ahead of time, since the raw artichokes tend to oxidize, turning dark and affecting the delicate taste. Alla Collina eliminates any possibility of this happening by preparing the salad right there in the middle of the dining room.

At a station set up in the entrance, the maître d' picks a perfect artichoke, trims it, and constructs the salad using two types of cheese, celery, and a drizzle of bright green Tuscan olive oil. He also adds a lot of showmanship as well as skill, which is also kind of the reason I love this place so much.

Ristorante Alla Collina Pistoiese
Via Amedei 1
Milano
+39.02.8645.1085
Open daily; lunch and dinner.

Cassoeula at Osteria dell'Acquabella

It's hard to find a more charming place than Osteria dell'Acquabella. Located in the Porta Romana neighborhood, this corner location is warm, cozy, and inviting. Floor to ceiling windows let light flow onto the terra-cotta floors, exposed bricks, and wood paneling. A big red Berkel slicer and vintage scale, sitting on the long counter, wins my heart.

Although this restaurant has a full menu year-round, for me it's the place I go to in the dead of winter to properly enjoy a massive plate of cassoeula. A Milanese variation on the French cassoulet, it's definitely a winter dish. And on a subzero snowy day in Milan (which happens more than you'd think), it is just what the doctor ordered.

The last time I was there I was alone. But that didn't stop me. And can I tell you how happy it made the owner? Here I was, an American woman, on her own, for lunch on a Wednesday. I'm sure he was thinking

"Oh, she's going to order a salad and then a half portion of bean soup or something." So when I said I'd take the cassoeula, he did a double take. "Are you expecting someone else?" Nope. Just me. Thank you.

I can see why he was a bit worried. Cassoeula is basically a huge plate of meat. Like cassoulet, it is a mixture of cuts: a pig's foot, a pork chop, and three kinds of sausage: cotechino, regular sausage, and then something he explained was *salsiccia di verza*, or "cabbage sausage." It's a special, lean sausage that is used for this dish, because the other cuts (including a huge amount of pig skin) are so incredibly fatty. The thinking is that you eat that lean sausage along with the cabbage, which has absorbed much of the pork fat.

And then, lest you miss out on any of the fatty, "porky," "cabbage" juices, there are two thick slices of grilled polenta to soak it up.

I admit, it was too much for me to get through alone. And if you do plan on ordering it, you might want to think about sharing. But I did manage to eat a bit of everything, which definitely gave me strength to face the sleet and slush outside.

Osteria dell'Acquabella

Via S. Rocco 11
Milano
+39.02.5830.9653
Tuesday–Friday: lunch and dinner.
Saturday only lunch. Closed Sunday.

Ossobuco at Testina

Red-checkered tablecloths, exposed brick walls, Thonet chairs, and wine-filled shelves make this a cozy, welcoming spot. The menu sticks closely to Milanese tradition. They always have some version of *mondeghili*, which are basically deep-fried meatballs. The day I was there they were served as an antipasto, along with grilled peppers, with a pool of red wine reduction. Many of the tables were starting out with a huge platter of their famous cured meats, including their own house-made mortadella served with *gnocco fritto* (fried dough) and *insalata russa*.

If you're eating in Milan and can't decide between a primo and a secondo, then ossobuco is the way to go, which is what I always order here. A huge portion of tender, slow-cooked meat, atop a bed of perfectly cooked *risotto alla milanese* and covered in a slightly sweet gremolata of slow-cooked onions and carrots.

The place is always crowded with local Milanesi, which is no wonder, since their tasting menu, which is four courses and costs 35 euros, is a great deal. And even though they are a relatively new place, they stick to the traditional weekly Milanese schedule by offering *bollito misto* (mixed boiled meats) on Tuesday; *busecca* (tripe) on Wednesday, *cassoeula* (Milanese version of cassoulet) on Thursday evening and Sunday lunch; and fried baccalà on Friday.

Testina

Via Abbadesse 19
Milano
+39.02.403.5907
Daily; lunch and dinner.

Vitello Milanese at Trattoria del Nuovo Macello

Even though this place is called "trattoria," and it's out along an empty street with a gas station for its nearest neighbor, don't let the looks deceive you. This is a restaurant with a capital *R*. While the interiors have remained comfortingly traditional—with a long steel-topped bar flanking the main room and original terrazzo floors—the menu is creative and sophisticated. And while I usually stick closely to the old-fashioned and traditional, I make an exception here for the Cotoletta del Nuovo Macello.

Many of their dishes are reinterpretations of Milanese classics, rethought and taken up a notch. The antipasti sound Old World—snails, nervetti, and anchovies with butter—but all are taken on a spin.

But what has brought them fame, and why most people go here, is their *Cotoletta del Nuovo Macello*. On the menu it comes with a bit of a warning: "thick-cut veal chop cooked rare and served, at our discretion, with or without a bone." Now, if you're used to ordering *vitello milanese* in Milan or anywhere else in the world for that matter, what you are expecting is a slice of veal, pounded thin, then breaded and fried. There is never a bone in sight and certainly no chance of being served even pink, much less rare.

But the version at Trattoria del Nuovo Macello is, like all they do, far from traditional. The chop comes to the table proudly bearing its bone, which rises vertically up from the slate platter. The cut is at least an inch and a half thick, breaded and fried to a crisp on the outside. The interior is indeed rare, and the entire thing is covered in a flurry of fleur de sel. It is as far from any cotoletta experience as you can get, but ever so much better. It is more like eating a veal chop, that had been pan-fried first. The interior is tender and flavorful, the outside crisp and salty, and the accompanying sauce, of carrots and cardamom, is the perfect slightly sweet balance.

Trattoria del Nuovo Macello

Via Cesare Lombroso 20
Milano
+39.02.5990.2122
Monday–Friday; lunch and dinner
Saturday; dinner only. Closed Sunday.

And Five Great Settings . . .

Risotto at Trattoria Temperanza da Abele

Milan does old-fashioned with style. While Trattoria Temperanza da Abele is not the only old-fashioned trattoria that pairs vintage interiors with traditional well-made food, it is certainly one of my favorites. Located a bit out of the center, the otherwise empty street is located in a decidedly residential neighborhood. In other words: far, far away from the circus around the Duomo.

Like most traditional trattorias in Milan, the main room is taken up on one side by a long, original counter. Glistening enamel green and stainless steel, the bar is stocked with liquor and wine, a gleaming espresso maker and is the command post for the friendly staff.

The three dining rooms are understated and almost anti-style, but in a good way. Dark green wainscoting provides coziness, as does the wooden furniture.

Another thing I love about Abele? The menu changes daily and is always posted on their website in Italian and in English. They always have 3 antipasti, 3 risotti, and usually 4 or 5 secondi to choose from, which always include one white meat, one red meat, one game, one fish, and one tripe or baccalà as well as a selection of two cooked vegetables and four salads. So, something for everyone.

Although almost every restaurant in Milan does risotto, and does it well, this is where I go for my fix. It's nothing fancy, but always intensely seasonal, working in whatever the chef has picked up at the market that day. My most recent springtime visit brought me *Risotto alla Borragine*. Made with wild borage, the risotto was bright green and speckled with garden fresh peas and asparagus, and was just cheesy enough to balance out the entire dish.

It's a bit of a taxi ride to get here, but it's easy to take the metro to the Pasteur stop, which is only two blocks away. And once you get there? It's probably a side of Milan you might never have seen. With food of course. And locals.

Trattoria Temperanza da Abele

Via Temperanza 5, Milano
(metro stop MM1 Pasteur)
+39.02.261.3855
Open Tuesday–Sunday; dinner only.
Call after 3:00 p.m. for reservations.

Latteria di San Marco

When you're in Milan you can't help but realize that this is a chic town. But the levels of chic can be deceptive. Of course there is the whole fashion thing, and even the taxi drivers have a certain sense of style that you would never see in Rome. But then there is another side to chic, one that's not so obvious and that lies just below the surface. Never flashy and almost always understated, it's a difficult one to pin down.

When I was in Milan recently talking to a transplanted Florentine he was trying to explain this concept to me, in terms that I could understand: restaurants. "You've got restaurants like Cracco and Breton," he said, citing Michelin-starred places that garner a lot of attention. "But those aren't the truly chic places. The chic places are the ones you'd never suspect. Like the Latteria."

I've known the Latteria for years, just like everyone else. The owners, Arturo and Maria, have been cooking up the same hearty, dignified simple food for the last few decades. The interiors couldn't be simpler, nor the food. And that, evidently, is where the chic factor lies. "You've got to be pretty sure of yourself, and make a conscience decision, to decide that this is the type of place you want to be. It's the complete lack of pretension that defines this kind of chic."

Well, the Latteria couldn't be simpler. And that is, in fact, what has always appealed to me. Recently I realized I hadn't been for a while and so wanted to stop by to take a few photographs for my app. It was 11:30 in the morning, and I wasn't even sure they'd be open. But when I pushed open the door and peered through the empty front room, I could see Arturo manning the pots in the back kitchen.

I had actually interrupted his lunch, but not only did he encourage me to take as many photos as I wanted to, he insisted I sit down with him for a bowl of minestrone. So we sat, and chatted (mostly about alchemy, which is his passion but also about his lack of interest in dining out anywhere else in Milan) over bowls of steaming soup. "It's a kind of ribollita" he explained, crumbling bits of bread directly into the broth.

Eventually a few more people stopped by, an antique book dealer and the post man. No one came to eat, just to sit, chat, and hang out.

If this is Milanese chic, then I'm all for it.

The menu changes every day, depending on what Arturo finds in the market and

what he feels like cooking. They don't take reservations, and you are expected to take your leave once you finish eating, to make room for the next person. Everything is cooked in silver pots and pans, which is one of Arturo's inventions (remember the whole alchemy thing?). And the prices, for the simple food, are on the high side. But this is a historic piece of Milan, and like stepping back in a bygone era. Kind of priceless.

Latteria di San Marco

Via San Marco 24, Milano
+39.02.659.7653
Monday–Friday; lunch and dinner.
Closed Saturday and Sunday.

Erba Brusca

Erba Brusca is about as far away—both literally and figuratively—from the hubbub of central Milan as you can get. It is located south of the Navigli area, just outside the city limits.

If you feel you need a day in the country, but don't really want to leave Milan, then this is the answer. Erba Brusca opened about seven years ago, and bills itself as *"orto + cucina"*: vegetable garden + kitchen. And, in fact, the real pleasure is the possibility of dining in the midst of a cabbage patch. The two-story building is located along the Alzaia Naviglio Pavese (a canal) and, once through the book-lined front

room (which must be very cozy all winter long), the building opens out onto a covered pergola, which gives way to a riotous garden full of herbs, flowers, birds, and vegetables.

The menu, overseen by Alice Delcourt, is rigorously seasonal, and the tastes and colors are directly influenced by the herbs and tones directly outside her kitchen window. My most recent meal was tinged pinkish purple, in the garden and on the plate. I started with a beet risotto, its bright color, flecked with parsley, chives, and coriander from the garden, and offset by a swirl of tangy yogurt. Even our chicken liver crostini were topped with a riot of purple cabbage salad.

If you feel you don't quite want to leave this paradise, don't worry. There are a few sling chairs set among the radishes and carrots in the garden, for a post-prandial nap before you head back into town.

Erba Brusca

Alzaia Naviglio Pavese 286
Milano
+39.02.8738.0711
Wednesday–Sunday; lunch and dinner.
Closed Monday and Tuesday.

Galli

It's somehow very comforting to think there are still places where ladies in white caps sit at tables hand-dipping and

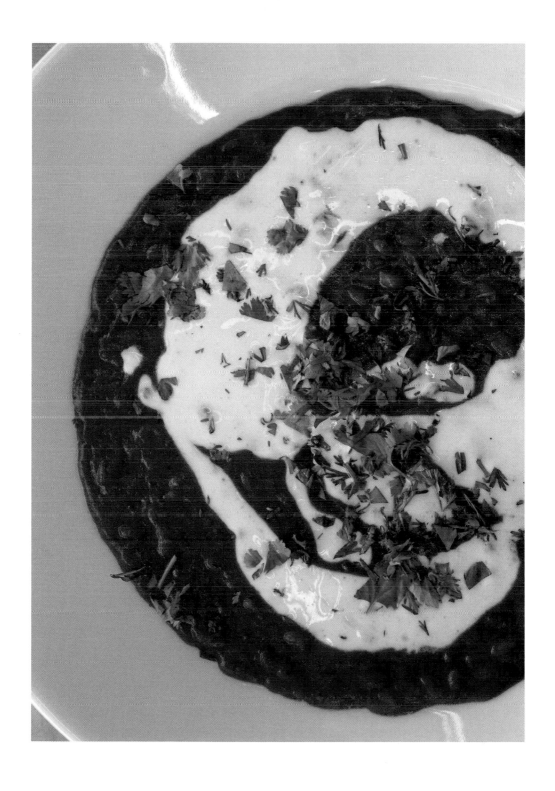

wrapping chocolates and that there are still stores where you know you will always be able to find candied violets.

When I want to pick up a bag full of candied violets or rose petals, I head for Galli. In business since 1911, they are still producing confections (because there is no other words that better describe these delicacies) that shine, glisten, and make you think a horse and carriage should be waiting outside to take you home.

While I indulge in seasonal treats like candied chestnuts in the winter, there is one thing I can count on year-long: the beautiful, jewel-hued fruit gelées. Coated in sparkling sugar, the chewy, sweet/sour candies come in all the colors of the rainbow. My favorite are the bright orange mandarin. I get an old-fashioned paper bag full of them, and gobble them up all by myself.

Galli

Via Victor Hugo 2, Milano
+39.02.864.64833
Monday–Saturday: 8:30 a.m.–8:00 p.m.;
Sunday: 9:00 a.m.–1:00 p.m.

Marchesi

Thank god some things never change. Actually, in the case of Pasticceria Marchesi, a pastry shop founded in 1824, you can thank Miuccia Prada. In the face of a changing landscape in Milan, Prada recently bought one of the city's treasures to help preserve this slice of Milanese history.

The small corner store retains all of its original Old World charm. The original windows display cakes and pastries, while the interior is divided into two spaces. Join Milanese for a standing breakfast at the bar. Grab your pastry from the small case near the cash register, and order yourself a perfect cappuccino or espresso.

A squadron of ladies dressed in pale green dress coats keep the cases at the other end of the shop filled with pastries, chocolates, and their famous panettone.

Marchesi

Via Santa Maria alla Porta 11, Milano
+39.02.862.770
Tuesday–Saturday: 7:30 a.m.–8:00 p.m.;
Sunday: 8:30 a.m.–1:00 p.m.
Closed Monday.

Rules for Eating in Milan

- **Transportation:** Milan is a big city. It is spread out over a large area and there is not one neighborhood that is the "center" like Rome or Florence. But public transportation is excellent (buses, trams, and the metro) so don't be put off by heading far for a meal. It will lead you to neighborhoods you might not otherwise explore.

- **Style:** Milanese are stylish. There is no way around this. If you want to fit in, leave your shorts and flip-flops at home.

- **Aperitivi:** The Milanese have perfected the art of the *aperitivo*. Although I don't list any places here, there are many on my blog and app. It's the best place to hang out over a Negroni or Spritz, and many of the bars offer excellent buffets that turn happy hour into dinner.

- **Authentic:** One of my favorite parts about dining in Milan is that it's so easy to get away from the touristy places. There just aren't that many tourists! And once you get away from the Duomo area, you'll find that almost all your fellow diners will be either Milanese, or other Italians in town for business.

Artichoke Salad

Serves 1

Although I often make artichoke salad at home, the salad prepared table-side at Alla Collina Pistoiese in Milan is different from any I've ever had. Restaurants hesitate to serve this dish because the artichokes will oxidize so quickly, turning dark and looking unappetizing. I solve this problem at home by using lots of lemon juice. But the problem with that is that the lemon juice hides the delicate taste of fresh, raw artichokes. In Milan, they solved the problem by eliminating the need for lemon by getting the freshly sliced artichoke to the table minutes after it had been prepared. The lack of acidity means the flavor of the artichokes is bright and clear, and is enhanced by the buttery addition of Gruyère and Parmigiano Reggiano.

1 fresh artichoke

2 tablespoons grated Gruyère cheese

2 tablespoons of grated Parmigiano Reggiano

⅓ cup thinly sliced celery heart

Salt

Extra-virgin olive oil

Shaved Parmigiano Reggiano, for garnish

Freshly ground black pepper, for finishing

Trim the artichoke by removing all the outer tough leaves and trimming away any dark green from the bottom and stem. Cut the artichoke in half, lengthwise, and remove the choke with the tip of a knife. Slice the two halves, lengthwise, as thinly as possible.

Place the two cheeses in the middle of a plate.

Place the celery and artichokes on top

of that. Add salt to taste, a healthy pour of olive oil, and toss gently to mix.

Top with freshly cut shavings of Parmigiano Reggiano and freshly ground black pepper and serve immediately.

Asparagus Bismark

Serves 1

I'm not really sure where the name of this dish, which pairs eggs and asparagus, comes from. But it is one of my favorite things to order in old-fashioned restaurants all over Italy. Each one has its own special spin, but this recipe is actually my own. Rather than steam the asparagus, as is traditional, I prefer to roast mine. And also, I use a little trick of adding grated Parmigiano to the bottom of the frying pan before I fry the eggs, which results in an extra-crispy cheesy bottom.

8 asparagus stalks

Olive oil

Salt

3 tablespoons unsalted butter

½ cup grated Parmigiano Reggiano, plus more for serving

2 large eggs

Freshly ground black pepper

Preheat the oven to 350°F (180°C).

Trim the asparagus and place on a baking sheet. Drizzle with olive oil and toss with your hands to make sure they are coated. Sprinkle with salt and place in the preheated oven. Roast until tender and the tips start to brown, 15 to 20 minutes. Remove from oven, but leave on the warm baking sheet while you prepare the eggs.

Melt the butter in a small frying pan over medium heat. When the butter has melted, add the grated cheese, making sure it covers the bottom of the pan. Immediately crack two eggs into the pan. Season the eggs with salt and pepper and cook until the whites are set but the yolk is still runny. The cheese on the bottom should begin to brown around the edges.

Place the asparagus on a plate and, using a spatula, gently place the eggs on top. Sprinkle with additional grated cheese and enjoy with a piece of crusty bread.

CHAPTER SIX

A Crash Course in Parmigiano Reggiano

If there is one Italian ingredient that people outside of Italy take for granted it is Parmigiano. Although, of course, by calling it Parmigiano I'm already lending grandeur and importance to something that many people mistakenly refer to as parmesan cheese.

Do we have to have the whole green can full of sawdust discussion? Yes, I'm talking about the pregrated stuff that you grew up with, which, as it turns out, is way worse than we ever thought it was. Did you follow the whole "wood pulp as fillers" thing that was discovered in 2012? Cellulose, was used as an anti-clumping agent. After an investigation it was found that less than 40 percent of the product was actually cheese, and of that 40 percent not any of it was actually Parmigiano. Many were a mixture of other cheeses— Swiss and cheddar—as well as a soupçon of cellulose. Even though, of course, they were labeled "100 percent Grated Parmesan." That is at the far and scary end of the parmesan spectrum, but even some of the more popular brands that actually contained real Parmigiano, that I won't name here, contained up to 8 percent cellulose.

Gross, right?

But this is a story about the wonders of true Parmigiano, and less about the perils of processed food. It's often difficult to know what's going on with your food unless you are willing to bring along a microscope and take samples to a lab, which kind of takes the fun out of things.

It's much easier to just step back and look at the bigger picture, which of course starts out with cows and milk. That is what I did recently during my crash course in Parmigiano Reggiano.

Parmigiano Reggiano: The Real Thing

Parmigiano Reggiano was not always the big wheel of yellow cheese that we know today. There were many dairy farmers making a local cheese from cow milk, but each had a slightly different method. It wasn't until relatively recently, in 1934, that the Consorzio del Parmigiano Reggiano was formed. And so the fight to claim the name Parmigiano and differentiate it from parmesan or any other imitator was on. The struggle dates to World War II when there was a U.S. embargo against the importation of Italian products (that whole Mussolini thing). Seeking to fill the grated cheese gap, producers in the States invented their own version, naming it parmesan. Enter the bright green can.

Italian cheese makers realized that their best bet for protecting themselves—and their cheese—was in numbers. And so they banded together to form the Consorzio del Parmigiano Reggiano. The Consorzio, or Consortium, sought to define the characteristics that made their cheese special, and establish minimum requirements that assured a high standard of quality. In other words, they branded.

What is amazing about the Consorzio is that it has allowed cheese production to go on at a very small and artisanal level. The Consorzio is made up of about 340 dairies located in the regions of Parma, Modena, Reggio Emilia, Mantova, and Bologna. Each of these dairies produces a very small number of wheels per day—an average of 8 or 10 wheels. So rather than codifying the process so that big industry could step in to increase production, they went in a completely different direction. The Consorzio instilled rules that made it almost impossible to ramp up to an industrial level, and so made sure that the time-honored ways of doing things were preserved in the name of quality.

Rules for Real Parmigiano Reggiano

- The milk must come from the region defined by the Consorzio.

- The milk is not pasteurized.

- No additives are allowed.

- The cheese must be made in specific copper kettles.

- Each and every single cheese must be checked by the Consorzio before receiving approval and the firebrand which marks each cheese.

Diving Deep into Parmigiano Reggiano

Most of what I've written so far is something I've known for at least the last twenty years. Although it may be new to you, it's just part of the background knowledge of information that has accumulated in my head over the last two decades—which might lead you to believe that I'm some sort of Parmigiano expert. Frankly, even I thought I was pretty well informed. But during a recent five-day trip to Emilia-Romagna I realized that I knew nothing. Well, not nothing, but a lot less than I thought.

First of all I have to admit something that is shameful but true. I had never ac-

tually visited a *caseificio* (dairy) to see how Parmigiano was made. So there was that.

Also? Like most other people—even those who already searched out true Parmigiano Reggiano—I pretty much judged what I bought, ate, and cooked with by its age. Going anywhere from 12 months to 24, or even 48, months old, the age was reflected in both the price and the taste. But beyond those labels of age and the distinctive branding on the side of the wheel that covered the "what" and the "where" of the process, I had pretty much ignored the "who" side of things. As it turns out, I wasn't the only one.

If you remember from a few paragraphs ago, I mentioned that the Consorzio established some ground rules for Parmigiano Reggiano production. But ground rules are called that for a reason. They are near to the ground. In other words, while establishing the minimum that was required to be labeled Parmigiano Reggiano (and actually, those rules are very strict) there was no way to distinguish individual producers who not only adhered to these requirements, but went above and beyond. And even among those who were making their cheese in exactly the same way, there was no real recognition that, among the finished wheels, there were huge differences in taste, texture, and aroma.

Now, if you're really into cheese and used to going into almost any store and seeing at least six different kinds of pecorino, or twelve kinds of goat cheese, from various

locations, each with its own flavor profile, this may seem odd. But next to those various *pecorini*, you'll be lucky to see, at the most, three kinds of Parmigiano Reggiano. And the only difference on the label will be the age, and usually no comment of the dairy, or the cows, or the location.

I was in Reggio Emilia purely because my friend Ari was frustrated with this state of things. While he had numerous types of almost every other cheese he carried in his deli Zingerman's, in Ann Arbor, the fact that they could never get a handle on specific producers of Parmigiano Reggiano was driving him crazy. Luckily he can be a very persuasive person, and so after numerous conversations with the Consorzio, he persuaded them to help him discover and promote the differences between various producers, rather than just focus on what unites them.

A couple of things I learned during our time with the Consorzio:

- Eighty percent of Parmigiano Reggiano is sold to stores through intermediary dealers. This means the stores are never aware of who is producing the cheese.

- Since the dairies are selling through a middleman, who must make a profit, there is no incentive to increase quality. As long as minimum quality control is met, then that's fine. There is actually a reason for this. The Consorzio is supported by the producers. Each cheese maker contributes 6 euros per wheel to the Consorzio. And since all are created and represented equally, the thinking was that no one producer could be singled out and promoted by the Consorzio. And, at the same time, since Parmigiano Reggiano was being represented by the Consorzio to the world, individual producers never saw the need to promote their individual cheeses.

The event that really shook up the Parmigiano world was (no pun intended) the earthquake of 2012. Remember when you saw those stacks and stacks of wheels lying broken on the floor in huge piles? The outpouring of support for the producers inspired people to contact the dairies directly, to buy some of the broken cheese from them, bypassing the usual middlemen.

And guess what? They discovered that some of the cheeses they were buying directly—even though in theory it carried the same label as what they were buying in the supermarkets—were infinitely better, and that there were real and tangible differences from producer to producer.

This also had the effect on the producers themselves who realized that they could sell directly to the public, without going through the big distributors.

At first the Consorzio was wary. Since it's made up of mostly older members, they were against change of any kind. Their thinking was "Things may not get better, but at least they won't get worse."

But there are important signs of change. One of these was the publication of a first-of-its-kind book, *Guida al Parmigiano Reggiano*, by Slow Food in 2016. This is the first book that actually reviewed 132 blind samples of Parmigiano Reggiano. Not only did they publish their tasting notes, but they provided the background story behind the dairies, including the types of cow, types of feed, and production level. This was huge.

At the beginning, some of the producers didn't really understand or want to be part of the process. Since they had to submit their wheels of cheese for free, some of them actually sent in their worst cheese. (true). But the upshot is that now all of the producers want to be part of this project, not only to distinguish themselves from the rest, but, hopefully, to make it onto the list.

How Parmigiano Reggiano Is Made

Parmigiano Reggiano is made in the time-honored way from cow milk. Ninety-eight percent of the cows are Holstein-Friesian, a breed known for its huge production levels. But a small number of producers use heritage breeds, including brown cows (*sola bruna*), red cows (*reggiana*), and a very rare white cow.

Regardless of the type of cow, each one is milked twice a day, and the milk from the cows is delivered to the caseificio after each milking. The evening milk is delivered to the caseificio immediately, with no pasteurization, and is then left to sit, overnight. The following morning, the evening milk is skimmed of the cream, which has risen to the top. The skimmed milk is then added to the product of the morning's milking, which is whole (not skim) and is also not pasteurized. It is this mixture of both milkings (one skim and one whole) that then makes its way to becoming Parmigiano Reggiano.

Each caseificio has anywhere from one to fourteen copper kettles, each of which holds about 1,100 liters of milk. The number of kettles is limited to the number of master cheese makers on hand. According to the strict rules of the Consorzio, each *casaro* (master cheese maker) can oversee a maximum of seven kettles. So the bigger caseifici tend to have at the maximum of fourteen kettles, with two master cheese makers overseeing production.

Observing the process is incredibly exciting to watch. Each of the massive kettles is sunk into the floor, where it is heated from below by gas-fed steam heat. The milk mixture is then warmed up in each kettle and the starter, which is made from the previous day's whey, is added, along with natural rennet.

After about 10 minutes the milk has transformed into a beautifully silky mas-

sive curd. The cheese maker then takes a large wire tool and begins to break up the curd, to begin the separation of what will become cheese from the whey. A machine then takes over, to continue this process for a little while longer, over heat, to break up the curd even further. When the curd reaches a precise acidity level, it is allowed to fall to the bottom of the cone-shaped kettle where it forms a solid mass. This stage is critical and only the casaro can make the decision to proceed to the next step. He goes from kettle to kettle, reaching in and pulling off a piece of curd. He looks at it, pushes it with his fingers, squeezes it in his palm, and once he thinks it's ready, then the wheels can be made.

And now comes the dance. Taking a pair of wooden dowels, the casaro attaches a piece of cheesecloth. He then reaches down into the very bottom of the kettle and begins to pull up the massive curd from the depths. As it emerges from the cloudy whey, it is wet and shiny and looks like a giant mozzarella. He then balances the dowels on the edge of the kettle to allow the curd to drain a bit more, while he goes on to the next kettle.

Once the curd has reached the appropriate firmness, after about 10 minutes, the casaro now must make the cut to divide the big curd in two. Using a long knife he carefully levels the curd and then cuts it decisively down the middle. Each newly formed curd is then caught in its own cheesecloth, and the casaro gently rolls it back and forth, and finally you can begin to see the shape the final wheel will take.

Now that the cheese has been formed, the curing and aging begins. The first step is to put each curd into a straight-edged form, lined with cheesecloth. They are carefully attended to for the rest of the day: clothes are changed, and the cheese is flipped as more and more whey leaches out. Finally, in the evening, the cheesecloth is removed and is replaced with a plastic stencil bearing the well-known pin-dotted imprint of Parmigiano Reggiano. This plastic stamp marks the still soft cheese not only with the brand but also with the date and place of where and when it was made.

After a few days continuing to drain, the wheels are taken out of the forms and placed in a salted brine bath. The wheels float around in this salty bath for another 24 to 28 days, with the salt leaching out more moisture from the cheese, while at the same time entering the cheese itself providing flavor.

Once out of their bath, the cheeses are moved to storage rooms where the salt continues on its journey to the heart of the cheese, helping to form the crystalline structure.

Finally, it is time for aging. Walking into an aging room filled with wheels of Parmigiano Reggiano is an experience like no other. The wheels are stacked on pine shelves in enormous warehouses where the shelves can go up 30 feet. Thousands of wheels, as far as you can see. How long the cheeses stay here, going through seasonal changes in temperature, can last anywhere from 12 to 24 months, although special wheels are often aged for even longer. The majority though, come to market at 18 months.

But before they get anywhere near a store, they must be inspected by the cheese inspector. The consorzio sends its inspector (who must have no personal ties to any cheese-making family) to check on the wheels when they reach the 12-month date. Each wheel is taken off the shelf and placed on a special stool. Using a small wooden hammer, the inspector gently taps the cheese around the circumference as well as on the top and bottom. He holds his ear nearby, listening for telltale sounds of hollowness or air bubbles, which would disqualify the cheese from being sold as Parmigiano Reggiano. If this happens (and it is a costly occurrence if it does) the tattoo of pin dots imbedded on the side are scraped off. The cheese is still edible, and can be sold as generic grating cheese, but it can no longer be sold as Parmigiano Reggiano, and cannot be exported as such. But if the cheese passes inspection? It receives one more branding: the Consorzio's certification.

Parmigiano Reggiano: The Rules for Buying the Real Thing

- Never buy anything that is labeled "Parmesan."

- Never buy anything pregrated, even if it is called Parmigiano.

- Try, if possible, to buy a piece cut freshly from a wheel.

- Look for the branding on the rind. If there's no rind, then chances are it's not the real thing.

Grana Padano

A lot of people think that Grana Padano is the cheaper version of Parmigiano Reggiano. A lot of people are wrong. Although Grana (as most people in Italy refer to it) is similar in many ways to Parmigiano Reggiano, there are a few very big differences. Although both cow milk cheese are processed in the same way that results in a granular type of cheese, the ingredients and location are the main differences and naturally affect the final product in terms of both taste and texture. Like anything cheese related, the story begins with cows. Cows producing milk destined for Grana are allowed to eat silage, which can result in the milk being contaminated with spores that aren't supposed to be there. This means that preservatives need to be added, which affect the final taste of the cheese. That said, there is a *Consorzio for Grana Padana DOP*, which guarantees a high standard. And while many people throughout Italy buy Grana Padano as the cheaper alternative to Parmigiano Reggiano, no one in the areas where this cheese originated would ever think of substituting one for the other.

Grana does have its uses and is one of the most popular cheeses used in Italy. And the Grana Padano folks are especially prickly when anyone compares the two, to the detriment of Grana. In fact, a few years ago, when a popular soap opera character read the lines "Crap! I bought Grana instead of Parmigiana Reggiano!" they were sued by the Consorzio di Grana. So let me be very clear: Different, but equal, cheeses.

How to Eat Parmigiano Reggiano

- Make sure it is at room temperature.

- Make sure you grate it as you need it.

- Break it, don't cut it.

One of my favorite ways to enjoy a truly great Parmigiano Reggiano is to nibble on chunks. It's also one of my favorite things to serve with drinks. Here in Italy a sure

sign of a luxurious cocktail party is a half-wheel of Parmigiano Reggiano hollowed out, and refilled with chunks of the cheese.

But there are chunks, and there are chunks. One of the distinctive character istics of Parmigiano Reggiano is its crystalline formation. And this nubbly, bumpy texture is what you want to preserve when you cut the cheese for eating. If you've never seen an entire wheel of Parmigiano being opened, it's well worth looking up on YouTube.

In the meantime, when dealing with your own manageable hunk-o-cheese, here is the drill:

- If you are going to be cutting a lot of Parmigiano in your life, it's worth investing in a Parmigiano knife. The double-edged, short, dull blade is heart-shaped and comes to a stubby point. You grab the knife by the wooden handle then insert the stubby blade into the cheese about an inch or more from the edge. When the blade is about a ½ inch into the cheese, pull the blade toward you, breaking off the piece of cheese sort of like a piece of ice falls off a glacier. You should end up with a very irregular chunk of cheese, with bumpy, rough sides that perfectly show the crystalline formation of the cheese. What you want to avoid is straight, smooth cuts. You are not looking for cubes here, but misshapen chunks.

- While you can certainly eat them as is, a truly decadent treat is to drizzle them with aged Aceto Balsamico Tradizionale or else a drizzle of a full-flavored honey and some nuts.

- **Fun fact:** If you do go to all the trouble of searching out and buying a chunk of Parmigiano Reggiano, you want to enjoy every last bit. Including the rind. While it might be hard to eat, it is not only edible but full of flavor. Keep those rinds and use them the next time you make minestrone or broth. Just throw them in, and they will mostly dissolve, adding a ton of flavor.

- One of the revelations I had this past year, during which I had the chance to spend several weeks in Emilia-Romagna, was the way people cooked with Parmigiano Reggiano. I had the great opportunity to spend time in kitchens with women who use the cheese so often in their cooking that they each owned their own electric cheese grater. But when it came to add the cheese to any dish, they would first specify the exact age of the cheese needed (and sometimes it would be a combination of two different aged cheeses) because, depending on the age, it would react differently to different cooking methods. Some melt more easily, some emulsify, etc. And then, before deciding the quantities, they would have a taste of the Parmigiano on hand. "You have to taste it first, otherwise how will you know how much you need?"

RECIPES

Frico

Makes about 38 fricos

Although this recipe originates in Friuli, using Montasio cheese, I often make it with Parmigiano Reggiano. And while most recipes suggest using a frying pan, I am lazy at heart and since I'm usually serving these to a crowd, I find the oven is the way to go.

3 cups grated Parmigiano Reggiano
1 tablespoon flour

Preheat the oven to 350°F (180°C).
   Line two baking sheets with parchment paper.
   Mix the grated cheese with the flour.
   Using a tablespoon, place spoonfuls of the mixture onto the parchment paper, spacing them 3 or 4 inches apart. Using the back of your spoon, flatten out the mounds.
   Place one sheet in the oven for 4 to

5 minutes. Keep a close watch, since you want them to melt, start to bubble, but definitely not turn brown.

Remove the baking sheet from the oven, and slip the next one in; this speeds things up.

Let the frico cool a few minutes, then, using a spatula, gently take them off the sheet and transfer to a rack to cool off completely. Once completely cool they will become crisp.

Note: I often add either a teaspoon of cracked black pepper or red pepper flakes to the cheese mix.

Sformato di Parmigiano with Caramelized Pears

Serves 6

This recipe comes from my friends at La Vecchia Dispensa Aceto Balsamico. As Roberta says, "It's a way to highlight two of the best ingredients from our region." I love it since it's easy to make for a dinner party while being elegant and very impressive.

Roberta was very insistent about using 30-month-old Parmigiano Reggiano. And in fact, all the cooks I spoke to were always very specific in the age of the cheese, rather than who it came from. This has to do with the physical changes the cheese goes through as it ages that make it adapt to different types of cooking techniques. Older is not always better. In the case of this Sformato, 30-month-old Parmigiano Reggiano is key for achieving a smooth emulsion.

This recipe uses two different kinds of Aceto Balsamico. Aceto Balsamico di Modena—the less expensive kind—is used to caramelize the pears. Aceto Balsamico Tradizionale di Modena—the expensive kind—is used to drizzle over the finished dish.

1 cup (300 ml) heavy cream

3½ ounces (100 grams) 30-month-old Parmigiano Reggiano

4 large eggs

1 ripe, but firm, pear

2 tablespoons granulated sugar

2 tablespoons of Aceto Balsamico di Modena, plus more for drizzling

Six ½-cup molds or one 6-cup muffin tin, buttered

Preheat the oven to 320°F (160°C).

Put the heavy cream, Parmigiano Reggiano, and eggs in a large bowl. Using a hand mixer, beat together until smooth.

Divide the mixture among the buttered molds and place them in a large roasting pan, filling it halfway up with boiling water.

Place the pan in the oven and bake for 40 minutes.

After 40 minutes, turn off heat, open the oven door, and let the flans rest for another 10 minutes.

While the flans are cooling, caramelize the pear: Slice the pear thinly. You can leave on the skin if you'd like, since it helps keep the slices whole.

Heat a nonstick frying pan over medium-high heat. Add 2 tablespoons of water and add the pears. As soon as they begin to brown, sprinkle them with the sugar, turn them over, and cook them on the opposite side.

Reduce the heat to medium. Drizzle with 2 tablespoons of the Aceto Balsamico di Modena and, keeping over the heat, let it evaporate.

Invert the flans onto individual serving plates. (You may need to run a knife around the rim of each mold.) Arrange a few slices of pear next to each flan. At the last minute, drizzle each flan with Aceto Balsamic Tradizionale.

Visiting a Parmigiano Reggiano Dairy

Visiting a dairy where Parmigiano Reggiano is made is an eye-opening experience. There are many tour operators who organize visits in the various areas where the cheese is produced. If you want to go on your own, the Consorzio has a very useful website listing the dairies and their contacts: www.parmigianoreggiano.com/where/guided_tours_dairies_1/.

CHAPTER SEVEN

A Sense of Place and a Bowl of Farinata

The Soul of Florence

If you've been to Italy, then there is a good chance you've been to Florence. You may have even been there more than once. But even if you think you "know" this ancient city, and have "done" it, chances are you have rarely ventured out of the picture-perfect postcard that is bordered by the Duomo and the Accademia at one end and the Ponte Vecchio at the other. Am I right?

And if you do "know" Florence, then you "know" it is just about as full of tourists as things get. Which is why, these days, I have a complicated relationship with the city. I love Florence with all my heart, but I also have a way of approaching it that is a bit different from everyone else's. And of course, this has to do with food.

I moved to Florence as a graduate student in 1988. And I'll say, right up front, Florence was not my first choice. Ever since I had lived in Rome as a child in the 1970s, I had been trying to figure out a way to get back there. An Italian dissertation subject seemed like a good plan. And it almost worked. I envisioned a topic that would take me back to the ancient city. But then I fell in love with the art of sixteenth-century grotto design (I know, it seems an odd object of desire) and so my academic path led me straight to the Medici archives in Florence, and two years dividing my time between the dusty volumes in the basement of the Uffizi and my darling frescoed apartment near the Bargello museum.

There I learned to translate sixteenth-century terms for building materials into English, gathering information that would lead to my dissertation. Although I eventually abandoned my career as an academic in favor of writing magazine articles and books, for the first fifteen years or so I kept my professional focus on architecture and design. Which helps explain why there are some words that, in the course of my professional career, I've learned directly in Italian.

When I was writing mostly about design and architecture words like *grondaia*, *altana*, and *davanzali* (gutter, balcony, and windowsill) often came easier in Italian than they did in English. As my focus shifted almost completely to food, there continue to be certain edible phrases that spring to mind first in Italian, then in English. Yes, I've become one of those annoying ex-pats who pepper their English conversations with words like *carciofi* and *lievito naturale* rather than just bending my brain to say artichoke and yeast.

But there are certain Italian phrases that I would never, ever think of using in English. Phrases that for me are so weighted in my Italian mentality that they just don't occur to me to even think of them if I am speaking or writing in English. For instance *colpo di freddo*, or "hit of cold" that is the bane of every Italian's (including my own daughter's) existence. It's what happens when you get hit by a cold draft. Evidently you run the risk of dying. It's a completely Italian thing, and so really doesn't translate. These phrases go beyond simple translation. Especially when it comes to food and culture.

I was thinking about all this recently when an Italian friend used the phrase *buon rapporto qualità prezzo*: "Good value for your money." I know there are probably some people who use this phrase in English to refer to restaurants. Not me. "Good value for your money," when used in English with reference to a dining experience makes me think of all-you-can-eat breadsticks at Olive Garden.

In other words, the phrase, in English, in my mind, has more to do with quantity than quality. In my Italian friends' minds I believe 100 percent that quality is just as, or more important than quantity.

Anyway, this complicated story was meant to say that I was thinking about all these issues—quality, quantity, and price—when I began thinking of this chapter on Florence. And I have to admit that I don't use the phrase, in either language really, when describing a restaurant. In fact, although I know full well that some restaurants are expensive and others less so, it's not ever the first thing I think of. Because for me there is another element that has a complicated relationship with both price and value and quantity and quality that is usually the defining element of whether I fall in love with a place or not.

For instance, I recently went to a Michelin-starred restaurant in Torino. The 90-euro, six-course tasting menu can probably be defined as extremely good *rapporto qualità prezzo*. But, I did not fall in love with the place, despite the Ginori china, the fresh flowers, and (I have to admit) the huge quantity of good food for that price.

It made me realize that the transformative experiences for me in restaurants these days have as much to do with culture and people and an undefinable element that makes me feel like I'm part of something bigger than just sitting down for a meal. Yes, there is certainly food involved, and it has to be good food. But there is also so much going on that has to do with people, places, and things that add to my element of not only contentment and satisfaction but also a kind of complete bliss that makes me feel that all is right with the world.

I did not have this kind of moment at the Michelin-starred restaurant. Not by a long shot.

I do, however, have it at several quite ordinary, working-class restaurants on the outskirts of Florence.

Sabatino

Sabatino had been on my radar a long time before I actually made it there. Since it's located just outside the gate of San Frediano—and so at least a 20-minute walk from wherever I usually am—my laziness almost always won out. Also? Whenever I had phoned, they always said I didn't need a reservation, and that I should just show up. That kind of thing always makes me nervous.

One of the reasons I'd always wanted to go there is because it is my friend Judy's husband's favorite place. Andrea grew up in the San Frediano neighborhood, and it was just "where he went," which sounded like the kind of local place I usually love. And while Andrea never specifically talked about the food, it was the "idea" of the place that stuck in my head.

When I finally went, several years ago, I decided to arrive early, to calm my "no reservations" worries. Since they open early for lunch, I figured I would get there as close to noon as possible to assure myself getting a table. It was a completely glorious day in Florence. Bright blue skies and a

crisp, cold wind as I walked over the Ponte Santa Trinita and down Borgo San Frediano. Once I was through the massive medieval Gate of San Frediano, and onto the Via Pisana I had a hard time actually finding the place. Tucked into the corner where two nondescript buildings came together at right angles, I finally spotted two men heading into a doorway—with dogs. And in fact, the almost nonexistent sign read "Trattoria Sabatino."

Once in, I felt that I was in some sort of *circolo*, or private club. The big open space was full of tables for eight, lined up against the walls, cafeteria-style. When I told the woman, who finally noticed me standing there that I was dining alone, she led me to a plastic-covered table where two other women were already seated.

Just so you know, I eat in restaurants alone a lot. I don't mind it at all, and usually actually love the quiet time. I eat my food, people-watch, and am pretty content with my own company. I never, and I mean never, strike up a conversation with strangers.

But I didn't actually feel as if I was in a restaurant. As I said, it felt more like a private club, or home even. And not talking to my table mates seemed not only rude, but impossible. I soon learned that they were mother and daughter, and that the daughter stopped by every day to pick up her mother, and her dogs, to take them all for a walk, stopping by Sabatino to eat lunch. My first question, of course, was about the dogs. I

asked if she had photos. At which point she just lifted the edge of the red-checkered tablecloth and there they all were. Behaving perfectly. As if they came here all the time—which they did.

As I looked around, I realized that the dogs weren't the only regular customers. Except for one table of French tourists, everyone else looked like they had been coming here almost every day, all of their lives, to have lunch, catch up with their friends, and then head on their way. Some had their dogs. Some were with elderly parents. Some, like my table mates, had both.

At that point Andrea, who had first told me about Sabatino, walked in. He looked at what I had ordered—a plate full of stewed leeks and another full of greens and squid—and somehow felt he had to justify his attachment to this place to me. "The food is OK," he said. "But I come here mostly for the conversation."

And as he continued on to his table to meet some childhood friends of his, I continued digging into my very good food but also chatting with my new friends and their incredibly cute dogs. For me, getting a chance to meet new people, hear about their lives, share my own stories—all while eating bowls of warming, hearty well-made food—with dogs to boot? How do you figure that into some sort of formula of *rapporto qualità prezzo*? For me, in this ever-changing world and even more rapidly changing Italy, this kind of experience, which has everything to do with gathering around a table over traditional food is, in fact, priceless.

But just in case you are interested in the prices? They are some of the lowest I've seen in Florence. Pastas cost 4,20 and my plateful of *seppie in zimino,* cuttlefish and greens, was 6,20. The leeks, stewed slowly in olive oil with a bit of tomato cost 2,70.

So yes. There is, in fact, a *"buon rapporto qualità prezzo."* But, as Andrea pointed out to me, it's not about the food.

Da Burde

I first visited Da Burde about fifteen years ago while I was working on a photo shoot in Florence, for a magazine article. It was in the heyday of magazine life. Back then publishers actually paid a writer to wander around a city with not only a photographer but also an assistant and stylist. And a car and driver.

When it came time for lunch I, of course, had my short list of where I thought we should go (I am bossy that way). But the driver insisted he knew better. And, in my experience, drivers do almost always know best.

So we headed out the Via Pistoiese in our shiny black Mercedes. Leaving ancient Florence behind, we drove past all those modern apartment buildings that ring the outside of old Florence. But every so often there was the odd *villetta*: small, elegant two-story, turn-of-the-century villas that spoke of another time when this road, leading to Pistoia, was practically in the countryside and the places along the road were actually prime pieces of property.

Da Burde is located right on this busy road, and has been in its current location since 1927, after having moved from a previous location down the road where they had a deli and simple trattoria since 1907.

I have to admit right here that I had a soft spot for this restaurant before even putting anything in my mouth. The front of Da Burde is still a store and bar, and sells everything from pecorino and prosciutto to cigarettes and coffee. The backroom, where the real eating goes on, seems frozen in time, remaining simple, with no halogen lighting or designer furniture to distract from the food. The only clue that something is up is the appearance of rather sophisticated wine goblets at every table. And, in fact, as I learned, while all appears to have been stopped in time, the Gori family—and especially Andrea Gori—have upped the ante quite a bit from the original humble origins, but not in any flashy way. Instead the restaurant has one of the best and most interesting wine lists in town while the dishes on the menu remain 100 percent rooted in tradition.

Since that first fateful trip over fifteen years ago, I've been back many times. Whenever Domenico and I are in Florence, we make it a point to go here. And no, we do not have a car and driver. (The life of a blogger isn't quite that of a circa 1995 magazine

writer.) Instead we happily hop on the number 35 bus from Santa Maria Novella, which drops us at the front door after an easy 15-minute ride.

This is the place to indulge in hearty Tuscan dishes. I almost always order one of those thick Florentine soups. It is also where I discover traditional dishes that I had never heard of. I recently had an amazingly green bowl full of *farinata di cavolo nero*, a dish that is usually hard to find in restaurants. It's a kind of cross between a bowl of soup and a plate of polenta, with the green coming from a massive quantity of Tuscan kale. A drizzle of bright green olive oil was poured at the table.

Domenico instead usually opts for another soup, *ribollita*, prepared how it should be—thick enough to eat with a fork.

Although you should definitely have a look at the wine list, if you are feeling like you just can't decide, the wines by the glass are always great. We had two glasses of Le Macchiole, a Bolgheri Rosso, which the waiter kindly left on the table just in case.

For our main course Domenico, again, is always predictable. If he sees bollito he orders bollito. While up in Emilia-

Romagna the bollito comes on its own little cart, at Burde it comes in its own little pot. A small brass-handled aluminum pot full of broth, bones, meat, and vegetables was brought right to the table. Slices of tongue, veal, turkey, and knuckle were nestled in the steaming broth, which served to keep the sliced meat both hot and moist. To the side: all the appropriate condiments: pickled onions, homemade mayo, and salsa verde.

I had another Tuscan classic: *la francesina*. It's similar to the Roman *picchiapò*, in that it's made with leftover boiled beef. But here the onions are the protagonists. And, in fact, my thickly sliced beef came to the table smothered in sweet, stewed onions.

Dessert was a homemade pear and hazelnut tart. I tried to ask the girls in the kitchen for the recipe, but the owner came by and nipped that in the bud real fast.

After lingering over our coffees, it was time to head back to town. As we were paying, at the counter in the front, we asked if they also sold bus tickets. "Yes, we do," said the owner, "but not to you," and handed us two bus tickets, on the house. How cool is that? When is the last time your restaurant paid for your transport? (I have a feeling that maybe he felt guilty for not giving me the recipe?)

Trattoria Tullio a Montebeni

One of the great things about living in a city in Italy is that it's usually very easy to get out of them. The sprawling, endless suburbs you get in the States don't really exist here. One minute you are in a city then the next—wham—there are sheep running across the road.

I have to admit it helps if you have a car, or have friends who have a car. During a recent weekend in Florence, Domenico and I decided to do what most Florentines do for Sunday lunch, and head to the hills. While we could have taken a bus to a small village like Fiesole, we got the chance to go a bit farther afield since my friend Judy and her husband, Andrea, agreed to pick us up in their car for a day in the country.

We drove out the Porta Romana and immediately started climbing. Our first stop was just five minutes out: Piazzale Michelangelo, which is a pretty perfect place to get a sense of how Florence is completely surrounded by green hills. It was so clear—and so cold—that we could even see snow to the North.

But we weren't headed that far. Our destination was Montebeni, just past Settignano. But even though we traveled just 9 kilometers, the change from stone-paved streets to olive tree–filled fields was so quick, and so drastic, that it felt like a mini vacation—which is, I guess, the main point of a Sunday lunch in the country.

The other main point? To eat. And the minute we walked through the doors of Tullio we were greeted by a literal wall of meat: a heaping pile of *bistecche fiorentine*. "They take them out of the fridge the night before," explained Judy. "So that they come to room temperature before being grilled."

So, while there was never any doubt about what our main course would be, we had trouble deciding what to have first. Andrea and Domenico shared a platter of *Pici* with sausage. I, instead, couldn't wait to try *Tortelli di patate*, a specialty of the area. I'd never had the potato-stuffed ravioli before, since they rarely show up on menus in town. The fat dumplings are stuffed with potatoes, and topped with a meat ragu, a bit of which also makes its way into the filling, to slightly stain it pink.

Judy instead ordered a plate of *pecorino fritto*, thick slices of breaded and fried pecorino cheese, cooked until gooey in the middle and served on top of rounds of fried pears. Brilliant, right?

Steak is the real reason everyone comes here. And they make a real show of it. Not only do you pass the "wall-o-meat" on your way to the dining room, they bring you a tray full of raw steaks to choose from. Then, when yours is ready, it is wheeled to your table, and cut into thick slices before your eyes. There is never any talk about how you would like it cooked. It's always

served extremely rare, and is extremely good. Like mind-blowingly good. I'm not a huge meat eater, but we were all fighting over the bone at the end. (Andrea won.)

As if that wasn't enough, we also ordered one portion of *Frittura dell'Aia. Aia* means "courtyard" in Italian, and this refers to the small animals that farms raise in sheltered spaces. So this was a fry-up of chicken and rabbit, with a few lamb chops thrown in for good measure, as well as a tangle of deep-fried onions, eggplant, artichokes, and potatoes.

One slice of very good apple cake to split, and four cups of very strong espresso before we headed back over the hills to Florence

How to Escape

- **Rent a car for a day:** It's not that hard, especially in Florence. Nor is it very expensive. And with smartphones these days, you don't have to struggle with maps on the dashboard.

- **Learn to take the bus:** The bus system is very reliable, and connects Florence to smaller towns all over Tuscany. The different lines all stop near the Santa Maria Novella train station. Busitalia bus station is the main one, but there are at least a dozen others (google "Tuscany bus routes"), which connect Florence to the rest of Tuscany.

- **Walk past through the Gates:** Florence was a walled city, and though much of the walls have come down over the centuries, most of the gates still stand. If you make the effort to walk beyond these gates, you'll find a whole other side of Florence you didn't know existed.

RECIPES

Fried Pecorino with Pears

Serves 4 to 6

There is a saying in Italian: *"Al contadino non far sapere quant'e' buono il formaggio con le pere"*: "Don't let the farmer know how good cheese is with pears." The meaning is that if the farmer knew, he would eat all the pears himself, and leave none for us. Tullio a Montebeni took this brilliant pairing and then took it up several hundred notches by frying not only the cheese, but the pears. Because, why not?

For this recipe you need a good *Pecorino Toscano*, about 2 months old. In other words, you don't want a heavily salty-aged pecorino, but something a bit softer and fresher.

> 6 ounces (300 grams) fresh Pecorino Toscano
> 1 firm, but ripe pear
> 1 cup bread crumbs
> 2 large eggs, beaten
> ¼ to ½ cup all-purpose flour
> Olive Oil, for frying

Cut the cheese into ½-inch slices, trimming the rind off.

Core the pear, but leave the skin on, and slice it into ½-inch wedges.

Pour the oil into a deep, heavy-bottomed pot until it comes up about 2 inches and heat over medium-high heat 375 to 380°F.

In the meantime, dip the cheese slices first into the egg, and then into the bread crumbs, making sure you get a good coating.

When the oil has reached temperature, gently slip the cheese into

the oil, and fry them, over medium-high heat, just until the crumbs start to turn golden. Gently lift out the cheese with a slotted spoon and transfer to a paper towel–lined plate to drain.

In the meantime, add the flour to the leftover eggs. Add just enough to form a pancake-like batter. Stir well. Dip each of the pear slices into the batter, and fry in the oil for several minutes, until golden.

To serve: place the fried pears on a plate and top with the fried cheese.

A Sense of Place and a Bowl of Farinata: The Soul of Florence   97

Farinata di Cavolo Nero

Serves 4 to 5

Most recipes for *Farinata di Cavolo Nero* result in a kind of soupy polenta with chunks of vegetables and leaves of Tuscan kale. Instead, I prefer the way it is served at Da Burde. And even though the restaurant keeps its recipes close, I found their method for the resulting bright green farinata in a video on YouTube where the chef, Paolo Gori, showed how it is done.

> 1 bunch cavolo nero, Tuscan kale
> 1 medium red onion, diced
> 2 carrots, diced
> 2 celery stalks, diced
> 1 cup celery leaves
> ¼ cup olive oil
> Salt
> Freshly ground black pepper
> 2 cups cooked borlotti beans, with their cooking water (see Note)
> 1 cup (150 grams) polenta (see Note)
> High-quality extra-virgin olive oil, for drizzling

In a large pot, bring 8 cups of water to a boil.

Strip the leaves off the kale stems, then cut the leaves crosswise into strips; you should have about 3 cups. Place

the kale and celery leaves into the pot of boiling water, add salt, and bring to a simmer.

In a separate pan, heat the oil. Add the vegetables and cook over medium heat until completely softened, being careful not to let them burn or brown. Season to taste with salt and pepper.

Once the vegetables have cooked through, add the contents of this pan to the pot with the kale. Using a handheld immersion blender, puree the contents of the pot, being careful not to burn yourself with the hot liquid.

Next, using the immersion blender, completely puree the beans with 1 cup of their cooking liquid, and add them to the pot.

Increase the heat, stirring to ensure that the bean puree doesn't sink to the bottom of the pot and burn. Gently pour the polenta in, stirring it the entire time with a whisk. Once the polenta is incorporated, reduce the heat, and let it simmer for a half hour, keeping an eye on it so it doesn't burn.

To serve: ladle into bowls and drizzle with your best extra-virgin olive oil.

Note: To cook beans: Sort and rinse the beans under cold running water. In a bowl large enough to hold the beans when they double in volume, soak the dried beans in cold water to cover by 2 inches overnight. The next morning, drain the beans and put in a pot with 4 cups fresh salted water. Cook slowly until completely tender. Depending on the beans you use, it can take anywhere from 40 minutes to 2 hours. Keep checking until tender.

Note: The quantity of polenta depends on how thick you want your "soup." Some people like it very thick, almost like polenta. With this amount you will have a more liquid consistency.

Where to Eat

Sabatino
Via Pisana 22R
Florence
+39.055.225.955
Monday–Friday: 12:00–2:30 p.m.;
7:15–10:00 p.m.

Da Burde
Via Pistoiese 6R
Florence
+39.055.317.206
Monday–Saturday: 12:00–2:30 p.m.;
Friday also for dinner: 7:00–11:00 p.m.

Trattoria Tullio a Montebeni
Via Ontignano 48
Fiesole
+39.055.697.354
Tuesday–Friday; dinner only.
Saturday and Sunday; lunch and dinner.

CHAPTER EIGHT

Hunting for Truffles

Umbria Part One

f someone told me that one day I would have too many truffles, I would have checked to see if they had a fever. Too many truffles? Is that like having too many oysters? Or too much champagne? Is that really a thing?

Now, however, that I live in the land of truffles, I've discovered that it is, in fact, a thing. And that thing is good

Let me backtrack a bit. When I say that I live in the land of truffles, I don't mean Rome, obviously. I'm referring to our home in Umbria. And while I've always loved truffles, it was in Umbria that I learned that truffles are not always meant to be consumed in thin slices in rarefied restaurants, but something that you could actually order up at a truck-stop diner.

I first learned about local truffles from my neighbor Marisa, who lives down the road from us, on a working farm. Since the day we moved in, she would gift me things like a goose or rabbit, a dozen eggs, or a bag full of freshly harvested wild chicory. But one day she came over with a sack of truffles. Needless to say, I was shocked.

A word about these truffles. When most people think of truffles they imagine pale slivers being shaved off a precious tuber in an expensive restaurant. As the waiter shaves, you are mentally adding up just how much that heavenly pasta or risotto will cost. And cost it does. But those are usually white truffles from Alba, in Piemonte, or black truffles from Perigord in France, and are quite a different animal from what Marisa was handing over.

As I took the precious gift from her hands I was a bit taken aback by the cold. The plastic bag was frosty and closed with one of those twisty metal things. Not very ceremonious for what I thought of as a priceless tuber.

"*Sono scorzone.*" "They are scorzone," Marisa explained, implying that they were nothing to get that worked up about. But even frozen, and even through the bag, I could smell their intense aroma. "They're good for pasta, but put them in the freezer right away, that way they will stay fresh."

What I had was a pound of summer truffles (*tuber aestivum vitt*). And as I soon learned not all truffles are created equal. As it turns out these truffles are readily "findable" all over Umbria, from the end of May to the end of August. And the thing that makes them easier to find compared to their more expensive fall and winter cousins, is their intense smell, which also makes them perfect for cooking. While the more prized varieties may have a more intense taste, the aroma of the summer truffles stands up to heat, which makes it a favorite with chefs both local and not. But you do have to use quite a few to make an impact—which explained Marisa's gracious gift of plenty.

To get the full effect you have to use a heavy hand. The locals know this, and you will never see them shaving them onto anything, unless it's as a final garnish. They use them by the handful, and treat them almost like a vegetable. An expensive vegetable, but a vegetable.

Truffle Hunting

As it turned out, my life as the recipient of truffle gifts was only just beginning. While I put up with hunters with guns traipsing through our property on their way to shoot rabbits, pheasants, and the odd boar (it's part of the local traditions, I've gotten over it), I actually welcome the truffle hunters. First of all: cute dogs. While truffles used to be hunted by pigs, today all truffle hunters use dogs to sniff out their harvest. And if the "real" hunting dogs are skittish and intensely focused on their prey, truffle dogs are a completely different story. They are often coddled and have close working relationships with their owners and cozy up to random humans (errant American women going gaga over their cuteness included). So I'm always up for a visit from a truffle hunter.

Also? Most of the truffle hunters that I run into on or near our house are doing it for the fun of it. They are not professional truffle gatherers and so are not only willing to chat about their hobby, but almost always dig into their pockets to hand over a half-dozen lumpy, muddy orbs.

While I, too, am the proud owner of a cute mutt, little did I know he had anything in common with his working brethren.

Until one day, when Pico was eight years old, he decided, out of the blue, that he was a truffle dog. At least for two days at the end of August. One day, coming back from his early morning walk on his own on our property, he returned to the back door with a huge truffle in his mouth.

For real!

And then, two days later, while our gardener was digging up an old bush, Pico came running over, started digging, and came up with three more truffles.

After that burst of energy, Pico has pretty much taken it easy since then, mostly napping on various couches and certainly not out truffling, which is actually a good thing, because we don't have a truffle license. Like any other form of hunting, truffle hunting is tightly controlled.

There is an exam and specific tools to use so that the grounds are not damaged.

Getting back to the whole pig thing: no, there are no pigs rooting around for roots. It's a dog-eat-truffle world in the Umbrian countryside, and teaching your dog not to eat the truffles, but just show you where they are, is the aim. Truffle dogs are much prized in Italy, as are the areas where truffles are found. In fact, whenever I tell Italians this story about Pico, they sort of look over their shoulder, and then whisper back to me, "You really shouldn't tell people this story." Why? Evidently someone might swoop in and kidnap my pooch. Since he's mostly on the couch asleep I think we are pretty safe from any potential malfeasance.

But truffle dogs are a very big deal and while the Lagotto Romagnolo is probably the best-known breed, it's mostly sought after since it is easy to train. Hunters in Umbria will start training dogs as puppies, teaching them to go after the scent

of truffle, rewarding them with chunks of cheese or hot dogs (which taste infinitely better than the lumpy black things they dig up). Most hunters will tell you that while male dogs have a better nose, females are easier to train.

Driving around Umbria in the fall, you are likely to see cars parked randomly by the side of the road, left by hunters as they head into the woods to search. And there is a lot of hunting that goes on in the wild. But these days there is quite an industry—especially in Umbria—of truffle groves.

No, truffles aren't growing on trees. But they do tend to grow under specific types of trees. Oaks mostly. Truffles are actually a type of mushroom that grows underground in a symbiotic relationship with roots of trees. In Umbria they are most often found beneath oaks, and not far from Spanish broom. Not too long ago, European researchers realized that the spores of truffles could be inoculated into the roots of host trees. The trees are then planted—much like a fruit orchard—except in this case the "fruit" is beneath the ground, and you still need a dog to help you find them.

Eating Truffles in Umbria: When and What

Umbria produces more truffles than any other region in Italy. But what and how you eat them depends on when you visit. With over ten varieties of truffles, you'll most likely come across the following:

Nero Pregiato
November to March

This is the truffle you are most likely to end up eating in Umbria. *Nero Pregiato* translates as "Esteemed Black," and it is famous for its intense aroma as well as for its persistent flavor, which actually becomes stronger with cooking. Although most are about walnut-size, they can grow as big as an orange. The skin is black and rough, and the pulp is dark to violet colored, with thin white veining.

Tartufo Bianco (White Truffle)
October to December

Most people think that white truffles come only from the area around Alba in in Piedmont. They are mostly right. But some do in fact grow in limited areas of Umbria where the earth is more calciferous. But if there are white truffles found in Umbria, chances are you won't be eating any there. They are so highly prized that they almost always get shipped out immediately to waiting chefs as far away as London who can pay the highest price for them. I have never once eaten a white truffle in Umbria over the course of twenty-five years.

Scorzone and *Bianchetto*

These are the two less prized, but most common, truffles in Umbria. (A bag full of *scorzone* was what my neighbor handed over). Both are harvested in summer and fall. The *scorzone* has a strong intense aroma and is often used to make sauces for pasta or else added to pork when making truffled cured meats. The *bianchetto* grows beneath leaf cover, at very shallow depths. Its pulp is very light colored (*bianco* means white) and has a slightly garlicky odor.

When in Italy . . . How to Truffle

- **Truffle Oil:** Just say no. This applies to anywhere, at any time. Truffle oil is not your friend, and 99.9 percent of the time it has absolutely no truffle in it, but is just a chemically generated facsimile. And while it might smell good at first, it almost always has a weird and funky aftertaste. Better to make your own truffle butter (see recipe for gnocchi on page 106). There are a few companies that do make real truffle oil, but it's a very difficult process and almost never achieves the intensity of true truffles.

- **Truffle Sauces:** In Umbria truffle consumption is not the precious "bring it to your table and weigh it" kind of experience. Truffles are often processed into sauces, along with wild mushrooms, and often preserved in jars. These sauces find their way not only onto pasta, but onto pizza and crostini as well. Although slightly more expensive than other dishes, it is not going to break your budget.

- **Buying Truffles:** Since fresh truffles are an agricultural item, in theory you can't bring any back home with you if you are traveling to the USA. You can, however, stock up on jarred or packaged truffles. I mentioned the sauces above, but you will also see whole truffles, in jars, that are packed in a water and salt mixture.

- **Truffled Stuff:** One of the most delicious truffled delicacies is *Pecorino al Tartufo*. Small wheels of sheep milk cheese are flecked with dark bits of truffle that infuse the entire cheese with their earthy flavor. And if you see boar sausages with truffle? Buy them. Many types of salami are flavored with truffle, but in my opinion the marriage between boar and truffle is the best. Another of my favorite treats is truffle honey. Slivers of truffle are suspended in yellow honey, infusing it with a heavenly aroma and taste that pairs perfectly with aged pecorino.

RECIPES

GETTING THE MOST OUT OF TRUFFLES

Gnocchi with Truffles and Cheese Fondue

(adapted from San Pietro a Pettine)
Serves 5

If you're going to truffle, you might as well completely indulge yourself. Heaps of truffles paired with potato gnocchi is always a good thing, but add way too much butter, cheese, and cream, and it becomes mind-blowing (and pants-bustingly?) good. This recipe comes from San Pietro a Pettine, which sources their own truffles.

A final note: It's hard to give a quantity for truffles. Not only do truffles vary in degree of strength, they also vary in cost. So use as many as you can afford or think you need. For this recipe 2 truffles will do.

Fresh truffle (as many as you can afford)
½ cup (1 stick/113 grams) unsalted butter
3 pounds (1.2 kilos) russet potatoes
¾ pound (400 grams) all-purpose flour
1 large egg
Salt
½ pint (240 ml) heavy cream
½ pound (200 grams) taleggio cheese, cut into small squares

The night before, grate some of the truffle into ½ cup of softened butter and mix it well. Place in a nonreactive bowl. Wrap it tightly in plastic wrap. Let sit at room temperature for at least 24 hours to develop flavor.

Wash the potatoes but do not peel them. Put them in a pot large enough to hold them and cover with salted cold water. Place over medium-high heat, reduce to a simmer, and cook until easily pierced with the point of a sharp knife.

Drain the potatoes and let them cool just long enough to not burn your fingers. Peel them while still warm, and pass them through a ricer or food mill into a large bowl.

Add the flour, egg, and salt, and mix until you get a mixture without lumps. Be careful not overmix.

Form long rolls of dough, rolling them out on a floured work surface. Let them rest a few minutes while you prepare the fondue.

Heat the heavy cream over a low heat, then add the cheese. Once melted, add a bit of grated fresh truffle.

Cook the gnocchi in boiling salted water, adding a handful of gnocchi at a time, and when they rise to the surface, scoop them up with a slotted spoon, letting the water drain away.

Add them to the fondue to reheat, using a bit of the gnocchi cooking water to loosen the sauce if needed. Add 3 to 4 tablespoons of truffle butter and stir in. Serve topped with grated white truffle.

Black Summer Truffle Pasta

Serves 6

- 6 black summer truffles (scorzone) (each one about the size of a walnut)
- 1 small garlic clove
- 2 anchovies
- ¼ cup olive oil
- ½ teaspoon salt
- Freshly ground black pepper
- 1½ pounds (750 grams) fresh fettuccine
- 1 tablespoon unsalted butter

A few hours before you are going to make the pasta, roughly chop all but 2 small truffles and put them into the bowl of a food processor. Add the garlic, anchovies, olive oil, salt, and pepper. Process until a smooth paste forms; it will probably stick to the sides, so keep scraping it down. You may have to add a bit more oil. Transfer to a large bowl and cover with plastic wrap. Let sit at room temperature a few hours, to allow the flavors to develop.

Thinly slice the remaining 4 truffles.

Bring a large pot of salted water to a boil, and add the pasta. When the fettuccine is done (this takes only a few minutes if the pasta is fresh), drain, reserving 1 cup pasta water.

Add about ½ cup of pasta water to truffle paste in the bowl, quickly stirring to loosen it up. You may need to add a bit more water. You want it to be sludgy/saucy.

Add the drained fettuccine, and toss well, adding the butter, and more pasta water if you think you need it.

Sprinkle the sliced truffles on top. Traditionally parmesan cheese is never served with truffle pasta.

Where to ... Truffle Hunt in Umbria

One of the places I've run around chasing after some very adorable truffle dogs who were chasing after some very fragrant truffles is at San Pietro a Pettine. Most recently I spent an April day there with Molly, a very friendly female blond Labrador and her partner, a male Lagotto Romangnola. There was also a painfully cute Jack Russell puppy named Pepe who was more interested in playing than anything else. I had a feeling that it was going to be quite a while until he settled down to the real business of finding truffles.

The truffles we were after were the black variety found in Umbria. Even though it was spring-like weather, the truffles we found were still the black winter truffle, *tuber melanosporum vitt.* We were also lucky enough to have have a few white spring truffles as well, *tuber albidum pico.* Since San Pietro a Pettine actually has a truffle plantation (where oak trees are inoculated with truffle spores to encourage a regular harvest) they are able to stretch the seasons out.

Depending on the weather and season San Pietro a Pettine can organize not only truffle hunts but also a truffle-laden lunch to follow.

San Pietro a Pettine

Localita' San Pietro a Pettine
Trevi, Umbria
+39.0742.386.637

Eating Truffles in Umbria

There are far too many restaurants in Umbria that serve truffles to list here. My favorite places in many of the bigger towns are listed in my app, *Eat Italy*. There are, however, a few that stand out:

La Palomba

Via Cipriano Menente 16
Orvieto
+39.0763.343.395

➤ Their signature dish, *pasta all' ascaro* sounds like a recipe conceived in truffle heaven. It's basically handmade pasta—in this case, thick, chewy flour and water umbricelli—tossed in sauce of egg yolks, pancetta, Parmigiano, and heaping quantities of black Umbrian truffles. Yes, basically carbonara by way of truffle.

Ristorante Umbria

Via San Buonaventura 13
Todi
+39.075.894.2737

➤ I never say no to a truffle with a view. And the leafy terrace at the Umbria looks out over the entire Tiber Valley. Ristorante Umbria is, I think, the very first restaurant I ever went to in Todi. That's because, for a long while, it was just about the only place in town. Although there were a few smaller places, and then eventually a pizza place or two, the Umbria was pretty much it, when it came to fine dining in this hilltop medieval town. While much has changed (there are many other restaurants now) the Umbria thankfully remains the same. The aforementioned terrace is divine, but the cozy dining room inside, with its open fireplace, is just as charming. This is the place to order tagliatelle or umbricelli (handmade local pasta) with a thick truffle sauce.

Taverna del Lupo

Via Giovannni Ansidei 6
Gubbio
+39.075.927.3291

➤ This traditional restaurant is a favorite in Gubbio. The stone-vaulted ceilings, stone fireplaces, and framed paintings are an appropriate background to indulge yourself with any of their truffle dishes, which run from antipasti through main courses. Their crispy lasagna, smothered in a flurry of truffles, is a signature dish and one of my favorites.

CHAPTER NINE

From Farm to Table

Umbria Part Two

communicate about food in all sorts of ways. There are my books, one of which you have in your hand. There are also my blog and apps. And then there is the whole social media thing. For the most part all of these are a mixture of words and images. About six years ago I also started making small videos. Food related, obviously. And mostly about the process of either making a specific dish, or producing or growing an ingredient.

But want to know what one of my most popular videos on my YouTube channel is? "Feeding Baby Goats." And that is pretty much what is on this video that has gotten over a half-million views. It is about hungry baby goats being fed.

But, of course, the story behind those 3 minutes of video tells a much richer and complex story than an incredibly cute meme.

The video was shot at a small goat farm in Umbria, Fattoria Il Secondo Altopiano, which is located in Sugano, just outside of Orvieto. And the way I first discovered it has everything to do with the miracle of social media.

You know when you get something stuck in your head and it just won't leave? Could be a song that runs through your mind while you're trying to work. Or a "to-do" list that swells at 3:00 a.m. when you're trying to get back to sleep. Well, I got something stuck in my head that refused to leave. It was a photograph of some cheese.

You're probably thinking "Elizabeth lives in Italy. Cheese? That happens daily." But this cheese was not your normal hunk of Parmigiano Reggiano or yet another globe of glistening mozzarella. The cheeses that kept bouncing around my head were daintily presented, beautifully wrapped, ash-dusted, perfect little goat cheeses. And they weren't an expensive treat imported from France. They were (or so my friend on Facebook said) from a little goat farm outside of Orvieto.

And even though my friend Vincenzo had been telling me about this farm for about six months, it blended into the background (people tell me about farms and/or cheese all the time). At least until he posted that photo. Beautiful goat cheeses produced so close to home? That I had to explore.

And if you're wondering why I got all kinds of excited, it is because while Italy has an awful lot of extraordinary sheep (pecorino) and cows' milk cheese (parmigiano, for example), goat cheese is still

pretty rare. Especially the "French" kind that was taking up Vincenzo's feed. And so, seven years ago, I headed into the hills between Orvieto and Lago di Bolsena, to see for myself.

The first time I visited it was a good thing I had Vincenzo leading the way, since it is extremely isolated. And for a reason. The piece of land where the farm is located was one that took the owners a long time to find. "We were actually looking for something that hadn't already been a farm," explained Emanuele. "We knew we wanted to be organic from day one, and so finding something pristine, and not too near to other farms that weren't organic, was our goal."

Emanuele runs the farm together with his wife, Alessandra. Alessandra is from Rome and Emanuele is from Sicily and they came up with the idea of starting this farm as a way to make a living and stay in the countryside, while running a sustainable business. Emanuele, a veterinarian, and Alessandra have created a slice of paradise where goat cheese just happens to be the happy outcome.

The farm is about 15 hectares and the goat shed and cheese-making facilities are right in the center. Built almost entirely of wood, the barn shelters an ever-expanding herd of goats. Along with the entire farm, the goats are raised organically and biodynamically and treated homeopathically when possible.

The reason I decided to include this

farm in this book is because I think it represents the next chapter in Italian agriculture. Although Italy is still an intensely agricultural country, like any other country in the developed world, the system is changing. Families that lived in farmhouses and worked the farms for big landowners in a system known as *mezzadria* have long since given over to a system that favors large-scale production. That means that the beautifully restored farmhouses that I've been writing about for most of my life (in my first six books) are almost entirely used as second vacation homes for either city dwellers or foreigners.

And so the families that ran small- to medium-scale farms in the countryside are dying out. Partly from competition from larger-scale farmers, but also because the current generation finds it more comfortable to leave the farms for successful careers elsewhere that don't involve the backbreaking work that farming entails. But there are signs that this is changing. And the fact that Emanuele and Alessandra chose this life, over an easier one located in a city, is emblematic of these changes.

While I'm thrilled that this goat farm exists for all the social and economic rea-

in red peppercorns, poppy seeds, or sesame seeds. Others are covered in ash and aged for a few weeks. Still others find their way down into the tufa stone cellar to age for months, becoming truly complex, rich, and outstanding.

Farming in Umbria

From my house in Umbria I've been able to see the changes in farming firsthand. One by one the fields have become fallow as my older neighbors pass away and the new generation either lacks the skills or will to farm, or just sells the entire farm.

That said, there are still farms that manage to make a go of it. And these farms usually have some sort of retail business attached to them, which makes them both easy, and delicious, to visit.

Granarium

It's hard enough to find a good bakery these days, but when you find one that also grows their own wheat, mills it, and then bakes it into delicious breads, cakes, and savory treats, it seems like a small miracle.

Granarium, created by the Lucarelli family, is located in the plains near Bevagna, in the middle of fields full of wheat. The wheat from the farm is threshed into grain that is stored in silos behind the mill. The only means of preservation is movement and air: there is no refrigeration involved. As the grain is needed, it is brought

sons I've just discussed, what I'm even more excited about is the cheese itself. Because not only is this type of goat cheese unique in this part of the world, it's just purely amazing cheese by any standard. Emanuele, who is in charge of both the breeding of the goats as well as the cheese making, is constantly experimenting and improving both his herd as well as the cheeses he is making. They are, for the most part "French-style" cheeses. Many are sold within days of being made, fresh white and creamy cheese formed into shapes and then rolled

inside and stone mills grind it into various grades of flour. Then, in the room next door, natural yeast is added and the loaves of bread are formed and baked in wood-fired ovens. Finally, the bread reaches the public in the darling store in the front. The entire cycle—from field to table—taking place in one estate.

This type of set up is extremely rare, and is the only one I know of in Umbria, and I actually don't know of any other place that goes from seed to bread, organically, by one family. In fact, it was extremely difficult to obtain the permits to even open this type of operation, since they were not simply a farm, or simply a mill, or simply a bakery. But the Lucarelli family persisted and managed to create something completely unique.

Their aim was to reconnect the links along the broken chain. Signor Lucarelii: "Up until one hundred or even fifty years ago, a baker would buy his flour directly from a mill, and so know what flour he was getting and how it changed from year to year. Just as the miller dealt directly with the farmer who grew the wheat, dealing with the vagaries of weather and able to adjust. And the person at the end of the chain, the consumer, would buy their bread from the same baker for most of their lives. They would have long discussions about the bread itself: how long it took to rise, if there were any problems, or if a batch came out particularly well. All of these personal contacts and interactions were an integral

part of the loaf of bread which came to the table. Our hope is to recapture that essential fact of life before it is too late."

The owners are very proud of what they have created, and very generous with their hard-earned knowledge. The entire farm, mill, and bakery is open to visits. In addition to selling bread, and other baked goods, they also sell their flours as well as legumes all grown on their farm.

DieciNove Microbrewery

Part of the trend in microbreweries in Italy can be directly tied to the crisis in small-scale agriculture. A younger generation may not want to carry on the back-breaking—and financially unreliable—work of running a farm. But many are attracted to a career that is somehow related to the land. One outlet is wine making. But the investment and skill to produce a great bottle of wine is prohibitive. A more attractive alternative has turned out to be craft beer.

The equipment and tools needed to produce beer, along with the skills, are relatively accessible. And the will to put a local spin on brews has made this a way to keep a new generation tied to the land in a way that is more flexible.

Umbria has proved to be a fertile ground, literally and figuratively, for this trend. Go into any supermarket and you'll most likely see some local brews lining the shelves next to the Peroni and Nastro Azzuro. An even more enjoyable way is to visit some of the microbreweries that have popped up.

DieciNove is a perfect, and delicious, example of these small-scale initiatives. Located in a ground floor space on a steep and narrow street in the medieval town of Spello, the brewing goes on in the back (you can see it through glass windows) and the tasting out front.

Like many of these small enterprises, they try to work with local ingredients when possible, to make their brews speak of location. I particularly liked their some-what sweet Ambrata, made with local honey and figs. And the Bianche ai Fiori di Sambuco, using elderflower blossoms, was dry and floral.

Visiting Farms in Umbria

Since most of these are actually working farms, they are not the easiest places to find or get to. But if you are persistent, it's well worth the effort. My daughter Sophie and I conduct tours to some of these places (www.ElizabethMinchilli.com) as does my good friend Jennifer McIvaine (www.life italianstyle.com/).

Angelucci Farm

Societa' Agricola Fratelli Angelucci
Voc. San Nicola 69
Loc. Collemancio
Cannara (PG)
+39.0742.724.26

➢ Angelucci is a fully functioning farm, which also has several rooms where you can stay. You can go there for a visit, as we did, petting as many of the animals as possible (piglets, goats, sheep, donkeys, kittens) before going inside for a pasta-making lesson. And, of course, lunch.

Fattoria Il Secondo Altopiano

Sugano di Orvieto 05010
www.ilsecondoaltopiano.com
+39.328.569.6223

➢ There is no easy way to give directions here. If you go to the website, there are directions, in Italian, that you can print out.

The cheeses from Fattoria Il Secondo Altopiano are also available in nearby Orvieto at:

Granarium

Via Madonna della Pia 14, Bevagna
+39.0742.361114
Open daily 7:00–1:30 p.m.
Call ahead to arrange a tour.

Gastronomia Arene

Corso Cavour 101, Orvieto
➢ Goat cheese from Fattoria il Secondo Altopiano available here.

Birrificio DieciNove

Via S. Angelo 12, Spello
+39.0742.847.494
➢ Not really a farm, but this microbrewery makes their beer on site, right in the middle of Spello. Extremely easy to find!

Goat Cheese and Kale Salad

Serves 4

Kale, or *cavolo nero* as it's known in Italy, is almost never used in salads. Italians tend to have a fear in general of raw or undercooked vegetables. And the thought of chopping up cavolo nero for a salad makes most Italians I know shake their head in bewilderment at my crazy American ways.

For this salad I also use another one of my non-Italian secret weapons: chives. I believe chives are one of the

great underused salad ingredients. Whenever possible I use a huge bunch in any salad I make. And by huge bunch I mean at least a ½ of a cup chopped. Everyone LOVES my salads. Even people who say they don't like salad love mine. And I am 100 percent convinced it's the chives.

5 cups chopped salad greens (I use endive, but romaine will do fine), washed and chopped

3 cups chopped cavolo nero or Tuscan kale, well-washed

1 bunch fresh chives (½ cup finely chopped)

¼ cup raisins

¼ cup toasted pine nuts

1 cup crumbled fresh goat cheese

For the dressing

2 teaspoons Dijon mustard

1 tablespoon honey

¼ cup olive oil

2 tablespoons red wine vinegar

1 tablespoon high-quality balsamic vinegar

Salt

Freshly ground black pepper

Place all the salad ingredients in a large salad bowl.

Whisk the mustard and honey in a small bowl until well blended. Slowly drizzle in the olive oil, whisking to emulsify. Add the salt and pepper, then add vinegars and stir to incorporate.

Pour the dressing over the salad, toss, and serve.

Torta al Testo

Serves 6 to 8

I admit that I'm not a frequent baker of bread. It's something that takes both skill and patience. But I do like to make pizza, and in Umbria there is a type of flat bread that lands somewhere between bread and pizza that I actually do like to make: *Torta al Testo*. And when I have flour from Granarium, this is how I often use it.

Torta al testo is a kind of griddle bread made throughout Umbria. The thick doughy circle gets its name from the circular pan on which it is made. The *testo* is a griddle-type pan that was originally made of stone and placed in the embers to heat and cook the pancake-like bread. Nowadays most cooks use a cast-iron pan on the cooktop.

The recipe changes from cook to cook. The basic recipe is flour and water, with a pinch of salt and maybe some olive oil. Originally an unleavened bread, most home cooks now add some sort of leavening agent (yeast or baking soda) to lighten the dough. Every cook has their own method for cooking it as well.

My recipe comes from Paola, a local cook whom I have known for about thirty years now. She not only cooks for my friend Laura, but is also the cook who is called in when a group of local hunters shoot down a wild boar. She not only turns the boar into a *cinghiale alla cacciatora*, but whips up a batch of torta al testo to sop up every bit of the sauce. Another way that torta al testo is used is sliced open, while still hot, and stuffed with sautéed garlicky wild chicory.

As she always does, Paola put her own spin on this traditional recipe. Since she was making the bread for lunch, and only had two hours to let it rise, she used a higher than usual amount of yeast. Also, while most cooks carefully roll out the dough into a circle before laying it on the testo, Paola just grabs a chunk of dough with her hands, stretches it out much like a pizza, and lays it on top of the hot griddle.

2 pounds (1 kilo) type "00" flour

3 cups (700 milliliters) tepid water

¾ ounce (25 grams) fresh yeast
   (*lievito di birra*)

1 teaspoon sugar

¼ cup olive oil

2 teaspoons salt

Put the flour into the bowl of a stand mixer, fitted with the dough hook.

Measure out the tepid water and add the yeast and sugar. Stir well and, with the mixer running, slowly add to the flour.

When the water has been completely mixed in, add the olive oil and salt. Let the machine run for 5 minutes more.

Turn off the machine, remove the bowl, and cover the dough with a damp towel. Put in warm place to rise for about 2 hours, punching down the dough halfway through the rising time.

When ready to cook, heat the testo or cast-iron pan over high heat.

Using your hands, break off a piece of dough and stretch it out into a disk about a ½ inch thick. Place on the testo, patting it out to reach the edges.

Let cook and start peeking at the bottom after 5 to 7 minutes. When it is cooked through, and beginning to get golden, flip the torta over and finish cooking the opposite side. You can test doneness by taking a nibble.

Place in a cloth-lined basket. Eat while warm. If you are going to eat them later, wrap in aluminum foil and reheat in low oven.

CHAPTER TEN

My Olive Oil Story

Umbria Part Three

When I first had the idea for this book, I imagined that certain foods would lead to a discussion about specific regions: pizza in Naples, capers in Pantelleria, etc. Makes sense, right?

But there are certain foods that defy the rigid geographical boundaries between regions. Or, on the flip side, actually illustrate how one food can change so drastically from place to place yet still bear the same name. Add to this that the story of olive oil in Italy is not only one with a national identity but has also changed so much over the last thirty years.

So instead of finding one iconic olive oil to illustrate this chapter, I have instead opted to tell my own olive oil story, because it's probably the most surprising one I have. If someone had told me, in my youth, that I would be growing and pressing my own olive oil, I wouldn't have even known what olive oil was. Like most people my age, I grew up in a house that had a big bottle of Wesson Oil in the cupboard and a tub of margarine in the fridge. Olive oil, if it existed at all, was in a small bottle, dusty and forgotten after having been used to make some exotic dish like a Caesar salad. And my mom was actually an adventurous cook.

I can't even tell you that I had some sort of olive oil epiphany while pouring through the original Marcella Hazan volumes in my apartment in Florence. She never really talked about specific oils, and often added as much butter to dishes as oil.

It wasn't until I was down in Bari, visiting Domenico's parents, that the fact that olive oil was actually something that individual people made, entered into my thinking. It was Christmas time, and we were walking down the street on our way to pick up some last-minute gifts, and we kept running into Domenico's boyhood friends. One of them (sorry, can't remember the name, but they all had nicknames like Bibi, Pucci, Bobo . . . is that a Bari thing?) called us into his store (he sold menswear) and pulled out a 5-liter green tin full of olive oil (from beneath the tie display). It had come from his own trees south of the city, and he was giving it to us.

Domenico was all kinds of excited. And I wish that I could say it was the best olive oil I had ever tasted in my life, but it wasn't. I thought it tasted musty, dank, and just, well, bad. Domenico tried to explain that

that's the way olive oil tasted in Puglia. At the time, never having tasted anything but store-bought, industrial oil, I had to take his word for it.

In any case, my olive oil education had begun.

Learning About Olives

My big learning curve in olives came from two sources. Growing my own (see below) and attending a series of conferences all about olive oil in the '90s and early aughts. The change in the way we think about olive oil has undergone immense transformation in the last twenty years, and I was extremely fortunate to be part of a group that helped make that happen.

Oldways Preservation and Trust was one of the first groups to help spread the gospel about the health benefits of the Mediterranean Diet. At a time when dietary fat of any kind was being demonized, Oldways organized International Symposia that brought together journalists, writers, chefs, scientists, nutritionists, importers, and producers to learn, explore, and then go out to preach the various parts that make up the elements of the Mediterranean Diet.

Learning about olive oil was a big part of this. Over the course of several years I visited Greece and Spain and various regions throughout Italy, tasting different olive oils while also learning about their health

benefits. But it was the tasting that was the true education for me. I learned the differences not only from one olive variety to another, but how much the actual process of pressing can affect the final product.

Growing My Own

About thirty years ago we bought a house in Umbria. Set on 3 hectares of land, it came with about 120 olive trees. Like the house, the trees had been abandoned for about thirty years by the time we got to them. And just as we restored the house, we have also done our best to nurture the trees. But while they are beautiful to look at, they have never been the most productive of plants. Even though we've had them pruned and fed them lots of tasty manure over the years, their output is never reliable.

And then there's the fact that we are in Umbria. Some years there's a late frost that nips the buds off. Other times there are torrid summers that make the olives either fall off, shrivel up, or get attacked by bugs.

It's a miracle we ever get any oil at all. But we do. Not every year. But enough to keep us in oil that we've produced ourselves. In a good year we've gotten about 120 liters of oil. In a bad year, we've made do with last year's oil.

We usually try to do most of the picking ourselves. We invite friends over for a long weekend, and if there are enough of us, we can get quite a bit done.

The best part of the process is taking our olives to the mill. And this is something that I've realized most people don't know about olive oil. Even though a lot of people have their own trees, only big commercial producers have their own olive mills. Everyone else takes their olives to the local mill. It used to be that there was one guy in each village. But these days the process has changed so radically, with new machinery and methods, that there are at least six *frantoi*—olive mills—to choose from in our area.

Over the years we've tried almost all of them. From the simple local guy in the next village to the newfangled, state-of-the-art machinery in town. While I know the new places produce a cleaner, less oxidized and maybe more flavorful and stable oil, I still love heading down to the old mill down the road from our house. It's located in a small building on the outskirts of our village. As farmers hang out outside, the owner struggles to make the ancient machinery work for just one more year. Since all of the olives, olive paste, and oil are out in the open—not closed up in stainless steel machinery—there is an intensely pungent smell of olive oil mist the moment you walk in.

Here the olives fall into a hopper, get chopped up into paste, and are then spread on round hemp mats that are squeezed

under a hydraulic press. The liquid is then run through a centrifuge to separate the oil from the vegetable water.

The bright green drizzle of oil that comes out at the end of this complicated and archaic system always seems like magic to me. Catching a bit on a piece of bread that's been toasted on the fire? Biting into the fire-charred bread as freshly pressed olive oil dribbles down my chin? I think that is the answer to the perennial question people always seem to be asking me: What is your favorite thing in the world to eat? Freshly pressed olive oil from our own trees. A delicious miracle.

A miracle maybe, but is my olive oil the best olive oil? You would think that since I see the oil go from tree to bottle, and can control everything that can be controlled that my very own olive oil, would be the best, right? And that is what most farmers used to think as well. One of the things that still goes on at mills is the eagle-eyed farmer keeping tabs on the olives that he's harvested himself. Because everyone else's are inferior.

But really?

In the case of my own oil I'm not so convinced. And here's why.

Making high-quality olive oil is a time-consuming, expensive, and risky business. And the operative word here is "high-quality."

One of the most important factors in pressing olive oil is the time lapse between picking and pressing. Ideally, to get a high-quality olive oil, with low acidity, the time should be mere hours. Which is fine if you have a team of pickers at your disposal. But if you're like us, and are constrained by weather, logistics, and just the fact that we usually can't get anyone to help us pick, a week or more may go by between picking and pressing. Not ideal.

So while I love using my own olive oil, I also am a big consumer of other olive oils that are made with quality in mind. The olive oils that I buy come from all over Italy, and over the years I've come to realize how completely different the various regional oils can be. Back when I first tasted the olive oil from Domenico's friend in Bari, and didn't like it, it was because for the most part olives in Puglia (at least at that time) were picked much later in the season, and then left to mature before being pressed. This led to the musty smell and taste that I hated, but that Domenico (and other Pugliesi) found normal.

And, in fact, these days "new oil," with its bite and peppery taste, is what most of us are looking for. Yet, if you let an older farmer taste it, he would think you are crazy, since they might prefer the oil to be left to "mature" for at least a year before using it.

When in Italy . . . Olive Oil

Learning about olive oil is a miraculous and wonderful way to enter into a region. If you are lucky enough to be in Italy during harvest season, then planning a day to see olives being picked and then pressed in the mill is like nothing else.

A Week in Umbria with Elizabeth and Sophie

I run several week-long tours each year, and one of my favorite is the Week in Umbria tour, which takes place in October. During this week, besides eating our way through the region, we get a crash course in olive picking and olive oil tasting.

elizabeth@elizabethminchilli.com
www.elizabethminchilli.com

Olive Harvest in Tuscany

My friend Pamela Sheldon Johns is not only an accomplished chef and writer, she also owns and operates a farm in Tuscany and bottles her own extraordinary olive oil. She runs a week-long tour at Poggio Etrusco where harvesting alternates with cooking and eating.

Food Artisans
www.FoodArtisans.com
pamela@foodartisans.com

Day-Long Olive Oil Tastings in Rome and Sabina

All oils are different: There are five major olive varieties in Italy, and most oils are a blend of these. Lately though, single varietal have become trendy. To understand what kind of oil you like, the best thing you can do is taste them. There are even degrees in Italy now, that certify you as an official olive oil taster (much like a sommelier). My friend and colleague Johnny Madge is one of those officials, and we offer both a day in Rome workshop as well as a visit outside of Rome in the countryside.

Olive Oil Workshop
www.ElizabethMinchilliInRome.com
elizabeth@elizabethminchilli.com

Olive Oil Commandments

- **Always store your olive oil in a dark, glass bottle.** Although it may look pretty all green in that clear glass bottle, olive oil is damaged by light.

- **Yes, you can use olive oil for frying.** In Italy, where olive oil is the default oil, almost all home cooks use it for frying. I'm not going to suggest you use your expensive imported new oil to fry with, but I'm here to tell you that it's a thing.

- **Italians don't start out their meal dipping bread in olive oil.** They just

don't. And if you go into a restaurant in Italy and ask for a bottle of olive oil to dip your bread into, be assured that in most cases it will certainly not be their best oil.

- **Olive oil is a condiment.** While it may be rare for Italians to add salt or pepper to a dish at the table, olive oil is another story. Hearty soups, beans, and vegetables, almost always get a swirl of olive oil at the table. That is why there is a bottle of olive oil at your table. (But not for your bread, see above!)

Buying Real Italian Olive Oil

If you have any interest at all in Italy and/or olive oil, then I'm sure you've read something in the past few years about fraudulent olive oil. The degrees of fake olive oil vary from the oil not being really Italian to not being even made from olives.

The problem is partly due to regulation, or lack thereof. It is legally permissible to label a bottle of olive oil as being from Italy as long as it is bottled there. That means that many of the big industrial bottlers (and even smaller ones) buy oil much more cheaply elsewhere (Turkey, Morocco, Greece, Spain) import it to Italy where it is bottled as Italian.

Another version of olive oil fraud involves declaring olive oil to be extra virgin, when it is anything but. Sometimes the only way to distinguish the veracity of extra virgin is to submit it to a test to check on the acidity levels. Not really something you can do on you own.

How to make sure what you are buying is truly extra-virgin olive oil from Italy? One easy indicator is price. True Italian extra-virgin olive oil is expensive to produce and therefore expensive to buy. Even in Italy, where it is made, true extra-virgin olive oil can cost anywhere from 12 euros to 24 euros per liter, and sometimes much more. Once you export it to other countries, the price, of course, rises. So, if you see a cheap bottle of olive oil . . . well, you get what you pay for.

The only sure way to ensure that your olive oil is true to its word is to buy from a reliable vendor. I've been lucky enough to know many of the best and most trustworthy importers of Italian food.

Although I know there may be other importers, here are some of the online resources that I know personally and that carry olive oils that I know.

Zingerman's
www.zingermans.com

Formaggio Kitchen
www.formaggiokitchen.com

Gustiamo
www.gustiamo.com

Market Hall Foods
markethallfoods.com

Manicaretti (Wholesale importers)
www.manicaretti.com

RECIPES

It was difficult choosing specific recipes for this chapter since olive oil plays a major role in so many dishes, but one thing I have learned over the years is that quantities of olive oil in a sauce is not up for discussion. When I share a recipe for something as straightforward as tomato sauce, I inevitably get feedback that it just didn't taste that special. When I ask readers if they followed the recipe, nine times out of ten they tell me that they either left out, or cut way back, on the olive oil, since they are trying to diet. What they don't understand, and what took me a while to digest, is that the amount of olive oil in certain dishes does not just provide a vehicle in which to soften onions or garlic. It has flavor and provides texture and mouthfeel on its own. And so in a recipe as simple as meatballs, olive oil is just as important an element to the success of the dish as is the choice of meat and other seasonings.

There are, however, a few recipes where extra-virgin olive oil is the main ingredient and plays the starring role. These are the dishes I pull out when I have a bottle of bright green olio nuovo, just pressed and beyond fragrant.

Pinzimonio

I have a deep and abiding affinity with nonrecipes. You know, the whole smoke-and-mirrors thing that makes it seem like you are putting a lot of effort into something, when really, it's mostly just a bit of chopping and a hefty dose of styling?

Pinzimonio is one of my favorite nonrecipes. While Italians don't get to the table and start dipping bread into olive oil, they do like to dip raw vegetables. But the olive oil in this case is seasoned with salt, pepper, and a bit of lemon.

The word *pinzimonio* actually refers to the olive oil mixture. What you dip in—seasonal vegetables—can vary. Carrots and celery almost always make an appearance, as does fennel. Radishes are nice, and even thin slices of uncooked zucchini. The aim is to have a bright and colorful variety. It is a very nice winter alternative to a leafy green salad.

How you serve it is also important. In central Italy there are specific sets of dishes used just for pinzimonio. A big bowl or platter holds the vegetables in the center of the table, while each guest gets a small bowl full of dipping oil. Another ingenious way I've seen it done is to give each guest his own small jar, with a couple of inches of seasoned oil at the bottom, and the strips of vegetables stuffed in as a sort of edible arrangement. It makes for a very cute presentation.

This dish calls for the best olive oil you can get. It's all about the oil.

A mixture of fresh vegetables, such as carrots, celery, radishes, fennel, and bell pepper.
Extra-virgin olive oil
Salt
Freshly ground black pepper
Fresh lemon juice

Prepare vegetables by peeling, if needed, and then slicing into more or less regular pieces. Carrot sticks, celery sticks, fennel, etc., should be cut into 3- or 4-inch-long lengths, and about ⅓ inch thick. In other words, pieces easy to pick up and bite into.

If you are providing individual bowls for each diner (which I suggest you do, so that everyone can double dip with ease), put about 3 to 4 tablespoons of olive oil in each bowl, a teaspoon of lemon juice, ¼ teaspoon of salt, and a few grinds of black pepper. Use a fork to mix up before serving.

Arrange the vegetables on a platter or bowl in the middle of the table. If you think this sounds like some sort of vegan fondue party, you're pretty much on track.

Bruschetta

While Italians don't dip the bread from the basket into a bowl full of olive oil, they do enjoy olive oil-topped bread when it's toasted. This simple dish appears all over Italy and is called *bruschetta* in most places, but also *fettunta* in Tuscany. It originates as a poor dish. It was a way to use up leftover bread, and turn it into a meal. Although around Naples it is most often served topped with tomatoes (and is how most people enjoy it), the simplest version is prepared with garlic and olive oil.

6 slices rustic Italian bread

2 peeled garlic cloves

Extra-virgin olive oil

Salt

The bread should be sliced about ½ inch thick.

Ideally the slices should be toasted over a flame. If you don't have the grill going, then you can use an old-fashioned Italian grill that is placed over the flame of your cooktop (this is what I use). And if all else fails, your broiler or even your toaster will do just fine.

Once toasted, and while the bread is still warm, rub it with garlic. Place the slices on a serving platter, and drizzle liberally with the best extra-virgin olive oil you have. Sprinkle with salt and serve immediately.

White Bean Soup

Serves 4 to 5

This is my go-to soup whenever I am entertaining. It's easy, it's delicious, and who doesn't love bean soup? It's always good, but the level reaches new heights when you have a bottle of great olive oil to swirl on top. In fact, I'd go so far as to say that final swirl of olive oil is the essential element here.

You'll notice there are very few ingredients in this recipe. I don't use broth, but I do use dried beans, not canned. Although I have made it with canned beans in a pinch, it is infinitely better when you cook your own. Also, the resulting bean broth really adds to the soup.

2 cups dried cannellini beans

1 carrot, peeled

1 celery stalk

½ onion, peeled, but left whole

2 cups reserved bean cooking water

1 tablespoon kosher salt

⅓ cup olive oil, plus more for drizzling

6 garlic cloves, finely chopped

¾ cup chopped fresh flat-leaf parsley,
plus more for garnish

Soak the beans, making sure they are covered by 2 inches of cold water, for at least 6 hours or the night before.

Drain and rinse the beans, and put them in a heavy-bottomed pot. Add

enough water to cover the beans by 4 inches. Add the carrot, celery, and onion, and bring to a simmer. Stir in the salt, and reduce the heat to very low. Put the lid on, askew, and cook until the beans are very tender. It should take about an hour, but all beans are different. They should be very tender.

In another pot over low heat, warm the olive oil. Add the chopped garlic and cook briefly until fragrant; don't let it burn or even turn golden. Stir in the chopped parsley.

Strain the beans and bean water,

discarding the carrot, celery, and onion. Add the beans and their water to the pot. Increase the heat and let simmer for about 20 minutes. You may have to add a bit more water, but the soup should be thick. Taste for seasoning and adjust as needed.

To serve, top with a bit more chopped parsley and a generous swirl of olive oil. It is great accompanied by bruschetta (see page 133) and is often served by placing the bruschetta at the bottom of the bowl like a giant crouton and then ladling the soup on top of it.

CHAPTER ELEVEN

Rustic Sardinia and the Secret of Su Filindeu

My first trip to Sardinia was strange. It was one of the last times I ever agreed to go on a press trip, and I accepted the invitation because I'd never been to Sardinia and I desperately needed an excuse. Like many people who had never been to Sardinia, one of the few things I had heard about was the Costa Smeralda. This pristine stretch of coastline was developed in the 1960s by the Aga Khan and today stretches out over 20 kilometers and includes golf courses, nightclubs, luxury hotels, and the most expensive house prices in Europe. In other words: Berlusconi territory, which is where I was destined to go if I accepted the invitation.

Even though none of this sounded very appealing, the actual press trip promised more than a stay at a luxury hotel. There was a wine and food festival going on and so, at the very least, I thought I would get a chance to meet and talk to some interesting food producers. Long story short, the actual festival was a bust (more of a market to entertain wealthy guests of the hotels), but there was one 20-minute experience that gave me a glimpse into another Sardinia far removed from the ritz and the glitz.

During an otherwise tedious press conference to present a tourism initiative in the interior of Sardinia, I discovered *su filindeu*. In a far corner of the room a lone woman had set up a table, where flour, water, and salt were magically being pulled into the thinnest strands of pasta I had ever seen. I stood mesmerized, made a short video, and vowed I would somehow make it back to Sardinia to find out more about this pasta. My search eventually led me to one of the most remote and isolated areas of the island where I tracked down Paola Abraini, who kindly agreed to let me come to her home in Nuoro and have a lesson in su filindeu.

At this point, I had been thinking about su filindeu, and reading about it, for about two years. In the meantime, there had been a Jamie Oliver video floating around Facebook and so I assumed it was not that much of a secret thing. But as I drove around Sardinia the two days before my appointment with Paola, I had a curious reaction from any Sardinian I mentioned su filindeu to. They had no idea what I was talking about. I'd start to explain that it was thin pasta that was stretched by hand and then eaten in broth. Still a blank stare. So rare was this pasta that not even people who lived an hour away from the village had even heard of it.

Making Su Filindeu

Paola lives in the city of Nuoro, located in the central part of Sardinia, far from the sea. She had invited me to her home, an apartment on the third floor of a modern building, and into her small kitchen, where, over the course of a few hours, I had a crash course in stretching dough.

The dough itself is nothing special. Durum wheat flour, water, and salt. The trick—or rather skill—is knowing when the kneaded dough has reached the exact moment of elasticity to permit Paola to pull it into 168 thin strands.

Once the dough is the right consistency, Paola breaks off a piece and forms a 20-inch-long tube of pasta, about 3 inches in diameter. Making a loop of the dough, she holds the two ends in her left hand, securing them with her thumb. In the meantime, with her right hand, she gives a firm pull at the bottom of the loop, stretching the rope to twice its length. She then takes the bottom of the loop, swings it up, and places it back in her left hand, securing it again with her thumb. At this point, there are now four strands of pasta hanging from her hand. She repeats the process again and again and again, each time doubling the number of strands—which become thinner and thinner—until finally she has stretched the small piece of dough 8 times to result in 256 strands of angel hair pasta.

Although Paola made it look easy, stretching and stretching in no time, when I tried my hand at it, I got as far as 3 stretches before my strands completely fell apart. And although I tried to learn how to tell if the pasta was the correct consistency, that, too, proved impossible in such a short time. Every so often Paola would dip her hands in a small bowl of salt brine, sprinkling some of this on the dough. "It helps make it elastic," she explained mysteriously.

Once fully stretched, Paola then places the strands across a round piece of wood, measuring about 36 inches in diameter. Once she had covered the disk of wood with one layer, she swiveled the disk 45 degrees, so that the next layer would cross it at an angle. And finally, after that, the third and final layer of pasta, at a slightly different angle. This mesh of paper-thin pasta was then put on the terrace, in the shade to dry, becoming one unified sheet of crossed "strands of God."

One of the reasons no one I met had ever heard of this rare pasta is because Paola is one of only a handful of women who still know how to make it. Invented about three hundred years ago to celebrate a local holiday at a nearby sanctuary on an isolated mountain outside of Nuoro, today only Paola, and a few of her relatives, know how to stretch the pasta.

Paola learned how to make filindeu from her mother-in-law. (Who also happened to be her second cousin.) Her husband's mother had been making it for the twice-yearly festival of San Francesco di Lula ever since she was a teenager. "I was eighteen when they let me help them make the pasta that year," recalled Paola. "We made 400 kilos and I became obsessed with learning how to do it."

If Nuoro feels isolated, the Sanctuary of San Francesco is even more so. The twice-yearly festival is located about 30 kilometers away from city, outside the village of Lula, up in the mountains, at 446 meters altitude. The first festival takes place on October 1. Pilgrims gather at the Church of Madonna della Solitudine in Nuoro, and then, by foot, make their way to the Sanctuary in the hills, arriving the following morning. The second festival takes place over the course of ten days in May, and again attracts pilgrims from all over who come to celebrate the novena.

The pilgrims who come are offered nourishment in a very specific order. In the first room they are offered coffee and cookies, and then, in the next room, a bowl full of filindeu in broth. And finally, in a third room, a plate of the meat and potatoes that were used to make the broth.

The pasta is rarely served in restaurants, and only very locally. And if you do find somewhere that serves it, it is certain that either Paola, or one of her relatives, has made it. Paola apologized that she couldn't serve me a bowl of soup, but her apartment is very small, she had other things to do, and besides "It's quite time-consuming to make." Although making a bowl of broth seemed pretty simple after the acrobatic and slightly magical feat of stretching the noodles.

But Paola didn't leave me high and dry, since she had put me in touch with an *agriturismo* (a farm B&B) where she promised they would make it for me. And, in fact, as I left, she handed me a pack of filindeu she had made the previous day, already dried up, cut into manageable sheets, and ready to go. "Give these to Bastiano, he is expecting them."

Heading to the Hills

As we left Nuoro, and followed our GPS, we soon left the main superstrada and kept turning onto smaller and smaller roads. Thick forests full of oak trees, which produced cork, lined the road. I was astounded not only by the beauty of the rugged landscape but also by the fact that we saw few people. When we did get into traffic jams, they were more likely to involve sheep, than humans. After a while even the GPS stopped working. We hadn't even seen a sheep for at least a half hour. But it was beautiful and I figured, how lost could we get?

While our GPS never really kicked in, we did finally come across a sign: *Agritur-*

ismo Testone. And as our car climbed, the landscape became even more spectacular. Massive boulders, looking as if they had dropped from the sky and split in half, dotted the spaces between the twisted oaks. Eventually I spotted a cow. And then a few more cows and eventually a herd of sheep. We had arrived in one of the most isolated, and authentic, agriturismi I'd ever been to.

About thirty years ago, laws were enacted that allowed working rural farms to accept paying guests in a type of rustic hotel. This new category of hospitality would, the thinking went, allow struggling farmers to make additional income from tourists looking to experience farm life. While part of the regulations stated that at least 30 percent of the food consumed at the agriturismi had to be grown there, the category soon became a way for entrepreneurs to open country inns that didn't have to adhere to the regulations of more formal hotels.

But Agriturismo Testone is one of the true agriturismi. It doesn't just talk the talk, it walks the walk. It is a 100 percent working farm, and the 350-hectare (864 acres) estate has cows, sheep, free range pigs, and a huge vegetable garden. Its complete isolation means that the silence is total, and the feeling you have stepped back in time absolute.

I was happy that I had reserved so far in advance, since every one of the eight rooms were booked. As it turns out, Testone is known not only for its rustic charm, but for its warm welcome and delicious food as well.

After Bastiano and his son had checked us in, I handed over the package of su filindeu. "I usually only make this for special occasions" explained Bastiano. "But since you are only here for one night, and we have a full house, it seems special enough."

Although most of the sheep we had seen while driving are used to make pecorino cheese (Sardinia is one of the biggest producers of pecorino in Italy), Sardinians also eat the meat from sheep. While in Rome I was used to eating *agnello*, which is baby lamb, on Sardinia the meat is more likely to come from an animal that is older, and at the end of its milking cycle.

We were to have su filindeu the way it is prepared for the twice-yearly *festa*. Bastiano showed me how he made the broth, starting out with meat from a five-year-old sheep. Although I was expecting something strong and gamey, the broth was actually quite delicate and rich at the same time. The addition of a young pecorino cheese at the end, both thickened the broth and gave it a slight tanginess. And the su filindeu pasta? The massive sheets were broken into irregular shards and dropped in at the last moment, to cook quickly in the broth before coming to the table. The noodles themselves, although delicate and brittle, retained their mesh-like texture, merging with the meaty broth and cheese resulting in a dish that was a bowl full of comfort. It was not only delicious but also nourishing in a way that felt as if someone was taking very good care of you. Exactly the type of thing I would imagine a hungry pilgrim would be happy to receive. And exactly the type of thing I felt privileged to have eaten.

Hills of Honey

Great honey starts out with great flowers, and by great flowers I mean flowers that have not been exposed to pollution of any kind. These days it's getting more and more difficult to situate your beehives in locations that are not only far away from city fumes but also distanced from the pesticides and chemicals commonly in use in rural areas.

The hinterland of Sardinia, which is as far from the pollution of the modern world as you can get, is the perfect location if honey making is your thing. Luigi Manias decided it was his thing, and as luck would have it he was already in Sardinia. He was born and grew up in the small town of Ales, at the foot of Monte Arci.

Luigi learned honey making from his aunt, but explained that honey making used to be very common: "There was a census that dates back to 1800, and every town in Sardinia had at least one honey maker." Not only was honey a regular ingredient in cooking, but the wax from the combs was also needed to supply the local church with candles.

Luigi's approach to making honey is as natural as he can make it. Rather than roam around, moving his hives to be near specific flowers, he camps his out permanently on the slopes of Monte Arci. Although he leaves the rest to the bees, he still manages to make single varietal honeys that have been winning awards since the day he began producing them.

When I ask how he determines which honey comes from which flowers, he says it is completely dependent on the season and the weather. "Certain flowers come at certain times of the year, and so the honey follows. But if the weather doesn't cooperate, some years we miss out on certain honeys."

Many of the honeys that Luigi produces are only made in Sardegna. *Spina bianca* is from a type of wild artichoke that flowers in the spring. The blossoms of *cardo*, a wild cardoon, produce a floral honey that is yellow with hints of green. But the honey that I am totally addicted to, and which is only made in Sardinia is corbezzolo honey.

The *corbezzolo* (arbutus, or tree strawberry) grows wild. It is easily recognizable by its red fruit, which look a bit like strawberries. But the flowers are what is important. The tiny bell-shaped white flowers appear on the tree in the fall. And since fall weather can be a bit unpredictable, the honey is not always running.

Corbezzolo honey is unlike any honey you've ever had. At first taste it is sweet, but almost immediately the bitter kicks in and dominates. It is this bitter taste, which is quite strong, that make some people call this "honey for adults." The complex taste is extraordinary, and I sometimes just like a spoonful of it. The other thing I learned while with Luigi, is to put it in my espresso, which was a revelation.

But the best use for corbezzolo honey is atop the pastry known as *scadas*. *Seadus* is a pastry made with a lard-based dough. The pastry is stuffed with pecorino, fried, and then covered in bitter honey. The mixture of ingredients, textures, and flavors—salty and sweet, and bitter and crunchy, and soft and creamy—is as

full of contradictions and contrasts as Sardinia itself.

Pasta in Lamb Broth

Serves 6 to 8

Although you probably can't get your hands on filindeu, that doesn't mean you can't enjoy the dish with a different kind of pasta. The broth is made from *pecora*,

which is "mutton." Both mutton and lamb are sheep. A lamb is under a year old, and mutton is older.

- 4 pounds (2 kilos) mutton
- 2 carrots
- 2 celery stalks
- 1 medium onion
- 1 tablespoon kosher salt
- 1½ cups cubed fresh pecorino cheese
- 1 pound (500 grams) pasta
  (see Note)

Cut the mutton into 3- to 4-inch pieces, and trim off any big pieces of fat. Bring a large pot of water (4 liters/1 gallon) to a boil. Add the meat and return to a simmer. As the meat simmers, skim off the foam that rises to the surface. This will help keep the broth clear.

Once the foam is no longer rising, add the vegetables and salt. Continue to simmer, with the lid askew, for 3 hours.

When the broth is cooked, using a ladle, scoop about 2 ladlefuls of broth per person, into a smaller pot.

Bring to a boil, and add the pasta. When the pasta is almost done (if you are using angel hair pasta, this should take only a few minutes), add the cubes of cheese, and stir to melt them.

Serve immediately, making sure the

cheese hasn't sunk to the bottom of the pot.

Note: You can use a typical Sardinian pasta, such as *malloredus,* which is like little gnocchi. Or, if you want more of the effect of filindeu, use angel hair pasta, broken up into tiny bits.

Seadas with Corbezzolo Honey

Serves 20

1 cup (100 grams) all-purpose flour

1 cup (100 grams) semola di grano duro flour

½ teaspoon kosher salt

2 teaspoons (10 grams) granulated sugar

¼ cup (40 grams) lard

1 cup cold water

1 cup (200 grams) grated fresh sheep's milk cheese

Honey, corbezzolo if possible.

Peanut oil or lard, for frying

Mix the two flours together with the salt and sugar. Add the lard and mix with your fingertips until worked in; it should look like small peas. Don't overmix.

Add the cold water, up to a cup, adding just enough, a little bit at a time, until the dough comes together.

Wrap the dough in plastic wrap and place in refrigerator for about an hour.

Meanwhile, grate the cheese and mix it with about 2 tablespoons of honey if desired.

Roll out the chilled dough until it is about ¼ inch thick (do this in batches, keeping the rest of the dough cold). Cut into small disks using a 2½-inch-diameter cutter.

Place about a teaspoon of cheese in the center of half the disks. Wet the edges with a bit of water, then place another disk on top, pressing down the edges with your fingers. Using a fork, press the edges to seal well, making sure not to pierce the seadas with the tines.

To fry: Place a pot with at least 3 inches of peanut oil or lard over high heat. When the oil is at temperature (you can test it with a bit of dough), slip in the seadas and fry until golden on the outside, turning at least once.

Remove with a slotted spoon and transfer to paper towels to drain excess oil. You can eat as is (since there is honey inside already), but it's even better if you place it on a plate and drizzle with extra honey.

Note: If you are making these for dessert, prepare them at the very last minute, and eat while piping hot. Otherwise the cheese becomes hard.

Shepherd or Bandit's Dessert

Serves 4

This was a recipe that I kept hearing about, but never actually had while I was in Sardinia. The rugged, wild, and isolated terrain is a land that has traditionally been populated by both shepherds and bandits. Often isolated in the mountains for months at a time, the one thing they could usually get their hands on was honey. And so, to soothe a sweet tooth, honey was drizzled atop lettuce leaves. At least this is the story I heard. Although I'm not 100 percent sure how either a bandit or shepherd gets himself a head of lettuce. It's actually very good. Here is my version, which is more of a first course, than a dessert:

> 2 hearts romaine lettuce
> Honey, preferably Millefiori Sardinian
>   Honey
> High-quality extra-virgin olive oil
> Flaky sea salt
> Chopped toasted almonds

Cut the hearts of lettuce into quarters, place 2 on each plate. Drizzle with olive oil and honey. Sprinkle with salt, and then with chopped toasted almonds.

Where to Eat in Nuoro

Since there are only a handful of women who still make su filindeu, there are even fewer restaurants that prepare it. The following sometimes have it on the menu, but it's best to call ahead if you have your heart set on it.

Trattoria S'Hostera Nugoresa
Via N. Ferracciu 63
Nuoro
+39.380.701.4355
Closed Sunday.
➤ This homey trattoria is located in the center of Nuoro and has traditional cooking both from the area and other regions of Sardinia.

Il Rifugio
Via A. Mereu 28/36
Nuoro
+39.0784.232.355

Where to Stay in Sardinia

Agriturismo Testone

www.agriturismotestone.com

+39.0784.230539 or +39.329.4115.168

➤ Located about a half hour north of Nuoro, this is the ideal place to experience this rugged corner of Sardinia. If you ask nicely, Bastiano may make su filindeu for you.

Beach Day

Spiaggia di Su Barone

08028 Orosei Province of Nuoro

➤ I can't end this chapter without mentioning Su Barone. Although Agriturismo Testone and Nuoro are inland, this fantastic beach is only an hour away. Located on the eastern coast of Sardinia, it is a natural reserve located on a spit of land that is separated from the mainland by wetlands. After going over a bridge, you drive directly into a pine forest where you can leave your car before heading to the pristine beach that stretches for kilometers.

Where to Buy Honey

As I mentioned earlier, I am totally addicted to corbezzolo honey. It's not easy to find, and isn't actually produced unless the gods are willing and the weather cooperates. But when all things go according to plan, Gustiamo carries it in the States.

Gustiamo

www.Gustiamo.com

CHAPTER TWELVE

Naples

Where All Roads Lead to Pizza

know that people have a thing about Naples. And, for the most part, I'm talking about people who have never been there. They are scared. Scared of the chaos they've heard about. Scared of the crime they've read about. Scared of a place that appears to be a culture that seems completely apart from anything they think they know about Italy yet at the same time everything you think you know about Italy concentrated.

While they may be right about the confusion, mess, and crime, anyone who has ever visited knows the complete and utter charm of the unique and utterly seductive chaos that is Naples.

I have to admit, that it took me a while to build a relationship with Naples. For years it had to do mostly with logistics. Naples was not fun to get to. Up until about twelve years ago, the trains that ran to Naples (and frankly most of southern Italy) were decidedly on the shabby and slow side. And driving there? For years the stretch of two-lane autostrada between Rome and Naples was a nightmare filled with Neapolitans (who don't follow rules) and Romans (who think the rules are made only for their benefit) vying with trucks for full domination.

But these days not only is the highway a spiffy three lanes, the train has upgraded the cars and the tracks so that a day trip to the city from Rome takes just over an hour. Barely time to read the paper, but plenty of time for a day trip from Rome.

One thing I've begun doing is heading to Naples for lunch. While I've actually sat down at one restaurant and had a full meal, what I really like to do is make it more of a moveable feast. Especially when I've got a friend in who's never seen the city.

Of course, for me, the main event for any trip to Naples is pizza. Or Pizza; I feel that in Naples it deserves that capital P. Because it is Naples that gave birth to what we today know as pizza. Yes, I know there is a world-class archaeological museum to be seen, as well as new modern museums and infinite art-filled churches. But. Pizza. Right?

And I fully believe that pizza is the entry drug to a full-on addiction to Naples.

You may think you know pizza, but the pizza you will get in Naples is almost certainly much, much different than the pizza you are used to eating back home. Or even, for that matter, pizza you may have had anywhere else in Italy. So specific is the typology of Neapolitan pizza that the entire process has been recognized, certified, and defined by the stringent pizza police (aka *Associazione Verace Pizza Napoletana*).

Among the rules that determine whether or not you are certified as a true Neapolitan *pizzaiolo* are:

- **Yeast:** organic yeast with a low acidity.

- **Dough:** when stretched out, must be no thicker than .4 centimeters.

- **Cheese:** must be D.O. P. buffalo mozzarella.

- **Tomatoes:** must be either San Marzano, Corbarino, or Piennolo (all D.O.P.).

- **The dough has to rise at least 12 hours,** but usually longer.

So far, so familiar. Dough, tomatoes, and cheese. But how it's all put together and then baked? That results in something that may, at first glance, be completely surprising.

Pizzas in Naples are on the small side, each one is meant to be eaten by one individual. They are baked in extremely hot dome-shaped ovens, 900°F or even hotter. This means that the pizza is cooked extremely fast. Often usually anywhere from 60 to 90 seconds.

This fast cooking means that the crust around the edges puffs up right away, cooking quickly, as does the bottom of the pie, which is often speckled with what pizza

experts refer to as leopard-spotting. These dark spots, almost burnt, are what gives Neapolitan pizza its distinctive smoky and almost bitter flavor.

This way of cooking also means that the center of the pizza, where the tomatoes, olive oil, and the cheese hang out, is wet and almost soupy. It is definitely not what you would get in a Roman-style pizza, but it is (trust me on this) one of the best things about going to Naples.

A Word About Toppings

Toppings in Naples are a minimal thing of beauty. There are usually few of them (that is why the standards are so stringently regulated) and even when those few are applied, they are done with a light touch.

There are two classic types of pizza you'll see at every pizzeria you step into:

Pizza Marinara: This is pizza at its purest. Tomatoes, garlic, oregano, and olive oil.

Pizza Margherita: Named after a queen, this is the queen of pizzas with tomatoes, olive oil, fresh buffalo milk mozzarella, and fresh basil leaves.

There are many *pizzerie* that get fancy and creative with their toppings (and we'll get to that later), but even then, the amount is never overwhelming. It's all about the balance, and the toppings never ever overwhelm the crust. It's a partnership.

Where to Eat Pizza in Naples

Here is my list of favorites. I think it's a pretty good list, which will give you a good overview of the different types of pizza. Can you do it all in one day? You can if you want to. I did. Best to go with a friend, and a pretty empty stomach.

Da Matteo
Via dei Tribunali 94, Naples

➤ This pizzeria opens at 8:00 a.m. This means that you can have pizza for breakfast. Although it's worth stopping by Da Matteo for a sit-down pizza in their restaurant, this is where I get my pizza to go. The window that faces the street is where pizza becomes portable. The method for this is specifically Neapolitan and called *pizza al portafoglio* (wallet), or *libretto* (small book). When you go up to the window you will see anywhere from three to twenty small pizzas laid out on a metal tray. Don't be deceived. These are not pizzas that have been sitting there for very long. The pizzaiolo knows, from experience, how many pizzas he will sell at different times of the day. These are freshly made, and piping hot.

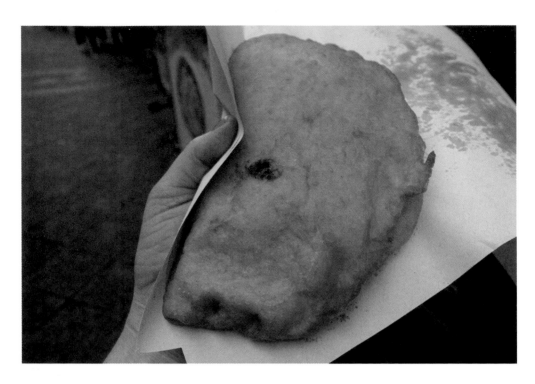

Pay for your pizza (only 1 euro!) and the pizzaiolo will place it on a sheet of parchment, then fold it in half, and then fold it in half again, with the paper forming a separation between the two halves, and a cone at the bottom. It's a bit tricky to eat, since your first few mouthfuls are mostly crust, but then you get down to business and at the end you are treated to a last bit that has absorbed all the juices of the tomato, mozzarella, and olive oil. At least the part that hasn't dripped down your chin, onto your hands, and hopefully not onto your shirt.

Figlio del Presidente

Via Duomo 181, Naples

➤ This is where I first experienced the wonder to man that is known as pizza fritta. It still remains my favorite. Pizza fritta is a bit of a misnomer, since it's actually more of a calzone fritto. It is a moon-shaped piece of dough, stuffed with just enough tomato and mozzarella to moisten and counteract the slightly sweet dough with savory. Because the dough is a bit on the sweet side, at least here. It's not donut sweet, but the fact that it's fried definitely brings donuts to mind. But maybe that is just my excuse to also include this treat in my Naples breakfast itinerary. Or second breakfast, since they open at 10:00 a.m. They, too, have a stand out front, which means that this pizza fritta is always to go.

Da Michele

Via Cesare Sersale 1, Naples

➤ If your idea of pizza in Naples was formed by watching Julia Roberts play Elizabeth Gilbert in *Eat, Pray, Love*, then you are already familiar with Da Michele. I actually remember when Liz (yup, I knew her when . . .) went down to Naples for the weekend and she really was completely blown away by the pizza here. As was I the first time I went. As are most people. But all this attention means that the long lines have gotten even longer. My advice: get there at least 20 or 30 minutes before they are scheduled to open. Since they open at 11:00 a.m. this may actually make it your third pizza breakfast of the day. (I told you this was not for the faint of stomach.) If you are there by 10:30, you have a pretty good chance of being seated right when the oven starts spitting out pizzas at a furious pace at 11:00. Otherwise it's a long wait in line.

Da Michele is a true old-fashioned sit-down pizzeria. And by old-fashioned I mean they serve only two types of pizza: Marinara and Margherita. The Marinara comes in three sizes (*normale, media,* and *maxi*) and the Margherita comes in two (*normale* and *media*) with the option of getting doppia mozzarella. Believe me when I say the normale, for 4 euros, is plenty big. Although it's not on the menu, the last time I was there I saw a local order a pizza with doppia mozzarella and NO tomatoes.

This is the place where you really un-

derstand that pizza is all about the dough. Think of the toppings as more of a type of condiment, that complements the dough. And the aim of the dough, which Da Michele slam dunks, is an incredible lightness. And, in fact, I would suggest you order the Marinara, with its incredibly intense "tomatoey-ness" with just enough oil, oregano, and garlic. Yes, it's big, but when you start eating it, you'll understand what I mean about the lightness.

Attilio

Via Pignasecca 17, Naples

➤ In a city full of pizzerias you can imagine there is a lot of competition with each place trying to distinguish themselves from the rest. And since I'm as much of a sucker for novelty pizza as the next person, I usually make time for Attilio. Besides being well-known as one of the better pizzerias, their specialty is for their pizzas with ricotta-stuffed crusts. The last time I was there I had *Sole nel Piatto* (Sun on a Plate). The main part of the pizza was mozzarella, mushrooms, and porcini, with the crust formed into little points (aka sunshaped) that were twisted by Attilio (the grandson of the original Attilio) into perfect little pockets around dollops of ricotta. It may sound like overkill, but it was anything but.

Starita

Via Materdei 27, Naples

➢ In case you can't decide if you'd like your pizza traditionally cooked in the oven or deep-fried, you can head to Starita and order a *Montanara*. This may be one of my favorite things in a city of favorite things. The pizza dough is first fried, then topped with a tomato-basil sauce, and just a bit of Parmigiano and fior di latte before being finished briefly in the pizza oven. It almost floats off the plate and into your mouth, it is so incredibly light and full of air.

The Pizza Stars

Pizza in Naples used to be a food for the masses, made with whatever was on hand. Flour, water, yeast, and toppings. There was no talk about where any of those ingredients came from. Both Gino Sorbillo and Enzo Coccia have been primarily responsible for not only the rise in quality of pizza, but for the extreme attention to specific ingredients used in making those pizzas.

Sorbillo

➤ If Neapolitan pizza is enjoying its place in the press at the moment, much of that has to do with the media-savvy Gino Sorbillo. He took what was arguably one of the best and well-known of the old-fashioned pizzerias in Naples and turned it into a phenomena. It was basically Gino who changed the view that a pizza was some sort of third-rate street food and taken it to be regarded as high-level cuisine.

The family pizzeria is located along Via dei Tribunali and today attracts hoards of would-be pizza eaters to a neighborhood that, thanks to him, is enjoying a rebirth. Even in the face of a fire (said to have been caused by his refusing to pay the local organized crime bribes) he has not only kept going, but kept getting bigger.

Although he serves the basic Marinara and Margherita, the menu changes a few times a year to include new and creative creations. Most of the pizzas are named for his extended family, and are variations on the classics, swapping in various cheeses, cured meats, and even types of tomatoes. All of the ingredients are carefully sourced, with the producers receiving credit on pizza descriptions.

Sorbillo has recently launched Lievito Madre al Mare, located along the seafront. Neither restaurant accepts reservations, so just plan on waiting.

Sorbillo
Via dei Tribunali 31, Naples

Lievito Madre al Mare
Via Partenope 1, Naples

La Notizia Pizzerie

➤ Enzo Coccia is often called the Professor of Pizza. It is Enzo, and his tireless inquiries into the mechanics of pizza that has led a new revolution in Naples in the exploration of new types of flour, toppings, and ways of cooking. He has three distinct restaurants located in the neighborhood of Vomero.

Pizzaria La Notizia 53
Via Michelangelo da Caravaggio 53, Naples
+39.081.714.2155
➤ This is Coccia's most traditional pizzeria where you'll find all the classics. Like most classic pizzerias, reservations are not accepted, but turnover is fast.

Pizzaria La Notizia 94
Via Michelangelo da Caravaggio 94, Naples
+39.081.1953.1957
➤ This is Coccia's experimental pizzeria, which is definitely more upscale. Reservations not only accepted, but required.

O Sfizio da 'a Notizia
Via Michelangelo da Caravaggio, 49/51, Naples
+39.081.7148.325
➤ His newest place is dedicated to fried pizza. It's a great place to go to share small plates of enormously delicious dough-based dishes.

Kalo' 50

Piazza Sannazaro 201B, Naples

+39 081 1920 4667

➤ Pizzaiolo Ciro Salvo is all about the crust. And his ethereally light dough at his pizzeria, Kalo 50, is considered, by many, to be the best in the new breed of pizzeria in Naples.

Last Bites

Before I get back on the train for Rome, there are two stops I make near the train station:

Sfogliatelle Attanasio

Vico Ferrovia 1-4

Naples

Closed Monday.

➤ I always leave enough time to wait in line at this small bakery near the station. They do one thing and one thing only: *sfogliatelle*. Those are the crispy crunchy ricotta-filled pastries that Naples is known for.

Bar Mexico

Piazza Giuseppe Garibaldi 72, Naples

➤ Naples has the best coffee in Italy. It's not just me that says so, it's just true. It may be the water, it may be the machines. For whatever reason, it's just the best. And in a city of good coffee, Mexico is often at the top of everyone's list. There are several locations throughout town, but the stopped-in-time location near the station is my favorite.

CHAPTER THIRTEEN

Gragnano

Home of Artisanally Dried Pasta

For some reason the entire pasta discussion has gone off the rails, at least outside of Italy. I'm not sure why, but there is this misinformed idea that handmade fresh pasta is better pasta. I have a feeling that it is a bit of a monster of our own creation. With the surge in interest in the handmade and artisanal when it comes to food, a misconception has developed that handmade pasta is better than any type of pasta that comes prepackaged. But there is a huge part of the pasta discussion that is almost always left out. And it is, I think, the reason why non-Italians tend to lean toward fresh pasta over dried (for more on the difference between fresh and dried see chapter 17).

When it comes to eating packaged pasta, most of the world is, in fact, eating mediocre to bad dried pasta. There, I've said it. I'm usually not in the habit of bringing any sort of negativity to the Italian table, but when it comes to the quality of dried pasta I have to take a stand.

I realize that most people have only ever eaten industrially made dried pasta, and so don't really know that anything else exists. To understand the difference, a bit of background is necessary.

Pasta in Gragnano

The one thing you've probably heard about pasta in Italy is that Marco Polo brought it here from China. This is almost certainly not true. Pasta has probably been going on in Italy for centuries, and may even date back as far as the Etruscans. But the pasta we are talking about, dried pasta, began its long road to our tables in the eighteenth century.

Dried pasta, unlike fresh pasta, is made from hard semolina, milled from durum wheat. Since this type of wheat grows in the south of Italy, in Sicily, and in Campania, that is where much of the first pasta-making industry developed. Particularly in the area in and around Naples, where the warm breezes off the hills assured that the pasta would dry, while the humid sea breezes ensured it would not dry too fast, and crack. This reliance on natural setting meant that tourists to Naples

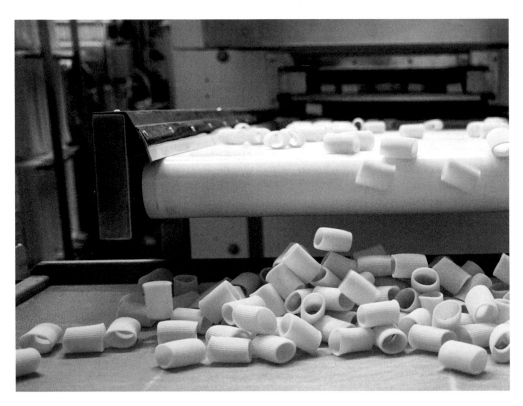

commented on the streets filled with rows of pasta drying on the streets, terraces, and even rooftops. Heaven, right?

But it was in nearby Gragnano that the first automation of pasta making took hold. The small town was perfectly situated for drying pasta, with the dry Ponentino western winds coming off the hills, alternating with the warm and humid Vesuviano winds coming from the sea. And it was here that the extremely time-consuming and strenuous process began to be automated. Dough made from durum wheat is extremely difficult to knead and it was here that the first kneading machines were made. It was also where the first presses that could extrude the unwieldy dough into various shapes were put into action on a larger scale. And so, it was from Gragnano that pasta began its way to becoming a more common food for masses, and not just a luxury for the upper class. Yet even though certain parts of the process were semi-automated, it was still being made by a group of family-run businesses that produced pasta in small batches, in an artisanal manner.

It was also in Gragnano that some of the first drying rooms were invented. These rooms combined heat with wind, imitating the natural breezes so that pasta could be made year-round, and not depend on the seasons. The progress in Gragnano sought to increase production while at the same time preserving the traditional methods, especially maintaining the flavors that were the result of the mountain breezes slowly drying local varieties of wheat over the course of several days.

As with all things, the process was adopted and industrialized and spread way beyond the pasta drying along the streets of Gragnano. It was not long before big companies all over Italy began to produce pasta on a much larger scale, ramping up production by not just using inferior ingredients, but mostly by speeding up the drying process. While these advances have made Italian pasta one of the biggest exports around the world, it has also turned it into something that is a far cry from the traditionally made dried pasta still being made by families in Gragnano and other parts of Italy.

While in Gragnano, drying rooms were invented to mimic the natural breezes so that pasta could be made year-round, big companies elsewhere in Italy left this far behind, speeding up the production to match demand. And this is how we now arrive at the fact that not all dried pasta is created equal. Instead of talking about which is better, dried pasta or fresh pasta, I hope by now you realize that it's more productive to be concerned with telling the difference between great dried pasta and the more industrialized brands.

I remember the very first time I cooked artisan-made dried pasta at home. We are all used to the great smells coming out of the kitchen when making pasta. But those aromas are usually from the sauce. You know, garlic, onions, and probably tomatoes. But when I put the bag of pasta in the water, the entire house filled up with a new aroma. It was the pasta itself, which was not merely a blank slate that would come to absorb the sauce, but a wheaty, earthy fragrance that wafted out into the living room bringing Domenico and our daughters, Sophie and Emma, running into the kitchen to ask what I was making and when was it going to be ready?

That first packet of pasta, given to me by a man from Puglia, who I met at a food fair in Torino, led me to visit many of the best pasta makers throughout Italy and, eventually, to Gragnano, the birthplace of the modern way of making artisan dried pasta.

What's the Difference?

I recently got the chance to go behind the scenes at two of the best pasta makers in Gragnano: Faella and Gentile. Both companies adhere to the older way of making pasta and their machinery produces relatively small quantities per batch: 1,000 to 2,000 kilos (2,200 to 4,400 pounds) of semola di grano duro is turned into a bit more pasta.

There are several factors that differentiate artisan dried pasta from the industrialized process. One, unsurprisingly is attention to ingredients, not only the flour but also the water. Another is, of course, the process itself. Here are the major factors that differentiate artisan-made dried pasta from industrial brands:

- **Texture:** Artisanal-made pasta is extruded through bronze dies (versus Teflon), which gives it a rough texture that better absorbs the sauce.

- **Temperature:** Artisanal-made pasta is dried at a lower temperature, which not only improves flavor but also gives it a completely unique texture: firm and chewy, that is never found in industrially made pasta.

- **Ingredients:** Artisanal-made pasta is made with just flour and water, with no extra colorings, preservatives, or additives. It is also usually made with high-quality flour, and special attention is paid to the water that is used.

- **Timing:** The importance of drying: This is probably the most important aspect of the process which differentiates the smaller, artisanal producers, from the industrial ones. Once the pasta is made, it is taken into drying rooms where, over the course of up to 48 hours, wind and heat gently dry the pasta (versus about 20 minutes of drying for industrial-made pasta). This is not an automated process, since the timing and temperature can depend not only on the shape of the pasta, but the quality of the flour that day as well as the weather. It is up to the master *pastaio* to decide exactly how to alternate air and heat, and it is he who decides when the pasta is ready to be packaged.

And if you have sometimes wondered why it is so difficult to cook pasta to that perfect al dente point, it is because the high heat used to dry industrial pasta practically precooks the pasta, affecting the final texture. This means that it starts out overcooked before it even hits the water.

Like many artisan-made food products in Italy, Pasta di Gragnano is recognized by an IGP label. The Consortium that monitors this process is the *Consorzio Gragnano Città della Pasta*. But like all such regulators, not everyone agreed with the rules. It's not that the rules were too strict, but that they weren't strict enough. Specifically, regarding the drying process, the Consortium states that the pasta must be dried from 6 to 40 hours, at from 40° to 80°C (104° to 176°F). That is a huge amount of leeway and, in fact, allows for the making of quickly dried pasta at high temperatures. All this to say that even if a brand of pasta is from Gragnano, it doesn't necessarily mean it is the best.

Try this at home:

If you don't quite believe me so far, in terms of the difference in taste and texture, then I have some homework for you. I'd like you to try one of the artisanal brands, and compare it to the one you usually buy at the supermarket. I realize this involves spending money. The high end pastas I'm talking about, by companies like Rustichella, Gentile, Faella, Martelli, and Cavalieri cost anywhere from $6 to $12 per pound, versus about $1.50 for a supermarket brand. Because the difference in taste, in texture, and in the finished dish is hard to describe here, you're just going to have to experiment yourself. I've provided a list of some of my favorite brands, and sources on page 169. And if you have time, and energy, try making two batches of pasta, one of your regular brand, and one of the better ones. Then dress them with a simple coating of olive oil. Let me know what you think. I think that people have gotten so used to the idea of cheap pasta, that they don't realize that there is an alternative that tastes completely different.

RECIPES

Spaghettone al Pomodoro

Serves 4 to 5

While I was in Gragnano, I had the great luck to not only visit the Pasta Gentile factory but also to hang out in the kitchen with Mamma Maria, the matriarch of the Zampino family that owns the company. She prepared various pastas for me to try. Naturally the sauces were simple, to bring out the pure taste of the pasta. My favorite was the spaghettone she made with a simple

tomato sauce. Spaghettone is Gentile's signature pasta, and is a toothsome thick strand of thick spaghetti measuring 2.7 millimeters in diameter. Since there are so few ingredients, the specific choice really does make a huge difference. For this sauce Mamma Maria, like most Italians, uses canned pelati San Marzano tomatoes. She actually follows these tomatoes from seed to can, but if you can't manage that see the resources below for the real thing.

1 pound (½ kilo) Spaghettone Gentile

¼ cup (70 grams) extra-virgin olive oil

1 smashed garlic clove

8 fresh basil leaves, plus more for garnish

One 26-ounce (750-gram) can San Marzano tomatoes

½ teaspoon salt

Parmigiano Reggiano, for serving

Bring a large pot of salted water to a boil. Add the pasta. While the pasta cooks (if you are using spaghettone, then it will take a while) make the sauce.

Pour the olive oil in a sauté pan large enough to hold all of the drained, cooked pasta. Add the smashed garlic clove and the basil. After 1 minute, add the canned tomatoes with their juice and salt. Turn the heat to high and cook quickly, for about 15 minutes, using a wooden spoon to break up the tomatoes.

Taste and adjust for seasoning.

Drain the pasta when it is just short of al dente, retaining 1 cup of the cooking water. Put the drained pasta into the pan with the sauce, and stir over medium heat to finish the cooking, until al dente. If the sauce seems too dry, add a bit of the reserved cooking water.

Serve garnished with fresh basil leaves and some grated Parmigiano Reggiano on the side.

Linguine with Pesto

Serves 4 to 5

I first came across *Pasta Faella* in Umbria. There is a store just off the autostrada, on the way up to our house, that sells about 2 dozen products from Campania. While most people stop off for a kilo of mozzarella di bufala, I make sure I stock up on Pasta Faella from Gragnano, which is almost impossible to find anywhere else. My favorite shape is their linguine, which I make all summer long with pesto made from our own basil. I also use local almonds rather than pine nuts, since they are not only cheaper but I also prefer their slightly less sweet taste. I substitute a bit of local sheep's milk pecorino for the Parmigiano to keep the local, and slightly more rustic, theme going.

1 pound (½ kilo) linguine Faella

⅓ cup blanched almonds

2 cups basil leaves, washed and dried

3 garlic cloves, roughly chopped

⅓ cup extra-virgin olive oil

½ cup grated Parmigiano Reggiano

½ cup grated pecorino (either from Tuscany or if you can get it from Umbria)

½ teaspoon salt

Freshly ground black pepper

Fresh basil leaves, for garnish

Preheat the oven to 350°F (180°C).

Spread out the almonds on a baking sheet and bake in the oven until lightly toasted. This will take 8 to 10 minutes, but watch them so they don't burn. Remove and let cool off completely.

Put the basil, almonds, and garlic in the bowl of a food processor. Process until the nuts and garlic are completely chopped up.

Add half of the olive oil, and half of grated cheese. Process until combined.

Add the remaining cheese and olive oil, and the salt and pepper and process until smooth.

If you are not going to use the pesto immediately, place in a glass jar and cover with a thin film of olive oil so that it remains bright green.

Make the pasta: Bring a large pot of salted water to boil. Add the linguine and cook until al dente. Artisan-made dried pasta like Faella takes much longer to cook than more industrialized pasta.

Drain the pasta, reserving 1 cup of the pasta cooking water. Place the pasta in a warm bowl, add the pesto, and stir to distribute. If it seems a bit dry, add some of the cooking water.

Serve with freshly grated Parmigiano Reggiano, and garnish with fresh basil leaves.

Variation: Replace some of the pasta with thin string beans. Add the beans, which have been trimmed, to the pot with the pasta when it is about 8 minutes from being done.

Visiting Gragnano

Pasta Gentile Factory

www.pastagentile.it

It's not always easy to visit food producers. There are many health regulations that prohibit the public from entering. And it also takes precious time away from the actual production schedule. Gentile has recently restructured an old mill into a new branch of their factory. Part of it is dedicated to pasta production and drying, and part of it is a store that features their products. There is even a small museum of old machinery. If you call ahead, you can arrange a visit. In addition to their pasta, the store also carries their line of canned goods, including not only tomatoes, but jams and pickled vegetables (artichokes!) as well.

What Pasta to Buy?

While Gragnano is intricately tied to the birth of high-quality packaged dried pasta, there are a few pasta makers from other regions in Italy who are making equally exceptional pasta. Here are some of my favorites to search out:

Benedetto Cavalieri, Puglia: This was the brand that first changed the way I thought about pasta. Located in Puglia. Not easy to find, but worth it.

Martelli, Tuscany: The bright yellow packaging distinguishes this family-run company. The production is small, but the taste is huge.

Rustichella, Abruzzo: This is probably one of the easiest brands to get your hands on outside of Italy. Located in Abruzzo, this family-run company has managed to grow while still producing high-quality, traditional pasta.

Gentile: This family-run pasta company in Gragnano can trace its business back to 1876. They make a variety of shapes including their signature spaghettone and hand-formed Fusilli.

Faella: Located right in the center of Gragnano, Faella is easily recognizable by their 1 kilo-size white and blue bags of pasta.

Where to Buy

Even in Italy the production from these companies is so small, that it's not easy to find.

In the USA many of these brands can be found from the following sources:

Zingerman's
www.zingermans.com
➤ Zingerman's carries both Rustichella and Martelli.

Gustiamo
www.gustiamo.com
➤ Gustiamo carries both Faella and Martelli.

Formaggio Kitchen
www.formaggiokitchen.com
➤ Formaggio Kitchen carries Rustichella.

Market Hall Foods
www.markethallfoods.com
➤ Carries Rustichella.

iGourmet
www.igourmet.com
➤ This online shop carries two of my favorite brands, Gentile and Benedetto Cavalieri.

CHAPTER FOURTEEN

Fishing for Anchovies on the Amalfi Coast

Not all anchovies are created equal.

I know, I go on and on about quality, but there is a reason. The way I cook, and the recipes I publish in my books and on my blog, often have just a handful of ingredients. And when your dish is made up of just four or five ingredients, if those ingredients aren't the best you can possibly find, it's going to affect the outcome of your dish. There is just no way around it.

And no more so does this quality issue matter than when it comes to anchovies. Most people tend to take those little jars for granted. (and those are the people who like them). But if you hate them? I have a feeling you've never really had great anchovies.

What a lot of people don't realize is that there are anchovies, and then there are great anchovies. One day when my friend Rolando was visiting for the weekend in Umbria, he arrived with a little jar of the fishies as a gift. I'm used to receiving bottles of wine, wheels of cheese, even guest soaps as hostess gifts. But a little jar of anchovies? Well, OK. He knows me well.

At lunch the next day, when Rolando served the anchovies as our first course, we all understood the power of that little jar. Rolando toasted rounds of bread, laid a thick slab of butter on top, and then gently draped each crostino with one perfect, glistening, slightly silver anchovy. As we bit into them, we all realized these were not the overpoweringly fishy, salty fillets that we were all used to, but a firm, almost sweet, explosion of the sea itself.

So transformative was this experience that I decided to head directly to the source, and followed Rolando down to the Amalfi Coast where we went anchovy fishing.

You think I'm being poetic, referring to anchovy buying as "fishing." But I'm not. We got on a boat and actually went fishing. And then I followed the fish from the water, to the processing workshop, and finally even got to watch them being stuffed into one of those little jars that had originally made its way to my table.

What I learned was that although the production of anchovy fishing may have increased over the last century, the actual process during which they make their way from sea to jar to table remains basically unchanged and is a method that dates back thousands of years.

Anchovies are fished throughout the world, but the best ones are generally considered to come from the Mediterranean. And one of the oldest towns where anchovy fishing has been going on for centuries is Cetara, on the Amalfi Coast.

As the sun set on the small fishing village we set out to see how it was done. The fishing takes place with the use of a *lampara*, which refers to the "lamp" or "spotlight," that is mounted on the wooden boat and mimics the moon, which the fish are drawn to. The light is turned toward the water, where the brightness attracts schools of anchovies. The anchovies, which feed during the day in the open waters, come into the shallows near the coast in the evenings.

As the fish gather, so do the boats, which string up a purse seine net in an ever-shrinking ring that draws in toward the point of light and the fish. In the last moments before the fish are caught, they are leaping and flying, trying to escape in a silvery, shimmering dance.

The net is hauled up, and the fish are immediately packed into ice. A few hours later, at first light, they are delivered to the processing plant where the first stage of the curing takes place. The fish, still cool and dripping with sea water, are unpacked by women who rip off the heads, and pull out the guts.

And if you're wondering, yes, it is always men who do the fishing (heavy lifting required) and women who do the processing (only delicate fingers need apply).

Once gutted, the fish are rinsed and then packed tightly into barrels, with alternating layers of sea salt. A weight keeps the fish compressed, and brine develops.

This curing process, which can take up to a year depending on the size of the fish, does several things. First and foremost, the salt leaches the liquid from the flesh of the fish.

How to tell if they are ready? It's a specific skill that is left up to the master salter. If the fillets are left too short a time, they don't have much flavor; too long and they can begin to ferment and lose their firmness. At the end of the curing the flesh has turned a rosy color and has a deep, rich aroma, but the fillets are quite firm.

Once cured, it's back to those ladies in the processing room. Rinsed of salt, each fillet is hand-boned, and laid, side by side, on linen sheets to dry overnight. In fact, if you look closely at the final fillet you can still see the imprint of the linen on the shimmering skin of each anchovy.

Once dry, they are packed into jars, by hand, and topped with olive oil.

These fillets are ready to use, but some are kept aside, bones intact, and packed in salt. This means boning and rinsing the fish at home, but many chefs swear that these have a superior flavor and texture and are, in fact, less salty than their oil-packed brethren.

We've all had bad anchovy experiences. Those anchovies that smell way too fishy and fall apart before you even get them out of the jar. It's most likely you paid a lot less for those as well. Some of the biggest productions of anchovies these days come from other countries and the lack of quality has to do with either using fish that aren't fresh and/or curing them too short a time. The fillets are also often dried in a centrifuge, which impacts the texture.

Anchovies: Salted or Under Oil?

It's up to you. If you're in Italy and happen into an *alimentari* (deli), you'll almost always see a huge tin of salted anchovies open. These are full of fillets and allow you to buy just what you need. This is what my mother-in-law does. She takes them home, and immediately puts them in a small bowl of water to soak. This allows the encrusted salt to come off easily. After about an hour, you rinse them under the tap, dry them off, and then gently take out the bones. It's fiddly, but not as hard as it seems when you get the hang of it. Using your thumbs, carefully insert them into the stomach cavity, pulling the fish into two halves. You'll notice that at this point the backbone, and most of the smaller bones, is attached to one side. Separate the two fillets and gently pry off and pull away the vertebrae, which should take most of the smaller bones with it. Once you've cleaned out most of the bigger bones, give it another rinse, dry it off, and it's ready to use. But the fillets benefit from a short soak in olive oil. Just place them in a glass bowl and let them sit for a few hours. This softens the flesh as well as adds the aroma of olive oil, which is always a good thing.

When buying anchovies under oil look for those that are packed in olive oil. And I usually tend to go for the jars, rather than the small flat tins, for the simple reason that you can reseal the jars after you use them. If you do buy them in the jar, and plan on storing the jar once opened, be sure that the fillets are covered with oil, so you may have to top the jar up.

Colatura: The Happy By-product of Traditional Anchovy Processing

I may not be very good at things like skiing, swimming, or running, but if there was an Olympic competition for multitasking I would win all the medals. I think it's become almost impossible for me to do just one thing, and one thing only. I realize that as a woman, wife, and mother that the multitasking gene is hardwired into my being, but I've proudly taken it to another level.

Since I started my blog, things like cooking, shopping, traveling, and general world-watching have now become officially work. My entire life is one big multitasking extravaganza, which is why I am so appreciative when I see multitasking in others.

When I was down in Campania learning how anchovies are caught and cured, I also learned how this complex and time-consuming operation has another delicious by-product: *colatura*. Anchovies also multitask. While the anchovies are being cured and getting ready for their entry into jars and onto our table, they are also producing this salty, magical golden elixir.

Although many people associate colatura with the ancient Roman fish sauce called *garum*, it is quite different. Garum was a fermented by-product of intestines and other nonedible fish parts. Instead, colatura is a much more straightforward process that involves no fish innards whatsoever.

When the anchovies are curing in their barrels for upward of a year, the salt in which they sit leaches the liquid out of the fish. When the barrels are finally cracked open, they are first tipped onto their sides, which is when the precious multitasking bears fruit. Rather than let the liquid run down the drain, the mixture of fish and salt and time is carefully caught, then aged in wooden barrels for yet another year.

The result is colatura, the most intense, fishy, and complex taste you can imagine. It is very concentrated, so a little goes a very long way. Down on the Amalfi Coast, I saw it used in many ways (on top of tomato salad was the most surprising), but my favorite way was a simple dish of pasta.

Cooking with Anchovies

There is a reason that chefs hold anchovies in their arsenal of flavor enhancers. The curing process of anchovies—a year or more under salt or brine—transforms the flesh and makes it a highly concentrated source of glutamic and inosinic acid. Don't worry if you don't know these words. The only thing you need to know is that those are two molecules that make us taste savoriness. In other words, it's that umami whammy that salt on its own can't deliver.

I always have a feeling that the people who say they don't like anchovies are saying that just because they think that anchovies are about the fishiest, strongest-tasting thing they can imagine. And even I admit, that, if you put an anchovy right into your mouth, with nothing else to buffer it, then yes, it's going to be fishy, salty, and intense.

But rarely are anchovies eaten like this. For anchovy addicts there is no better treat than bread slathered with butter topped with one perfect fillet. They also pair perfectly with mozzarella and potatoes. You see where I'm going here? Anything rich and/or starchy only improves with anchovies. In other words, a little anchovy goes a long way.

But there is another side to anchovies. This is when they give up their supporting role, and instead join other ingredients to be a backup. In this case, they disappear, melting into the dish to lend it a full, rich flavor that almost nothing else can bring.

Crostini with Anchovies

Makes about 12 crostini

This is barely a recipe, but there are two important points to keep in mind: The recipe requires great anchovies. Also? Wait for the bread to cool before placing the butter on top. You don't want the butter to melt, but to remain somewhere between cold and creamy.

1 baguette-type loaf of bread

1 jar high-quality, olive oil–packed, anchovies

Good-quality unsalted butter

Slice the baguette into ½-inch slices and toast (over a flame if possible).

Let the crostini cool off.

Cut the cold butter into ⅛-inch slices and place on top of cooled bread, using enough to cover.

Lay one anchovy on top of each, letting it flop over the sides.

Spaghetti con Colatura

Serves 4 to 5

- 1 pound (500 grams) spaghetti
- 5 tablespoons colatura
- 3 tablespoons of olive oil
- 1 garlic clove, thinly sliced
- ½ cup chopped fresh flat-leaf parsley
- Toasted, seasoned bread crumbs

For the toasted bread crumbs
- 2 teaspoons olive oil
- 4 slices dry bread, crusts removed
- 1 tablespoon fresh marjoram leaves
- ½ garlic clove, chopped

First make the bread crumbs: Place all of the ingredients, except the olive oil, in a food processor, and pulse until the bread has been chopped into rough crumbs.

To toast: heat a medium, nonstick frying pan and add the oil. Add the bread crumbs and using a wooden spoon, stir and toast until golden. Be careful since the crumbs will go from golden to brown very fast.

Prepare the pasta: Bring a large pot of salted water to boil and add the spaghetti.

Meanwhile, in a large bowl, combine the colatura, olive oil, the garlic, and 3 tablespoons of the chopped parsley. Using a whisk, stir vigorously to combine. Slowly drizzle in 3 tablespoons of cold water, whisking as you do, to emulsify.

When the spaghetti is al dente, use a fork to pick up the cooked, still dripping wet spaghetti from the pot and add to the bowl along with ½ cup of the pasta cooking water. Stir very vigorously to combine.

Add ¼ cup more of the chopped parsley and ¼ cup of the seasoned toasted bread crumbs.

Continue stirring vigorously, adding a bit more of the pasta cooking water. You will know it is done when a thickish sauce forms at the bottom of the bowl. It won't be a lot of sauce, but you will see that the olive oil and pasta water have emulsified. Taste and adjust for seasoning, and add a few more drops of colatura. Sprinkle with toasted bread crumbs before serving.

Potato Salad with Arugula and Anchovies

Serves 4 to 6

For this recipe, I usually use salt-packed anchovies, since they tend to have a firmer texture, and in this recipe, I actually like the bits of anchovy to stay intact. The anchovies stay firm and their fishy saltiness is the perfect pairing with this simple, starchy salad.

- 6 anchovies packed in salt
- ½ cup olive oil
- 1 pound (½ kilo) new potatoes

1 big bunch arugula or watercress, rinsed
 and chopped
Freshly ground black pepper

Prepare the anchovies: Rinse the anchovies in water, place them in a small bowl, and cover with cool water. Let them sit for at least a half hour or more.

Rinse and dry the anchovies and place them on a flat surface, such as a wooden board. With a sharp knife, gently slit open the belly, from tail to head (which isn't there actually). Using your fingers, gently flip the anchovy open. The backbone should stick to one side.

Using your fingers, gently pull up the backbone, starting at one end. Try not to pull up any of the flesh. It's a bit tricky, but you'll get the hang of it.

Chop the fillets into ¼-inch pieces and place in a small bowl along with the olive oil.

Scrub the potatoes, but don't peel them. If they are small, leave them whole, otherwise cut them in half. Place them in a steamer and cook until just done; this should only take 10 to 12 minutes.

When the potatoes are done (you want them cooked, but still firm), drain them well and place in a bowl. Pour over the olive oil and anchovies and toss to coat. While still warm, add the arugula, and toss. The warmth of the potatoes should wilt the greens. Season with freshly ground black pepper. Serve at room temperature.

Note: Of course, you could use anchovies packed in oil, too. I don't usually add any vinegar to this salad, but if you would like

yours with a bit more of a bite, then just whisk a teaspoon of white wine vinegar into the olive oil before marinating the anchovies.

Visit

The best way to experience anchovies at their very best, firsthand, is to go to the source. Although there are anchovy fisheries all over Italy and Spain, there is only one place that produces anchovies as well as colatura, and both have their own festivals.

Fishy Festivals

Notte delle Lampare
www.nottedellelampare.it
➢ The festival has been going on for almost fifty years and takes place every year at the end of July. The precise date is chosen in accordance with the phases of the moon, which affects the schools of fish. Cetara is a tiny fishing village and while there are a few hotels, most people come by boat for the festival. I was on a private boat, but there are special ferries available that leave from Salerno for the festival at 8:00 p.m., giving you the opportunity to observe the fishing up close. Afterward the ferry docks in the small port of Cetara. There you'll find a town festa where you can dine on freshly fried anchovies and other local specialties. There is also a lot of fun, loud, live folk music. During the festival don't even think of trying to drive here. There are only about six parking spaces in the town on normal days!

Festa della Colatura
www.colaturadialici.it
➢ This yearly festival is a newer event, aimed at promoting this little-known, traditional product. The Colatura Festival is a much more staid affair than the Notte della Lampara. Instead of live music there are awards given out as well as competitions among chefs to cook with colatura.

Restaurants

These are the three best restaurants in Cetara. It's hard to recommend one over the other, since they are all good, and all offer—more or less—the same versions of local dishes.

Acquapazza
Corso Garibaldi 38, Cetara
+39.089.261.606

San Pietro
Piazza San. Francesco 2, Cetara
+39.089.261.091

Convento
Piazza San Francesco 16, Cetara
+39.089.261.039

CHAPTER FIFTEEN

Eating Meat in Puglia

For anyone who has followed my trips to Puglia over the years, my seemingly constant talk about fresh fish comes as no surprise. In fact, say Puglia to most Italians and the first word out of their mouths is *pesce*: fish. Puglia, in case you aren't familiar with Italian geography, is the heel of Italy's boot. And because this is Italy, the boot in question sports a stiletto heel, which means that Puglia ends up having a higher coastline to inland ratio than any other region. So fish comes as no big surprise.

What does come as a shocker to many is the region's other, meatier side. Just a few kilometers in from the coast, fishmongers give way to butcher shops and a very specific and meat-oriented cuisine exists. If there is one thing I've learned over the years, it's the incredible difference only a few kilometers can make.

Yet even in the towns by the sea, meat has always been part of the local cuisine, especially in the more prosperous cities like Bari. I've been going regularly to Bari, the capital of Puglia, since I first met my Barese husband, Domenico, thirty years ago. And from the very first visit, I began to learn many of the recipes that would become standards in the Minchilli house back in Rome. Of course, most were Domenico's favorites, and his mother was more than happy to make sure I was able to feed her son, and eventually her granddaughters, properly. But if my meaty education both in Rome and at our home in Umbria involved learning to roast big cuts of meat, like porchetta and lamb, in Bari, in Rosa's kitchen, the recipes I learned tended to involve smaller cuts of meat.

In fact, one of the first recipes I learned was for *involtini*. Minimally seasoned and cooked in a light tomato sauce, I realized that the most important step in this recipe,

and all the recipes I learned, was a visit to the butcher.

When I first started visiting Bari there were several butchers to choose from. And while Rosa's relationship with her husband and sons was the most important in her life, her relationship with the man who sold her meat was also up there in the grand scheme of daily life. But it was a complicated relationship, with a push and pull that resulted in Rosa getting exactly what she thought was the best piece of meat in the store. I learned her technique by her side.

We would walk in, me behind a Sophie- or Emma-filled stroller, pushing aside the beaded curtain meant to keep the flies out of the spotless shop. And already Rosa was

eyeing the cuts of meat on display. And frankly? There usually wasn't much to look at. There seemed to be more sparkling expanse of stainless steel than marbled hunks of flesh. (I was used to the butchers back in Rome whose counters were usually groaning under the weight of so much meat.) "What shall we have today?" asked the butcher, who started to suggest different cuts, pointing them out. Instead, Rosa announced that she wanted to make involtini but that none of the meat on display would do for the thin slices of beef that would eventually get rolled up around a filling and cooked slowly in tomato sauce. At this point she looked the butcher in the eye and he promptly turned around, opened the walk-in fridge behind him, and came out with prized cut both of them knew was hiding in the back.

And then the complicated math would kick in, with Rosa figuring out precisely how much meat per person she needed, and not one gram more. The entire experience taught me a few things about eating meat in Puglia. Meat was considered a luxury, and rarely were big cuts bought and cooked for a family meal since that would result in leftovers, or waste. Dishes involving smaller cuts, like thin slices of beef rolled up and slowly cooked, were more common. And since the meat was so prized, the best cuts? They were kept hidden in the back, only brought out for those who knew the difference and could give them the respect they deserved

Over the years, I visited other butchers with my mother-in-law. Each butcher had his own specialty. The most obvious was the *polleria*, which sold only chickens and other fowl. There was another that was all pig. And then there was the one we never went to, the *Macelleria Equina*. During the first years, it was one of those words in Italian that went in one ear and never quite made it to my brain. (Maybe I was blocking out the fact that it was a horse butcher intentionally.)

I soon learned that this song and dance between home cook and local butcher was something that went on all over Italy. It was also, sadly, something that would soon disappear. When I first moved to Rome there were five butchers in my neighborhood of Monti. Today, there is one. The same fate, sadly, awaited the butcher in Bari: there is currently no butcher in my mother-in-law's centrally located neighborhood.

Fornelli

Yet in the rest of Puglia the situation isn't so dire. There are some butchers, located mostly in the Valle d'Itria, just south of Bari, and farther south in Salento, that have managed to not only survive but also to thrive. They are a type of butcher that is called a *fornello*. Definitely an urban phenomena, these butchers are located in the small towns that dot this area. *Fornello* translates as either "oven," or "grill," and

the butchers provide the service of cooking the meat for customers who have no access to a wood-fired grill. The drill is that the customer comes in, chooses their meat, and then, at a predetermined time, comes back and picks up their meal, ready to go. Eventually many of the fornelli added on rooms with tables. One butcher explained it to me: "Today people live in very small apartments, but maybe they want to invite people to a meal. My room serves as an extension of their home."

Most are not restaurants. There is no menu of pastas or desserts. There is often no menu at all besides the price list for the meat behind the butcher's counter. Always rough and ready, some supply plastic plates and cups and jugs of local wine as well as table service. But you still go to the counter and point to which piece of meat you would like to buy, and it is always by the weight.

There are a lot of theories about how these fornelli came into being. Some say it was a way that workers on farms, who were paid a daily wage, could stop by and buy a few pieces of meat that they could eat right away. Another theory is that they came about as the offshoot of festivals, providing a type of street food into the night.

Some of the most popular ones are (I know you're not going to want to hear this) horse butchers. I could easily have left this out of the book, since it contains some information that is sure to upset some people. But I do think that including the gritty, as well as the pretty, is important to understand a culture not your own. Rose-colored glasses are nice, but not very truthful.

But regardless of the type of meat sold and eaten, the cuts are almost always the same. A fornello is not where you come for a big steak. The specialty of these places are mostly small cuts, wrapped up around stuffings, and seasoned and cooked in the

fornelli. Not surprisingly, since the freshness is assured, carpaccio, or thin slices of raw meat, are also a specialty.

The method of cooking is very specific, and the term *fornello* refers to a wood-fueled oven. In some fornelli the pieces of meat are slipped onto wooden skewers and cooked inside the oven, next to, but not over, hot coals and flames. In this way, the fat from the meat and stuffing and/or wrappings does not drip down into the heat, provide smoke, and then change the taste of the meat itself. But many today are regular grills, with the skewers cooking directly over the coals.

Not all butchers in Puglia are also fornelli. But one thing almost all butchers have in common is the sale of prepared little tasty nuggets with names in dialect that change from town to town. I first came across these in the butcher in Bari when we came home one day with a small package of *gnumereid*.

A Primer of Fornelli Specialties

Gnumereid or *Gnumerieddi*: My personal favorite, these little tidbits are pieces of lamb organs (liver, lung, and kidney) seasoned with salt, pepper, and parsley and wrapped up tightly with intestine.

Bombette: Small involtini made with pork, stuffed with pancetta and cheese, and then grilled. It's the most famous of Pugliese meat-based, street food cuisine.

Zampina: Although this may look like ordinary sausage, it's a special Pugliese mix of veal with pork and sometimes lamb. The meat is seasoned with tomatoes, cheese, and herbs before being encased in natural sausage casing. The sausages are about an inch in diameter and then rolled up in a spiral and held in place with a skewer before being grilled.

Panzerottini: A regular panzerotto is a half-moon–shaped stuffed piece of dough, which is fried. Instead, in fornelli, panzerotti are made of meat. They are stuffed and shaped like a regular panzerotti, a half-moon, and then grilled.

Bombette and *Braciole Panate*: A variant of regular bombette or involtini, which are breaded before being grilled. These are a personal favorite of mine.

Carpaccio: Since you are buying your meat directly from a trusted source, this is often the place to order carpaccio, raw slices of beef or—a true specialty—horse.

Where to Eat Meat in Puglia

A fun thing to do is to go to an actual for-nello. These are almost all open only in the evening for dinner. Although the butchers themselves are open in the mornings, the fires don't get going until the sun starts to set.

Il Cavallino

Corso Cavour 21
Gioia del Colle (BA)
080.348.3740

➤ When Sophie and I began to research our meat-filled excursion into the Valle d'Itria, just south of Bari, this was the for-nello that everyone kept mentioning. Far from the summer crowds in Cisternino (see next page), Il Cavallino is busy year-round feeding locals as well as Baresi who make the 20-minute drive here. As the name would suggest, this is a butcher spe-cializing in horse meat. The butcher ac-tually oversees all the animals they raise, and so the meat is 100 percent local. Horse meat, in case you've never had it, is slightly sweeter than beef, and extremely delicate tasting. While Il Cavallino makes all of the usual delicacies to be grilled over their wood-fired grill and domed oven, one of their specialties is carpaccio.

Bar La Fontana

Via Monte Sabotino
Alberobello (BA)
380.369.6969

➤ Almost all fornelli are open only in the evenings. La Fontana is a delicious excep-tion. Since it is located in the incredibly touristy (but extraordinarily beautiful) town of Alberobello (the town with the cone-shaped buildings), it is also open for lunch. Walk up to the counter and choose your meat. I'm particularly fond of almost anything breaded. And like many fornelli, this is also the place to order cured meats. Don't miss the thinly sliced pancetta, dressed with salt, pepper, and olive oil. And yes, you can eat pancetta "raw" since it's actually not raw, but cured. Really. It's OK.

Cisternino

This whitewashed town, located midway between Bari and Brindisi, is fornelli central. If you are in the area, it's worth going by for a meat-filled evening stroll. The small winding streets of the whitewashed town become, in the summer evenings, an open-air restaurant with the perfume of grilled meat filling the air. Some of the fornelli worth mentioning are listed below, but if the lines are too long or something else smells good, keep strolling. You won't go hungry.

Al Vecchio Fornello
Via Brasiliani 18
Cisternino
080.444.6431

Pietro De Mola
Via Duca d'Aosta 3
Cisternino
080.444.8300

Michele's Bombette

Makes 10 to 12 bombette

One summer, while hanging out on the beach in southern Puglia with some of her friends on a camping trip, Sophie met some boys. While most blond-haired, blue-eyed girls would end up going to a club or bar, Sophie somehow wrangled herself an internship in a butcher's shop in a small town in Salento. While butchers are a dying breed in bigger cities like Florence, Rome, and even Bari, in the small towns of Puglia they were thriving. In fact, they were so busy that they needed help. And so, Sophie became, for two summers, Michele the butcher's apprentice.

One of Sophie's tasks was preparing the bombette, which are the porky version of involtini. They are usually meant to be grilled, and are often served at street fairs where the butcher will actually set up a grill on the street. The bombette are cooked on a skewer, but are then slid off into a paper cone, to be eaten while walking.

Everyone has their own special version of bombette, but the basic recipe is as follows: a thin slice of neck muscle (*collo*) seasoned with spices, filled with cheese and pancetta, and then rolled up tightly and cooked. Each butcher is known not

only for the quality of his meat but also for the special, inventive, fillings. Here is Michele's basic recipe, with some of his filling ideas.

> 3 ounces (100 grams) caciocavallo cheese
> 1 bunch of fresh flat-leaf parsley
> 1 pound (½ kilo) pork neck, cut into very thin slices; you should get 10 to 12 slices
> 6.5 ounces (200 grams) pancetta, very thinly sliced
> Salt
> Freshly ground black pepper

Cut the cheese into small cubes and set aside.

Remove the parsley leaves from the stems and set aside.

Prepare the meat by pounding each steak, using a meat pounder, until the meat is about ⅛ inch thick. Then cut each steak in two, so that you are left with pieces measuring about 5 x 5 inches square.

Assemble the bombette: Place 1 of the slices of pork on a flat surface. Season with salt and pepper. Lay a slice of pancetta on top, and then add a few cubes of cheese, followed by a few leaves of parsley. Roll it up, tucking the sides in so that the cheese can't melt out.

Bombette are almost always grilled, and this is most easily done by placing 3 or 4 bombette on a skewer. Grill over low to medium heat until cooked through and browned on the outside.

Traditionally the bombette are slipped

off the skewer and tipped into a paper cone, so that you can eat them while walking around. If you are preparing these for a party, it's a great idea to serve them this way as an appetizer before you get to the table. (If you are throwing a party anywhere near Cutrofiano, in Salento, Sophie's friend Michele will come by with his own grill.)

While pancetta and caciocavallo are the traditional fillings, Michele, has his own special fillings:

• pancetta, caciocavallo, and mushrooms (see Note)

• radicchio and gorgonzola

• arugula and grated Parmigiano

• mortadella and provolone

Note: The mushrooms and radicchio should be cooked first, in a pan, with oil and garlic.

If you don't have your grill going, you can either cook them in a 400°F (200°C) oven for about 30 minutes, or even in a pan on the stovetop with a bit of olive oil.

Involtini

Serves 4

Although I make involtini all the time now, I wasn't always an involtini master. In fact, I'd never really even heard of them until Domenico's mother made them for me on one of our first trips to Bari. If you're an Italian American, you probably grew up eating these (and probably called them *braciole*). Not me. I'd never really had them in Rome, since they are definitely from the more southern end of the Italian cooking spectrum.

Everyone has his or her own favorite recipe. They often include prosciutto and other types of cheeses. Some people make them big, some small. My mother-in-law's version, which I've never veered from, is pure and simple. The only "stuffing" is a bit of salt, pepper, parsley, olive oil, and grated cheese. While she tends to stick to Parmigiano, I sometimes substitute whatever hunk of pecorino I have at hand. It's easy to forget olive oil, but make sure you don't. It's the essential part of the filling that render the meat roll-ups tender and succulent. (If you go to my Youtube channel, you'll find a video of me making them.)

1 pound (½ kilo) thinly sliced beef
    top round
Salt
Freshly ground black pepper
½ cup grated Parmigiano or pecorino
1 bunch of fresh flat-leaf parsley
3 tablespoons olive oil, plus more as
    needed
4 cups crushed tomatoes
Toothpicks

Have your butcher slice the meat very thinly. Although most of the recipes I see in English call for veal, in Italy more

mature beef is always used. If you'd like to have leftover sauce to dress your pasta, double the amount of tomatoes.

Make each involtino by laying one slice of beef on a flat surface. Season it with salt and pepper, sprinkle some grated cheese (about a tablespoon), a few leaves of parsley, and a drizzle of olive oil. Roll it up and secure with a toothpick. Repeat with the remaining slices of meat and stuffing.

Heat the olive oil in a pan large enough to hold all of the involtini in a single layer. When hot, add the involtini and brown well on all sides. This browning is important since it will flavor the sauce. Season with salt and add the tomatoes, scraping up the browned bits from the bottom of the pan with a spoon.

Bring to a simmer and let cook for about 40 minutes or so. Add a bit of water if it gets too dried out.

The involtini are even better on the following day.

CHAPTER SIXTEEN

The Bari Chronicles

Eating Fish with Nonna

For the last twenty-five years whenever I mention to an Italian that I am going to Bari, nine out of ten times they respond with the rhyme: *"Se Parigi avesse il mare, sarebbe una piccola Bari."* Translation: "If Paris was on the sea, it would be a little Bari." It's just one of those phrases that most Italians know, and repeat, without ever really thinking about it or having any sort of opinion about how ridiculous that is. A small provincial city in the south of Italy being compared to The City of Lights. And frankly, they really don't have any basis to form an opinion because I can guarantee you that most of them are more likely to have visited Paris in their lifetime than Bari.

Bari is a provincial city in a far-flung province. And while Puglia has gained in popularity as a tourist destination over the last twelve years or so, Bari never quite makes the bucket list, which is sad because Bari is pretty fantastic.

Admittedly I am biased. I am, for all intents and purposes, an honorary Barese. And Barese are (as evidenced by that Paris comparison) proud of their city. Although Domenico left Bari at age eighteen, heading off for University and never moving back, his mother still lives in the home he was born in, which both of his grandfather's built. In other words: deep and strong roots, which have transferred, by marriage, to me.

There are many reasons I love going to Bari, not least of which is that Domenico's family home is located right on the Lungomare. The apartment is perched on the top floor of a building and the balconies literally hang out over the port. The sea is ever present. And as his mother often repeats: *"Siamo gente di mare"* ("We are people of the sea").

And that seawater running through their veins has evidently been passed along to my children as well. You know how cute it is when children just start to talk? Mimicking adults without really knowing what they are saying? Well, one of the first sentences my daughters learned, and knew full well what it meant, was *"Accattate le rizze."* Speak Italian, but still don't know what that means? Well, it's Barese dialect, and it's what we hear fishermen yelling every morning outside my mother-in-law's home in Bari. "Accattate le rizze!"

But it turns out my daughters weren't just blindly mimicking. They understood exactly what they fishermen were yelling.

"Buy sea urchins! Buy sea urchins!" While other kids their age were screaming for fish sticks or macaroni and cheese, Sophie and Emma just wanted all the raw sea urchins all the time.

I'm always fascinated by how tied Bari is to the sea, and how it is affected by its moods. Out of Nonna's window we watch the view change according to the season, weather, and even the time of day. Sometimes the sea is a limpid turquoise green and others it is a turbulent gray. The sky, too, can change from one moment to the next, with strong winds pushing through storms in the space of minutes.

But whatever the weather, we try to get out, and enjoy the sea at ground level. Once on the Lungomare (which was also constructed by one of Domenico's grandfathers), if we turn right, we head down for a long walk to the beach that is right in the city called *Pane e Pomodoro* (yes, it is called "Bread and Tomato Beach"). Instead, if we head left, we immediately reach the tiny port that is still the haven for the city's fishermen.

The great thing about this city is that the old fishing port is smack dab in the center of the city. Small wooden boats pull up beneath the massive bulk of the turn-of-the-century Teatro Margherita and the Banca d'Italia. As cars speed by on the Lungomare, fishermen pull out their fish-filled nets and empty them right onto the elegant paving stones of the sidewalk.

The market is there most days, with

fishermen selling things like sea urchins, mussels, and squid. But Sunday's market always seems to have way more actual fish (I think because the regular fish stores are closed that day), so it's the day I love the best.

A covered structure was constructed about twenty years ago, to serve as a formal fish market where the fishermen can sell their catch of the day. Massive, sturdy, intensely ugly concrete counters stand beneath the awnings to allow the fishermen to lay out their fish in style. Of course, the only thing those counters get used for is to maybe act as a place to rest empty beer bottles. (Peroni seem to be an essential element of a typical Barese fisherman's breakfast.)

There is probably a fee for using the counters, and so all the fishermen avoid them like the plague.

The real action takes place just a few feet away, directly on the sidewalk. This is where the fishermen set up rickety stands, propped up by empty crates and buckets, to sell what's just come off the boats.

While most of the catch will be weighed on ancient, handheld scales to be taken home and cooked up for Sunday lunch, there is the street food side to the market, too. Piles of prickly sea urchins, mussels, clams, and whelks are laid out on plastic plates, to be eaten on the half shell.

And let me say right here: No health inspector has ever gotten anywhere near these stands. The plastic plates are reused until they fall apart, hastily rinsed off after each use in the sea. There are no utensils, but the vendor will sell you a crusty piece of bread to use as a scoop if you ask nicely. Still, if you've ever had a freshly opened sea urchin, then you will understand why I don't blink twice about digging in. The mussels and whelks are just too scary, but, like my daughters, I can never have enough sea urchins.

Freshly opened sea urchins are like nothing else. To eat them you hold them delicately in one hand (remember, they are spiny) then, using a small piece of bread, you gently scoop up the bright, coral colored flesh, avoiding the dark bits which are bitter. It takes effort both to open them as well as to eat them, but the explosion of briny, salty, umami on the tongue is completely unique and absolutely addictive.

While nearby Bari Vecchia (see chapter 17 on eating pasta in Bari) is the domain of women, at the port it's all men. Although I go almost every time we are in Bari (for sea urchins if they are in season), I would never think of actually buying anything on my own. It's definitely a guy kind of place. I am tolerated, but barely acknowledged. Men are doing the selling, and men are definitely doing the buying. I have never seen a local Barese woman buying anything. It's the husband's job, evidently, and I'm not going to mess with that.

One of the main guy activities seems to involve octopi. Guys whacking or shaking octopi To actually cook an octopus it must first be tenderized. In Bari it's done three ways. You can either place it in a tub full of sea water and gently swoosh it back and forth. Or you can place them in a handwoven basket and shake it vigorously. The most exciting though are the fishermen who lay them on the concrete dock and whack them with a big wooden mallet. Wisdom has it that it breaks up the muscles and so results in a more tender octopus. Whatever the reason, it's worth heading down to the port if only to watch the octopi action.

Fishing for a Restaurant

Although we do our fair share of cooking at my mother in-law's home, when it comes to fish we love to go out. This is from a purely greedy point of view. Going out to a restaurant in Bari for fish means sitting back and enjoying an endless quantity of small plates that make up the antipasti.

One of our favorite places is Al Pescatore, located at the edge of Bari Vecchia, in the shadow of the Castello Svevo and only a few hundred feet from the waterfront.

Like most of my favorite serious fish restaurants, this one isn't much too look

at. Unless you're looking at your plate, that is. The interiors are bare and simple: white walls, unflattering neon lights, and usually a cold draft coming from somewhere. But if the weather permits, we opt for the terrace that wraps around the restaurant.

Whether you are sitting inside or outside the waiter will come to your table and ask a one-word question: "Antipasti?" The answer, in case you haven't figured it out, is *"Si."* He will then ask *"cotti"* or *"crudi"* (cooked or raw)? Again, just say *"Si."*

A word about *crudi*: If it was up to Sophie, we would have no limits as to the types and quantities of raw seafood that makes its way to the table. And in this she is showing her Barese roots.

While we draw the line at raw mussels (they actually do eat them down here), we do order and eat almost everything else. Bright pink scampi that swim around in a puddle of olive oil and lemon juice. Freshly shucked *noce*, a type of clam that reminds me of the littlenecks I used to get back home. And bright white tagliatelle—thinly cut strips of raw squid, dressed in nothing but the seawater they swam in on.

The cooked portion of the antipasto usually includes two types of shrimp. Huge, beautiful barely cooked *gamberi*, that are nestled in a pile of crisp and crunchy celery, tomatoes, arugula, and red onions. The all-time best version of shrimp salad ever.

The house specialty is *scamponi al ghiaccio*. Think shrimp cocktail on steroids. Mega scampi are cooked ever so briefly in boiling water, then immediately plunged into ice to stop the cooking. They are then brought to the table in a big bowl full of ice, which is mostly for dramatic effect but fun.

Massive bowls of mussels and clams, steamed just enough to pop open, always has us all dueling with chunks of bread to sop up the garlicky broth.

Like any good Barese, Domenico's favorite is the fried portion of our program. Lovely rings and tentacles of squid, of course, but also fluffy, creamy balls of fried crab.

The final dish is always a newer, fancier, version of shrimp salad. Tiny *gamberi* (baby shrimp), lightly floured and pan-fried, then tossed (still warm) with chopped tomatoes and arugula. A drizzle of balsamic seemed out of place at first, but the sweetness went perfectly with the hot, fried shrimp in a very exotic, non-Barese, but really good way.

Pesce con Olive

Serves 6

I was doing it all wrong.

Pesce con olive (fish with olives), was one of those dishes that Domenico mentioned from the very beginning of our relationship. Whenever I would buy fish, he would request I cook it this way. Every time he described it, it always sounded so . . . boring? Since Domenico's request was based on a childhood memory, I turned to the source of all Minchilli family food lore: his mother, Rosa. As far as I recall, she told me to put the fish in the pan and surround it with olives. A drizzle of olive oil, and then pop it in the oven, which I did. With many different kinds of fish. It was never bad. But it was never great. The fish got baked, the olives kind of dried out, and never really added anything as far as I could tell to the final outcome of the fish. What was the big deal?

Now, you have to know a few things about this story. First of all, I got the recipe from Rosa while talking on the phone early on in my marriage. So, maybe my Italian wasn't as good as it is now? Maybe I was missing something essential? Also, I never actually saw Rosa cook this dish herself, so had nothing to base it on.

Somehow, it never occurred to me to A) look up the recipe in a cookbook or online or B) ask someone else for their recipe.

So, there I was, making this kind of boring dish over and over again for years. Until one day I went shopping in Bari at the market for olives to make this dish. As we stood in line for our olives, and mentioned that we were making pesce con olive, I asked "were these the correct olives to use?" At which point, I'm sure you can imagine what ensued. Just about every other woman standing in line started chiming in about what type of olives we should use and how best to go about making this dish. First of all they all agreed that at least a few tomatoes were essential. OK. Also, that the entire fish—along with the olives and tomatoes—should be wrapped up, in *cartoccio* (aluminum foil), before heading to the oven.

Well, duh. Of course; this made perfect sense. Once wrapped up tightly in a little package with the olives and tomatoes, the fish came out of the oven perfectly cooked, moist, and fragrant with the briny olives. It all made sense—finally.

It only took me twenty-five years, but some recipes take more practice—and research—than others, I guess.

2 whole fish, about 2 pounds (1 kilo) each

1 bunch of fresh flat-leaf parsley

8 cherry tomatoes

1 cup briny green olives, unpitted

Olive oil (about ¼ cup)

Salt

Freshly ground black pepper

Make sure the fish vendor cleans the fish for you, by taking out the guts and removing the scales. But leave the head on.

Preheat the oven to 350°F (180°C).

Place one fish on a sheet of parchment paper or aluminum foil. Generously oil the fish, and season the cavity with salt and pepper. Stuff some parsley into the cavity, along with 1 olive or 2. Scatter half the olives around the fish, along with 4 of the cherry tomatoes, quartered.

Wrap up the fish creating a seal so that when it cooks, the steam doesn't escape. Repeat with the other fish.

Bake in preheated oven for about 25 minutes.

Take out and let rest for 10 minutes.

To serve, place on platter, open the packet, and debone the fish. Remove the bones and pour the juices from the parchment paper, along with the olives and tomatoes on top.

Cozze Gratinate

Serves 4 as appetizer

Although eating raw fish is almost a religion in Bari, even I draw the line at eating raw mussels. WAY too dangerous for me. But I do love mussels, as long as they are cooked, and since the fishmongers in Bari can open bivalves at the speed of light, ordering two dozen mussels, opened, is no biggie. But if your fish store won't do this for you, steam them just enough so that they open and you can take off the top shell.

2 dozen mussels, opened

1 cup fresh bread crumbs

3 garlic cloves, chopped

½ cup fresh flat-leaf parsley

¼ cup olive oil, plus more for drizzling

Salt

Freshly ground black pepper

Preheat the oven to 350°F (180°C).

Place the opened mussels on a baking sheet large enough to hold them all.

Put the bread crumbs, garlic, and parsley in the bowl of a food processor and whizz until parsley and garlic are mixed in. Transfer to bowl, add the olive oil, and mix with your hands until the crumbs are moist. Taste and add additional salt and pepper as needed.

Place a good amount of the bread crumb mixture all over the mussels. Drizzle abundantly with olive oil.

Place in oven and cook for 6 minutes, just until cooked. You don't want to overcook them.

Octopus in Its Own Water

Serves 4

I know many people are scared of cooking octopus, but you shouldn't be. Believe me when I say the most difficult thing about making octopus is finding one to buy. Once you've got that part out of the way, you basically just plunk it in a pot and cook it.

I learned how to cook octopus from my mother-in-law, Rosa. When she first explained this recipe, I thought she was leaving something out. It just seemed too simple: "You put the octopus in a pot, with some oil and a clove of garlic and then you cook it." I, of course, being a know-it-all, assumed she had made

a mistake. "You forgot to mention the water." "No, it cooks in its own water." And, in fact, that is the name of this recipe *Polpo all'acqua sua* (Octopus In Its Own Water).

When octopus cooks, it loses almost a third of its weight. In this recipe, the liquid that comes out of the octopus becomes the fishy broth in which it cooks. The trick with octopus is letting it cook long enough. It usually takes at least 45 minutes to become tender, but you can make sure by testing it along the way. The best way to serve it is in a deep bowl, surrounded by a puddle of broth. With, of course, as many slices of crusty bread as you need to sop it all up.

¼ cup olive oil

2 garlic cloves, peeled

2 pounds (1 kilo) octopus (you might need 2 small ones)

1 bunch fresh flat-leaf parsley, chopped

Crusty bread, for serving

I love the fishmonger clean the octopus for you. If you're buying a frozen one, it should already be clean. If you're using a large one, you should divide it, cutting each of the tentacles into separate "legs."

Pour the olive oil into a heavy-bottomed pot. Add the garlic cloves and the octopus. Turn on heat to medium, and cover the pot. Cook until done. This should take at least 45 minutes, but could take up to an hour. To test for doneness, just take one of the pieces out and cut a piece off and taste it. It should be firm, but very easy to chew.

To serve, place 1 tentacle or 2 in a deep soup bowl, top with a ladleful of juices and sprinkle with chopped parsley. Serve with crusty bread to sop up the juices.

Note: Once you've made the octopus this way, it is ready for any other dish that calls for octopus. A favorite antipasto in restaurants is a salad made with cut up octopus and celery, dressed with olive oil and lemon juice.

Eating Fish in Bari

Ristorante Al Pescatore
Piazza Federico II di Svevia 6
Bari
+39.080.523.7039
➤ See above for description.

Antiche Mura
Via Roma 11
Polignano a Mare
+39.080.424.2476
➤ If you are visiting Bari, then chances are you will be getting in a car and heading south to Salento. If you are, or even if you just want to get out of Bari for a day and

head to a beautiful village, then Polignano, about a 25-minute drive, is perfect. Polignano is just about the most picture-perfect town I can imagine. Honey-colored stone buildings alternate with whitewashed walls, all perched precariously on cliffs that jut into the aquamarine sea.

Antiche Mura is not one of the oft-photographed restaurants in Polignano that show terraces carved into niches dug into the cliffs above the sea. Located in the oldest part of town, not only does Antiche Mura not have any views but doesn't even have any windows. But that doesn't matter. The interiors, dug into the ancient stone and with a soaring vaulted stone ceiling, couldn't be more charming if they tried. Fish is the thing here, and like most fish restaurants, go for the antipasto. And please wait to order your next courses until you've finished your antipasto. It's a huge amount of food.

Fish Market
Lungomare Avaldo di Cvollalanza Bari
➤ If you're in Bari, the part of the Lungomare where you buy sea urchins is just to the south of the Teatro Margherita. The fishermen are there every morning, and have sea urchins in all but the hottest months. Is it safe to eat raw seafood here? Who knows?! I wouldn't eat a raw mussel, but I did eat a *tartufo di mare* (some other type of sea barnacle) one morning and I'm still walking.

When in . . . Eating Fish

- **Italians eat fish with the head on.** Get over it. The head is the best way to tell if the fish is fresh or not. So don't scream when the waiter comes by your table, putting the platter holding a raw 3-pound (1.5 kilo) branzino beneath your nose. Look it in the eye. Really, look it in the eye. If the eyes are clear and full (not dried and sunken), that's a sign of freshness. And trust your nose. If the fish doesn't smell good at this point, it's not going to get any better by being cooked.

- **To shell or not to shell.** When ordering *spaghetti alle vongole,* or with mussels, the bivalves will come in the shell. It is fine to use your hands to hold the shell to get the meat out. Again, this is a sign that the fish is fresh. Whether or not you take the meat out of the shells all at once, then eat, or do it as you go along is your choice. Domenico and I still fight about which makes more sense.

- **Cheese.** Just don't do it. When eating almost any pasta with any kind of fish don't add any kind of cheese. Unless of course it's spaghetti con le cozze in Rome and then you can add pecorino. Because any rule needs an exception, right?

CHAPTER SEVENTEEN

The Bari Chronicles

The Pasta-Making Ladies of Bari Vecchia

One of the most frequent questions I receive, when discussing Italian restaurants or recipes, is what I refer to as The Pasta Question. Inevitably, whatever the level of knowledge or experience of the person speaking, they will always ask the same thing: Is the pasta fresh? Or dried? As if that defines not only a restaurant's or dish's worth, but is the end of all conversations about quality.

When talking about pasta in Italy the dry versus fresh question should be the least of your concerns, because within those two types of pasta there is a myriad of differences that have little to do with quality, but instead allow you to explore the cultural and culinary history of a place. (For more on dried pasta, see chapter 13.)

I find that if I want to get a direct insight into where I am in Italy, I go straight to the pasta. The pasta that people make and eat changes not only from region to region, but also from town to town and sometimes from house to house.

Orecchiette in Bari

I learned my fundamental fresh pasta-making lessons over my many years of visiting Bari. Since we were in Bari, the lessons concerned the little ear-shaped pasta *orecchiette*. In the early years spent visiting my mother-in-law, I was under the impression that there was pretty much only one kind of orecchiette, and it was made in one specific way. Thumb-size orecchiette dressed with turnip greens and anchovies. (See my book *Eating Rome* for my attempts to re-create this iconic dish.)

It wasn't until I grew brave enough to question Rosa's authoritarian orecchiette laws and venture beyond her kitchen that I learned that while good, the small store where Rosa bought her freshly made orecchiette was not nearly the only place, nor necessarily the best place to buy pasta (heretical, I know, but I survived to tell the tale).

I am pretty sure my discovery of the pasta-making ladies of Bari Vecchia took so long due to another of my mother-in-law's rules. From the first time I visited Bari, Rosa warned me that the old part of town was not a place where a young woman on her own should venture. It was, or so I was told, dangerous, with men on scooters ready to whip the purse off your shoulder. And actually, I guess the stories were mostly true. But thankfully they are old stories since now those days have long since past, and the old part of town is not only safe but also full of bars and cafés as well as many of the original stores and places to eat. Yes. Gentrification –at least up to a certain point—has happened here, too.

But that is why it took me a good ten years to discover the street of the pasta-making ladies. Even though Bari Vecchia is a warren of small alleys and dead-end streets and passages, I pretty much thought I had seen it all. And even if I wasn't allowed to venture there on my own, under the protection of my male husband (that would be Domenico), we would always make our way to the cathedral of San Nicola di Bari, while

also visiting a handful of shops that sold handmade fishing baskets and terra-cotta cooking pots.

One day as we made our way toward a restaurant on the far side of the old section of town, we took a turn down a street I had never been on: Strada Arco Alto. As the name suggests, we passed beneath a stone archway (which was low rather than alto) and then onto one of the many pristine white flagstone-paved streets.

In Bari Vecchia, I had become used to peering through ground floor doorways to see entire families living their daily life in full view of anyone who passed by. While there are ground floor stores as well, most of these spaces are actually homes where people live. Televisions blare, meals are prepared and eaten, children take naps. You know, life. And since these homes are basically on the street, the streets are spotless. Housewives take pride in keeping the stones in front of their homes as sparkling as the ones inside.

But Strada Arco Alto was a bit different. Yes, there was the obligatory housewife mopping the street. But each little doorway had a makeshift table set up in front of it. When I got closer, I saw that the chairs and stools were actually supporting wooden framed drying racks filled with handmade pasta.

Orecchiette mostly, but also *capunti, cavatelli,* and *strascinati.* Some of the shapes were freshly made and drying, others were already packed up, weighed, and ready to go in plastic bags.

And inside the doorways? Women quietly working away in their kitchens, turning flour and water into mini masterpieces of pasta. Not just for their own families, but for sale to anyone who happened to be walking by.

Over the years I have come to know many of these women, but I usually head back to Signora Nunzia. Like many, I was first attracted to her huge personality. (There's a reason that she shows up again and again on YouTube.) But, of course, it is her skills at working flour into pasta that draws me in.

First a bit of background on this type of pasta. When most people think of fresh pasta (at least most non-Italians), they are referring to freshly made fettuccine. Long, silky ribbons of dough made with flour, water, and eggs. Orecchiette couldn't be more different.

The pasta that these women are making is a type of handmade pasta that is common all over the south of Italy. Although the shapes and names change from region to region, and even town to town, the one thing that distinguishes them is the use of durum wheat flour.

While I have just about given up on ever being able to roll out a sheet of paper-thin pasta that is common in central Italy (see chapter 4 on tortellini), the pasta shapes from this part of the world are somewhat

more forgiving. I say somewhat, because while I've long since mastered the art of making cavatelli, strascinati, and capunti, orecchiette are still a bit of a challenge. What all of these shapes have in common, though, is the way they are dragged across a wooden board.

The dough itself is more about brute force, than skill at stretching it thin. The flour used, and minimum water and no other liquid (like eggs) means that the dough is extremely stiff. Wrangling it for the 10 to 15 minutes required to activate the gluten and make the dough springy and bouncy to the touch means throwing your entire upper body into the action. But once the dough is made, the formation of the shapes is relatively easy. You break off a fist full of dough, and then roll it into a long tube, which you then cut into smaller pieces. Both the diameter of the tube, and the size of the pieces will depend on how big you want your final pasta shape to be.

Then the fun part begins. Depending on what type of pasta you are making, you drag the little pieces of dough across the wooden board, so that they begin to curl up on themselves. It seems hard at first, but is very easy to get the hang of. The most difficult shape, though, are orecchiette, in which a dull knife is used to stretch the dough. Then, using your thumb, a final flip turns the disk inside out, while still leaving a little lip around the entire thing. Or not. According to Signora Nunzia the turning of them inside out or not depends on whether or not you are from Bari or nearby Molfetta. (I told you pasta was a loaded subject.)

One nifty trick I learned while making cavatelli with my friend Fabrizia was a little hand-cranked machine that can spit out perfectly formed cavatelli. Thinking that it was some ancient invention, I found out that Fabrizia had ordered it on Amazon. I, of course, ordered one immediately, and I suggest that you do, too, since it is loads of fun.

Where to Eat Orecchiette in Bari

Terranima
Via Niccolò Putignani 215
Bari
+39.080.521.9725
➤ Terranima is almost like a museum of Barese food. If it's traditional and Barese,

Flour

The flour used in making the hand-shaped pastas of the south of Italy is called, in Italian, *semola di grano duro rimacinata*. This is not to be confused with semolina, which can be a generic term of any type of coarsely milled grain. In Italy it refers to a specific variety of grain, *grano duro,* which is hard durum wheat in English.

Both durum wheat and soft wheat belong to the Graminae family. Soft wheat is what is used to mill all-purpose flour in the U.S. or "0" or "00" flour in Italy. The final consistency is powdery (floury). Doughs made with soft wheat flour are very elastic and tough. It is most often used for cakes, cookies, and pizza as well as bread.

Durum wheat is known as "hard" wheat, since the grain is difficult to grind. The dough is much less elastic and quite tough and difficult to knead. This toughness is actually what makes it perfect for making not only these types of homemade pastas but also bread.

Semola di grano duro rimacinata is durum wheat flour that has been ground twice, to result in a finer, less coarse, although still somewhat granular, flour.

then you can find it here. The restaurant itself, though, is relatively new and the owner's obsessive quest for the local and traditional has made Terranima a temple to the concepts of Slow Food. But a temple where you eat really well. You can certainly look at the menu, but better to just put yourself into the owner's hands. That is how I first had orecchiette made with grano arso flour.

Today, orecchiette are made with durum wheat flour and eaten all the time. But up until before World War II pasta was still considered a luxury, and the typical Pugliese diet was made up mostly of vegetables. Pasta, made with flour, was a luxury. And for the poorest, who couldn't even afford flour, there was always gleaning the stubbles of wheat from fields that had already been harvested. Not only were there just stubbles left, but the stubbles had been burnt, the easier to turn back into the dirt. But in that short period post-burning and pre-plowing, poor farm workers would hurry across the field, gathering the burnt remnants of wheat, which they would then grind into what was basically burnt flour.

Fast-forward a few decades (or centuries), and no one is running out to the burnt fields anymore to augment their near-starvation serf diet. So what's a chef to do? A few flour mills have been producing a newer version of farina grano arso, a type of toasted grano duro (durum wheat) flour that reproduces the nutty, smoky flavor of the original. Without the backbreaking, stubble picking of course. And Terranima is one of the restaurants that always seems to have this dark variety of orecchiette on the menu.

Il Pescatore

Piazza Federico II di Svevia 6
Bari
+39.080.523.7039

➤ When we haven't filled up on the fishy antipasti, we usually order orecchiette or cavatappi topped with some sort of fish. This restaurant is only three blocks away from the street filled with pasta ladies, so you can combine a visit to both.

Nunzia Rino

Arco Alto, Bari (Bari Vecchia)
+39.393.251.8948

➤ By far the most authentic dish of orecchiette in Bari available to a visitor is in the home of one of the most famous orrecchiette-making ladies of Bari: Nunzia. Like many in Bari Vecchia, she has opened a clandestine restaurant where you can eat plastic plates full of freshly made, piping-hot pasta: dressed alla Barese with *cime di rape* and anchovies.

Where to Buy Orecchiette in Bari

Strada Arco Alto

➤ Bari is divided into two parts, the old part, and the new. Head into the alleyways of the old part, Bari Vecchia, to discover a past way of life. Arco Alto isn't the easiest street to find. The dead ends and winding streets may drive you crazy, but keep going until you find the street with all the tables out front.

Bottega del Tortellino

Via Cardassi 81
Bari
+39.080.554.2873

➤ If heading into Bari Vecchia proves too daunting, you can visit my mother-in-law's pasta source. Although it's called Bottega del Tortellino, what everyone is buying are orecchiette. And they offer orecchiette in every possible dimension: from teeny-tiny ones no bigger than your fingernail, to large flappy ones that they refer to as elephant ears. They usually have whole wheat versions as well as those made from grano arso. They are made fresh every day, but you can also buy them already dried out if you are traveling.

Homemade Orecchiette or Cavatappi or Cavatelli

Serves 5

1 pound (½ kilo) semola di grano duro rimacinata
Boiling water

Making the dough for these types of pasta is relatively straightforward. The most important thing, though, is to use the correct flour. I have learned to make this type of pasta from various ladies all over the south of Italy and they all use 100% Farina di Grano Duro Rimacinata. They never mix it with all-purpose flour ("0" or "00"). If you do go looking for recipes for this type of pasta elsewhere, online, many recipes call for a mixture of the two flours. This is, I think, because the resulting dough is easier to knead and work.

The dough made with 100 percent hard durum wheat is difficult to wrangle, but once you've done it, you'll see it's just a matter of brute strength. Be strong!!

On a floured surface make a mound of the flour. Using your hand, make a well in the center of the mound.

Heat 1½ cups of water to just below simmering.

Since the water will be hot, at the start of the mixing you may want to use a scraper or spatula or wooden spoon. Slowly begin pouring the hot water into the well of the flour. Using your hands or scraping tool, start bringing in the flour from the sides mixing as you go. Slowly add more water, and more flour, until all the flour is incorporated. Don't worry if it's still a bit crumbly.

Once it begins to hold together, use your hands to knead the dough. Keep kneading, up to 10 minutes or so, until the dough is uniform and springy to the touch. You won't have used all the water; that's OK. You want to use as little water as possible. Cover the dough in plastic wrap and let sit an hour before forming your shapes.

To make orecchiette: Break off a small handful of dough and roll it into a rope, about ⅓ inch in diameter. The dough should be pretty difficult to roll out. Using a table knife, cut the rope into ½-inch pieces. Now comes the fun part: Holding the knife with both hands, place your forefingers on either end of the blade, holding it almost parallel to the wooden board. With the long side of piece of dough in front of you, gently but firmly place the sharp end of the blade on top of the piece of dough. With even and gentle pressure, press down while at the same time dragging the piece of dough across the wood. The dough should curl up on itself, while also forming a small lip that is thicker along the edges. Now pick up the curled-up piece of pasta, and, using your fingers, gently flip the concave piece of dough inside out, so that inside of the curled-up piece of pasta is now the outside, bulging, part of the pasta. It should have a slight rim, and, in theory, it now looks like a little ear.

Don't worry if it takes you a while to get the hang of it. Be sure to look this process up on YouTube and watch it in slow motion. And definitely look at the videos produced in Puglia, where it is made in this traditional method. The dragging motion not only results in the combination of both thick and thin, it also provides the typical rough surface.

BEWARE: There are also very misleading orecchiette tutorials out there that advise you to take a ball of dough, put it in your palm, and just make a thumb print. This is not orecchiette!!

If you are too wary of attempting this, you can try one of the easier shapes like cavatelli, which dispense with the knife and just use your fingers for a tube-like shape. Or, even easier, buy one of those nifty cavatelli makers as I did! (See page 216)

Orecchiette Grano Arso with Broccoli

Serves 4 to 5

This is my own spin on the traditional *Orecchiette con le Cime di Rape*. When good-quality broccoli rabe or rapini is hard to find, I can always find a beautiful head of regular broccoli (which is known as Sicilian broccoli in Italy). If you can't find orecchiette made with grano arso flour, whole wheat orecchiette will work as well.

> 1 pound (½ kilo) orecchiette grano arso
> 5 cups broccoli florets, chopped into
>   1-inch pieces
> 5 tablespoons olive oil
> 1 teaspoon crushed red pepper flakes
>   (or to taste)
> 6 garlic cloves, finely chopped
> Salt

Bring a large pot of salted water to boil and add the pasta.

While the pasta is cooking, quickly steam the broccoli. It should only take 6 minutes, but do make sure it is cooked through. Better to err on the side of overdone, rather than have crisp broccoli bits in your pasta.

In a pan large enough to hold all the pasta and broccoli, heat the oil over medium heat. Add the red pepper flakes and garlic and stir for about a minute. Add the cooked, drained broccoli, stir, and season with salt to taste. Add a ladleful of the pasta water and stir to combine.

When the pasta is cooked just shy of al dente, drain, reserving a cup of the cooking water.

Add the drained pasta to the pan and stir over medium heat to combine the flavors and finish the cooking. Add a bit of the reserved water if it seems dry.

Serve with or without grated Parmigiano Reggiano or Pecorino Romano.

Orecchiette with Fava and Spring Pesto

Serves 5

Although I tend toward the traditional while in my mother-in-law's kitchen in Bari, sometimes I just have to change things up. During a recent trip, I decided to go beyond the usual orecchiette with broccoli rabe and anchovies, and instead doused the pasta with a heavy coating of "spring." I took bunches of mint, wild fennel, and parsley and whizzed them into the best pesto ever, with almonds instead of pine nuts. To make things even greener and springier, I barely stewed some tender fava beans with spring

garlic, which became part of the "sauce." Finally, a shower of snow white ricotta salata added tang and was just plain pretty.

For the pesto

1 cup fresh mint leaves

½ cup fresh flat-leaf parsley leaves

½ cup fresh wild fennel or dill

Zest of 1 lemon (only the zest, carefully taken off with vegetable peeler without any pith), finely chopped

2 garlic cloves, or 1 spring garlic, roughly chopped

⅓ cup peeled, raw almonds

½ cup fruity extra-virgin olive oil

½ cup grated ricotta salata cheese

Salt

Freshly ground black pepper

For the pasta

3 tablespoons olive oil

2 spring garlic stalks

1 pound (½ kilo) orecchiette

3 cups shelled fresh, fava beans (see Note)

½ teaspoon salt

Ricotta salata cheese

Place the mint, parsley, dill, lemon zest, and garlic in the food processor. Puree until well chopped. Add the almonds and puree until smooth. With the motor running, drizzle in the olive oil. Scrape the mixture out into a small bowl, and mix in the grated cheese by hand. Taste and season with salt and pepper as needed.

In a saucepan, gently heat the olive oil. Add the chopped spring garlic and let cook briefly over gentle heat. Add the shelled fava beans (in Italy, no one takes them out of their skin, just the large pod) and stir. Add the salt and about ½ cup of water, cover, and let cook just until tender. Keep tasting for doneness; they shouldn't take more than 10 minutes.

In the meantime, bring a large pot of salted water to boil. Add the pasta and cook until done. Drain, reserving some of the cooking water.

Place the pasta in a large serving bowl, add the fava beans, and stir gently. Add the pesto and stir gently, using a bit of the cooking water to loosen things up. When the pesto is well distributed, add the grated ricotta salata and lemon zest, stirring some in, but also letting some sit on the top since the white is so pretty against the green.

Note: Try to use small, very fresh fava. If you can't find tender small fava, then it's better to substitute fresh peas.

CHAPTER EIGHTEEN

Savory Sicily

For a region that is known for sun, my first exposure to Sicily was not auspicious. It was Christmas in 1972, and my family had just moved to Rome a few months earlier. Rather than spend the holiday break in the shadow of St. Peters (which would have actually been kind of nice), my father decided to take us on a road trip: to Sicily. My parents packed up the car and my sisters and me, and we headed south. Mostly we were worried how any presents could have fit in the back of the trunk of that tiny Fiat 124.

Autostrada to the port in Naples. Ferry to Palermo. Then a solid week of touring in what turned out to be the rainiest week ever on record for the island. The heavens opened. Torrential downpours. Flooding. In my memory—and those of my sisters—it was a horrible week. The three of us sat in the back of the tiny car, looking through rainswept windows, at a decidedly soggy landscape. And when we did manage to sightsee, it was crumbling Greek temples, dusty museums, and Baroque cathedrals. We still talk about it.

And that was pretty much my memories of Sicily until I was assigned a story about fifteen years ago for *Islands* magazine. As you can imagine with a magazine of that title, it was mostly about islands in the sun. And so my friend Laura and I set out to drive from one end of Sicily to the other. And guess what? It rained every single solitary day. We still joke about driving into Palermo and almost getting stuck in a lake-size puddle.

But don't worry, I finally went back. Many times over. And I finally found the sun. And happily not only did I find sun, I realized that when talking about Sicily the sun—or lack thereof—is one of the most important things there is.

Over the course of the last fifteen years, my trips to Sicily have included everything from treks through the lava-flecked vineyards of Etna to boat rides around the salt ponds in the lagoon of Stagnone. And if I needed an umbrella, it was only to protect myself from the bright, blinding sun that defines this island.

But there was one thing that was on my to-do list that depended on the Sicilian sun god like no other: the making of tomato paste.

Since the first trip I took to Sicily as a journalist I have been visiting the estate of Regaleali. And like many things in Sicily, it is not that easy to get to, but well worth the effort. In fact, even though I've been there at least a dozen times, I inevitably get lost. But not for long. That's also the nature of

Sicily. You usually get where you're going, even if it isn't by the most direct route. And yes, that is also a metaphor for all things Sicilian.

I had mostly been to Regaleali as the guest of the branch of the Tasca family that are wine makers. One of the biggest wine producers in Italy, Tasca D'Almerita's vineyards stretch over 550 hectares of idyllic landscape in the middle of the island. The estate is large, and I was always a guest at the Casa Grande, or big house. Constructed as a typical Sicilian *baglio*, the sturdy square building is built around an inner courtyard where magical dinners would take place.

Yet there was another building on the property that always drew my attention: Case Vecchie. And while Casa Grande, with its prestigious and ancient winemaking traditions was seductive, I was captivated by what was going on down at Case Vecchie.

This is where Anna Tasca Lanza started her cooking school in 1989. It's hard to understand just how radical an idea this was, now that we are living in the age of cooking schools just about everywhere. Back then, there were pretty much no cooking schools for amateurs in English in Italy. Hard to believe but true. Also, women like Anna Tasca Lanza—a lady of a certain social class—were not only not supposed to run a business, but certainly not one that put them in the kitchen. There were maids for that.

But Anna persisted, and in doing so, taught an entire generation of cooks and chefs about the joys of the Sicilian country kitchen. With the support of her parents, her little cooking school was soon the place that people like Julia Child, Alice Waters, and James Beard made a point of visiting.

By the time I heard of it, almost everyone I knew in the food world had been there at one time or the other. Yet somehow, whenever I visited the Regaleali Estate over the years, Anna was not there. And then, sadly, she passed away, and my window of opportunity was closed. Or so I thought.

Luckily her daughter, Fabrizia, has not only taken over her mother's school, but has continued to support the food artisans that provide the ingredients that are the fundamental core of the cooking she espouses.

During one of my early trips to Sicily, I had seen a photograph that had haunted me. It was a black-and-white image of the courtyard of Case Vecchie. The stone-paved area was covered with about ten rickety wooden tables. And on top of these tables, dripping onto the stones, were thick layers of tomato sauce. Eventually, with the power of the ever-present Sicilian sun, this liquid mess would solidify into an intense, deep red, tomato paste.

Even though the photographs dated to only a few decades past, during the 1960s, it seemed like ancient history to me. Of all the many processes I'd seen throughout Italy of preserving and transforming food,

this seemed not only the most simple and rudimentary but also the most glorious.

And then I found out that it was still happening, every single year when the tomato harvest coincided with the blazing hot sun of late summer. And so I made it my personal mission to join Fabrizia for this yearly ritual.

Easier said than done. While I should be used to the vagaries of nature, when you're on a book deadline and want to make sure you see something before your book is due, suddenly the quality of the sun—and the rain or lack thereof—take on an entirely different importance.

And then there is the whole Sicilian approach to scheduling. Let's call it "creative."

When I started talking to Fabrizia about coming to visit during the process she was all for it. But when I tried to nail her down on a date—I had to buy my plane ticket!—she was a bit more vague. "Yes, definitely come down," she said. "When the tomatoes are ripe would be perfect."

And that would be when, exactly?

"It should be the end of August. Or the beginning of September," she said, "that's if we, in fact, end up with any tomatoes."

But I insisted, and, being neurotic me, called almost every day at the end of August. And I finally got the go-ahead: Come quick, the tomatoes are ready!

While, over the years, I've gotten used to the whims of weather affecting grape harvests for making wine, I have to say that the attention to the perfect stage of ripeness when making tomato paste was something new. But then again the whole process of making tomato paste was new to me.

Not so new, however, to any other Italian I mentioned it to. When I said I was going to Sicily to watch tomatoes dry, rather than look a bit perplexed (like my American friends), almost all the Italians I mentioned it to got this dreamy look in their eyes, and then started mumbling something about their grandmothers and summer days spent swatting flies away.

The one thing I gathered from them is that no one did this anymore. While a lot of people do still put up jarred tomatoes or *passata* (puree), the long process of preserving tomato concentrate is almost nonexistent. When making other types of preserved tomato products, the ratio of produce to finished product is pretty much one to one. With concentrate, as I was soon to learn, the effort and time far outweighs the finished product.

When I arrived at Case Vecchie, the most backbreaking part of the work had already been done. A few hundred kilos of tomatoes had already made their way from field to crates, stacked up in the barn. When I went out to see the plants, I realized that I was OK with having missed out on this stage. The tomato "vines," in this case, were more like small bushes, low to the ground and sometimes trailing in the deep, rich earth. This is a variety of tomato

that, according to Fabrizia, doesn't even have a name. It's just the local tomato that has been bred over the centuries to survive with next to no water, and they pack a wallop of intense taste. These are not salad tomatoes, meant to be sliced and eaten in season. Instead they have been bred to produce a fleshy, dense meat inside, with next to no excess water.

The one thing they do have, when picked, is a tough, inner, white core. But the two days of sitting lets them ripen and the core disappears and becomes one with the rest of the orb. This essential step was made clear to me when we finally started to "process" our produce on its way to becoming concentrate. When you are about to start trimming a few hundred kilos of tomatoes, you appreciate the fact that there is no core to remove.

After sitting for two days, the tomatoes are washed and rinsed twice in cool water. They are then cut in half, any imperfections are removed, and tossed into a huge pot that is set to simmer over a gas flame. They are cooked just enough to break them down, at which point the seasonings are added. chunks of onion, garlic, and bay leaf.

Once the mixture has cooked for a few hours more, the pot is tipped out to drain through a cloth. And if you're wondering how such a massive amount of pulp is set to drain, they used an old tablecloth set over a crate that was set over a tub.

Then the whole thing gets put through a food mill, twice, to get rid of the skin and the seeds. What is left is set into large tubs to rest again overnight, inside in the kitchen At this point we were basically waiting for the sun to rise to begin the next step of the process.

The next morning, at 8:00 a.m., as I was on my way to the kitchen to grab breakfast, I passed through the courtyard where Giovanna, the housekeeper and cook, and her crew of ladies were setting up the wooden tables in the courtyard. They were using a hose to wash them down, scraping the surface with a spatula to make sure they were smooth and free of debris. The sun, even this early in the morning, was blazing hot and the tables dried in an instant.

I gulped down my breakfast of bread and fresh ricotta, and was ready to join in with the next step. With help from some of the men from the estate the huge tubs of tomato puree were lugged outside. Grabbing a 4-liter jug, Fabrizia dipped it into one of the vats and began to pour.

There is something very primal about watching the thick, red liquid pour out of the spout and onto the bleached wooden boards. My first reaction was "Oh my god, it's all going to run off the sides and onto the flagstones!" But years of practice means that Fabrizia, Giovanna, and the other women know just how much to pour, and how to do it. Although it looked at first like the entire table was covered, a 2-inch border of exposed wood rimmed the edge.

Now it was my turn to help (I wasn't

allowed to pour). Taking a metal soup spoon, I dragged it through the puree, exposing the wood below. My little rivers lead to the edge of the puree, and to the edge of the tables, allowing the tomato water to separate from the pulp, and run over the edge, off the table, and onto the pavement, which began to turn red with the juices.

And almost immediately the soupy puree began to change before our eyes. As much of the liquid ran off the table, just as much was beginning to evaporate in the heat of the courtyard. A thin crust formed, which we would stir back in with our spoons, while at the same time creating more rivulets.

Even after just 2 hours the change in consistency and taste was amazing. It was the sun that had given the tomatoes their incredible taste to begin with, and it was the same sun that was being harnessed to concentrate the already intense flavor even more.

The next three days were spent tending to the paste. And just in case you are looking for an antidote to the stress of your daily city life, may I suggest the tomato paste cure? Spending the next three days literally watching tomatoes dry was one of the most grounding experiences I've ever had. Each evening we would use a scraper to scoop up every last bit of paste and put it into bowls, because by the end of the first day the quantity had been so reduced that tubs were no longer necessary.

Each day we needed less table space until, by the last day in the sun, that massive amount of tomatoes had been completely reduced to a 2-inch-thick layer atop one single table. On the final evening, as the sun was setting, Giovanna came out of the kitchen, bowl on her hip, scraper in one hand, and began to make her way across the courtyard to put the paste to bed one last time. Before she got there, though, I swiped my finger across the board to take a final taste before I headed home to Rome. To me? It tasted like the sun, like Sicily itself.

Uses for Tomato Paste

A lot of people take tomato paste for granted. That small jar or tube of stuff that is called for in many recipes for Italian food, along with a tablespoon full of sugar. But if it's real *concentrato* (see below), then not only do you not need the sugar to balance the acidity (there shouldn't be any) but the concentrato is so good you can eat it on its own. A jar of good concentrato can add a whammy of umami as well as the brightness of tomatoes to almost any dish.

- My favorite way to use tomato paste is in minestrone. A few tablespoons will flavor the entire pot.

- When using tomato paste, it's always a good idea to dilute it first. Just place a few tablespoons in a small bowl, add warm water, and stir until it breaks up and dissolves.

- If you have really great tomato paste, then you can eat it straight up. In Sicily, they spread it on toast for breakfast, but you could easily make little crostini, smeared with a bit of concentrato and topped with a sprinkling of fresh herbs.

Preserved Vegetables: Dos and Don'ts

This seems as good a time as any to have the tomato talk. Your mother probably didn't sit you down and have this talk with you, did she? Well, she didn't have to. Up until recently where you got your canned or bottled or jarred tomato products from was not such an issue. But like all things food related these days, there are tomatoes and then there are tomatoes.

You are certainly aware that a tomato fresh from the vine (your own or your farmer's) at the height of summer, tastes like no other. But what you may not realize, when it comes to using tomatoes in the winter it is always preferable to use high-quality preserved tomatoes over mediocre and tasteless "fresh" ones. Always. Unless you are living in the southern hemisphere, the winter months are never ever a time to consume fresh tomatoes. They are watery, tasteless, and mealy, and, believe me, no amount of cooking down is going to change that. You can't concentrate what isn't there.

If and when you do grab that handy can or jar of tomatoes, like any product you have to know where it comes from and how it got there. Unfortunately in the last decade or so there has been as much food fraud in the tomato industry as there has in the olive oil business, it just hasn't gotten coverage in the press. Like the regulations governing the process of bottling olive oil, as long as the cans are sealed up in Italy, they can be labeled "Made in Italy." Even if the tomatoes come from China. In a recent investigation in Italy, it was discovered that highly questionable tomato concentrate was being shipped into Italy from China, watered down, colored up, and then packaged as "Made in Italy" tomato puree. Ew, right?

One way to tell if your tomatoes are what they say they are is to buy them from a reputable source. Price should also be an indicator. Real canned tomatoes from Italy don't come cheap, and, in fact, can be ridic-

ulously expensive. But once you taste them, the difference is mind-blowing.

When in Italy...
Cook in Sicily

Sicily is not always the easiest place to navigate on your own if it's your first time. One of the most enjoyable, delicious ways is to join a cookery tour.

Anna Tasca Lanza Cooking School

www.annatascalanza.com

info@annatascalanza.com

➤ Fabrizia continues her mother's school and has expanded the program. The programs last for three to five days and run from April to November. Fabrizia teaches many herself, but many are taught by visiting chefs, authors, or artists. She also has launched a "Cook the Farm" program, an intense three-month program.

Peggy Markel's Culinary Adventures

www.peggymarkel.com

info@peggymarkel.com

➤ Peggy was one of the first people to start bringing Americans to Anna Tasca Lanza's cooking school. Her week-long tour takes place in May and includes not only a five-night stay at Regaleali but also nights in Modica and Catania.

Judy Witts Francini

www.divinacucina.com

divinacucina@gmail.com

➤ Judy (aka Divina Cucina) has been leading culinary tours to Sicily for the last five years. Her food-filled weeks are based at the wine estate of Planeta and the itinerary changes depending on the time of year to include visits to local festivals.

RECIPES

Pesto alla Trapanese

Serves 4 to 5

Whenever I go to Sicily, I come away with recipes that change my way of thinking about ingredients. Pesto alla Trapanese was always one of those things I never really "got" when I read recipes. I fluently speak the concept of traditional pesto, but I never understood how you could add tomatoes to the mix and not have it turn into a mushy mess. I had always imagined a distant sort of raw tomato sauce cousin to the better-known, thick and pungent Genovese pesto.

Like regular pesto, basil plays a starring role, as does garlic. But the main thickening agent here are not pine nuts from the Ligurian coast, but Sicilian almonds (both toasted and untoasted).

Once these are crushed together with a bit of salt, garlic, and just enough olive oil to bind it, the tomatoes are added.

And here is the important part: just a few of the most intense-tasting cherry tomatoes are added. In Sicily this recipe requires local tomatoes that have been grown in the unforgiving harsh heat of Sicily. This results in a thick skin, minimal juice, and intense flavor. Cut in half, they are added to the mix and crushed until they are perfectly amalgamated.

Then, slowly, slowly, just as in regular pesto, the oil is drizzled in and mixed until the result is an extremely thick, pesto-like mixture of uniquely Sicilian flavors.

Like pesto from Genoa, cheese is involved. But instead of incorporating parmesan cheese directly into the mix, in Trapani a sharp pecorino is added in hefty doses atop the already sauced pasta.

Although the changes from traditional pesto seem minimal (almonds and tomatoes), the resulting taste is completely different. The almonds add a unique sweetness and the tomato's acidity makes it sing. The sharp taste of the sheep's milk pecorino balances out everything.

And like regular pesto, it's all about the ingredients. While you can get almonds and garlic year-long, the tomatoes and basil make this an intensely summer dish.

4 garlic cloves
¼ cup unsalted almonds (see Note)
1 bunch fresh basil
¼ teaspoon salt
⅓ cup olive oil
6 cherry tomatoes, halved
Freshly ground black pepper
1 pound (½ kilo) pasta
Freshly grated pecorino cheese
  (about ½ cup)

Put the garlic, almonds, basil, and salt to taste in a mortar and pestle. Add 1 tablespoon of the olive oil and mash until well blended. (You can do this in a food processor, too, just don't overmix.)

When everything is very smooth, add the tomatoes. If you are using a mortar and pestle be careful, since the tomatoes tend to squirt out juice. Mix until the tomatoes have become incorporated.

Slowly start to add the rest of the oil, mixing all the time so that the oil is well amalgamated. Taste and season as needed with additional salt and the pepper.

The pesto can be made ahead of time and actually gets better after a few hours. Just make sure you top it up with olive oil and cover it with plastic wrap so that the basil does not oxidize.

Bring a large pot of salted water to a boil, add pasta, and cook until done. Drain and dress with pesto.

To serve, place in individual bowls and top with grated sharp pecorino cheese.

Note: A lot of recipes call for peeled almonds, but here only almonds with their skin are used; some toasted and some not. I'd say you can use whatever is easiest for you as long as they are fresh and good-quality almonds. Just make sure they are not salted.

Pasta with Tuna

Serves 4 to 5

One of my favorite ways to cook is from the pantry. And having good ingredients—including tomato paste—makes this dish an easy, last-minute dinner.

¼ cup extra-virgin olive oil

1 small onion, thinly sliced

½ teaspoon salt

2 garlic cloves, finely chopped

3 tablespoons tomato concentrate

⅓ cup capers

¼ cup pitted black Italian or
　　Greek olives

2 cups high-quality tuna packed in
　　olive oil, drained

½ cup white wine

½ cup chopped fresh flat-leaf parsley

1 pound (½ kilo) spaghetti

Pour the olive oil into a sauté pan large enough to hold the cooked and drained pasta. Add the onion and salt and cook over medium heat until softened (about 8 minutes). Add the garlic and when it becomes fragrant, after about 1 minute, add the tomato paste and stir until it dissolves. Add the capers and olives, stir to incorporate, and then add the tuna.

Break up the tuna with a wooden spoon, and let it become flavored with the other ingredients. Add the white wine and cook until it evaporates.

In the meantime, bring a large pot of salted water to boil. Add the spaghetti and cook until al dente. Drain, reserving 1 cup of the pasta cooking water. Add the drained pasta to the pan with the sauce, along with the reserved cooking water. Stir, letting the cooking water bubble, reduce, and amalgamate with the other ingredients. Turn off the heat, stir in the parsley, and serve.

CHAPTER NINETEEN

Sweet Sicily

When people ask me for advice about traveling to Sicily, there is no easy answer. You would think that since Sicily is an island, that the advice I could give would be limited. But for me, Sicily is like an entirely separate country, and within that country each corner is different from the next. Do you want some of the most gorgeous coastline in Italy? Or maybe a rugged and isolated volcanic island? Do you want some of the most important and dramatic archaeological sites in the world? There is almost too much choice.

But if your taste runs on the sweet side, then the answer becomes a no-brainer. The southwestern corner of Sicily is like one big sugary extravaganza.

The towns of Noto, Ragusa, Modica, and Scicli are some of the most spectacularly, breathtakingly beautiful architectural confections in Italy. And I do not use the word *confection* lightly. The style and decorations of these Baroque palazzi and churches are like iced wedding cakes gone wild.

This string of towns date their history back to prehistoric times, and later even the Romans left their mark. The area, and particularly Noto, continued to flourish, especially under the Arab occupation, for centuries. Yet the current fairy-tale-like setting is due to a relatively recent disaster. In 1693 a massive earthquake struck this region and leveled entire towns. But rather than spell the final chapter in the history of this region, things just took a new turn. Evidently in the seventeenth century things moved much more quickly than they do in modern day Italy, and within a very short time the towns were completely rebuilt. This flurry of reconstruction attracted some of the most talented architects of the day, resulting in a homogeneous and extravagantly beautiful late-Baroque style that is unique in the world.

Noto

Of all the towns in Sicily, Noto is the most outrageously beautiful. If you're picturing the heavy, sometimes oppressive Baroque decoration of Rome, think again. The streets of Noto are lined with facades that are all froth and lightness. This is partly due to the material itself. Using local stone, the honey-colored palaces and churches are almost blinding in the strong southern sun. And rather than remain true to the ancient orders like Doric and Ionic, much of the architectural details take their cues from nature. Looking up, you can spy peasants' contorted features supporting a balcony or a bare-breasted beauty framing a window.

Like towns of any size throughout Italy, if you are in Noto on a summer evening you will soon be swept up in the *passeggiata*. When the heat of the summer's sun starts to fade, families, couples, and teenagers head out in force to stroll along the main street, Corso Vittorio Emanuele, to see and be seen, to socialize while getting some fresh air, and perhaps to have a pre-dinner snack. Noto, is no different in this respect. Come five o'clock the first pram-pushing mothers come out. By seven, waves of people are walking up and down the main street.

While much of the walking is purely social and pleasantly aimless, in Noto one of the main stops—especially on a warm summer evening—is Caffè Sicilia for a scoop of what is arguably the best gelato and granita in the whole of Italy, and pastries that perfectly embody all that is sweet and good in Sicily.

While there are certainly other pastry and gelato makers throughout Sicily and the rest of Italy, people in the know actually make a pilgrimage to Noto, not only for the architecture but also to sample Corrado Assenza's confections at the Caffè Sicilia. Biting into a piece of cassata or scooping up a cool spoonful of almond granita means

experiencing tastes and sensations that are as rich, complex, and history-filled as the surrounding palazzi.

There is a long tradition of sweet making in Sicily, which traces its origins to monastic orders. Monks and nuns became specialists in creating pastries as well as guarding the secrets of gelato making. To support their religious orders, the clever clergy sold their wares to wealthy patrons and so a tradition was born. Delicacies such as candied citrus peel and *pasta reale*—a paste made from almonds—became standards on which a whole genus of pastries is based.

Caffè Sicilia is firmly rooted in this tradition. Founded over a century ago, Assenza is the fourth generation to take the reins, inheriting the establishment from his mother's side of the family.

At first glance, there is not much to differentiate this caffé from others. The elegant interior was, until the '60s, the haunt of local nobility. By the '70s it was certainly the most elegant place to meet in town. Yet Corrado Assenza's changes were not about appearances, but all about taste. Basing himself firmly upon tradition, Corrado has created a repertoire of granite, gelati, cakes, pastries, honeys, and marmalades that are unique in Italy for their range and quality.

"We are always respectful of tradition," he explains as I take a large bite out of a freshly filled cannolo. The crunchy pastry has been freshly fried this morning, but only stuffed with the rich ricotta filling minutes before finding its way to my plate. The brittle crust gives way to a rich, smooth cheese with only the barest hint of sweetness. "It is all about the ricotta," explains Corrado. "We don't add chunks of candied fruit or chocolates, even though that may be part of the traditional recipe. Instead we focus on getting the best possible basic ingredients—in this case a batch of sheep's milk ricotta produced this morning—and bringing out the taste in that. It's a one-of-a-kind experience, seemingly easy to prepare, but only if you are vigilant in every step of the preparation!"

It is this attention to detail—sourcing, or even growing, the best ingredients possible—that is one of Caffè Sicilia's secrets. The almond granita, a cool and slushy delicacy, is an intense, flavorful burst in the mouth because these are no ordinary almonds. Only Romana almonds—an almost extinct variety known for their particular taste and high oil content—are used. He tries to encourage local farmers to grow the prized Romana almonds, although they can make more money growing more commercial varieties.

While many of the sweets are obviously based on tradition—*cassate, cannoli*, and the eighteenth-century *biancomangiare*—some take a seemingly more modern twist. "There is a big Arab influence in Sicily, especially in cooking" explains Corrado. "And one of the most fundamental elements is the mixing of sweet and salty, something that seems so modern, but really harks back hundreds of years." During my most recent trip there I dug into an icy cup of strawberry-tomato granita. Both flavors came through loud and clear, with the last of the season's strawberries providing a burst of sweetness that was balanced by the aftertaste of the first of the season's cherry tomatoes.

Modica

If I associate Noto with the almond, then Modica for me is all about chocolate. But if Noto is surrounded by groves of almond trees, the source of Modica's chocolate expertise—and ingredients—is much more exotic.

Chocolate first came to Sicily from the New World via the Spaniard conquistadors in the sixteenth century. One of the traditions to survive the earthquake, which leveled the town in 1693, was the tradition of using chocolate in both sweet as well as savory dishes. But it wasn't until the nineteenth century that the Antica Dolceria Bonajuto brought this unique form of chocolate to international fame. While much of the world was turning to chocolate emulsified with sugar and milk fats, adopting the processes known as conching and

tempering (think Cadbury), the Modica style of chocolate making remained closer to the original Aztec *xocolatl*, a cold process of turning bean into bar that resulted in a fruitier, somewhat bitter and decidedly granular bar. Another holdover from Mexico is the addition of spices from the New World, including vanilla and hot red pepper.

Today Bonajuto is the oldest chocolate maker in Italy, and continues this cold process not only producing chunky dark bars but also producing pastries that preserve the tradition of mixing sweet and savory.

Bonajuto is located just off the main Corso and its wood-paneled shop is a virtual museum to the carefully preserved way of making chocolate. They are also filled with actual chocolate, but you might not realize that it's also a pastry shop, unless you watch the locals stop by to either pick up their neatly wrapped packets of preordered pastries or to ask for a cannolo, which comes from the back workshop, freshly filled with creamy ricotta to order.

Even though I've been coming to Modica for intense chocolate fixes for years, I still love watching the sensual and physical process of making the bars of chocolate. Each tin mold is carefully filled with a perfectly measured amount of the grainy chocolate paste, then placed in a thick wooden tray. Once all of the molds are filled, the chocolatier grabs the tray by both hands and begins beating it in a rhythmic manner against the cold, hard marble counter. Five minutes of this cacophony forces the air bubbles up and out of the chocolate to make sure that each bar is smooth and glistening. Once the chocolate has a chance to settle, the paste solidifies, is popped out of its mold, and neatly wrapped by hand in thick sheets of paper emblazoned with the store's turn-of-the-century logo.

During my most recent trip I was happy to discover a pastry I'd never had before: *mpanatigghi*. And don't worry, I can't pronounce it correctly, either. These small dry pastries are actually based upon empanadas and the filling mixes both chocolate (not surprising) with ground meat (extremely surprising). The sweet was devised as a way to preserve meat, especially when traveling for long distances. Although I saw the actual process, and can assure you there is meat in those cookies, the final taste is overwhelmingly chocolate, although maybe a bit richer and fuller than usual.

How to Eat Granita

Seasonal Flavors: If you think you know granita and you've only ever had *granita di caffè*, then you don't know granita at all. In Sicily the granitas are tied to the season, so make sure you take full advantage of asking specifically for seasonal treats like peach, strawberry, and mulberry.

Regional Flavors: Different regions have different traditions. You'll find the best almond granita in Noto, pistachio granita (yes, that's a thing) near Bronte, and for a pure icy bombshell don't miss a chocolate granita in Modica.

Granita for Breakfast: The best way to eat a granita is in a cup with a side order of brioche. This is traditionally eaten for breakfast throughout Sicily where on a hot summer morning you'll see people scooping up fresh slushy goodness onto their eggy brioche before popping it in their mouth. There is something about the contrast of cold and room-temperature, sweet and yeasty, that is uniquely addictive. My favorite is the *Cappuccino*, prepared at Caffè Sicilia in Noto that tops the almond granita with a dollop of coffee granita.

Where to Eat in Southeastern Sicily

Caffé Sicilia
Corso Vittorio Emanuele 125
Noto
+39.0931.835.013
➢ See above for a full description.

Trattoria del Crocifisso da Baglieri
Via Principe Umberto 46
Noto
+39.0931.571.151

➢ Generally regarded as the best restaurant in Noto, after our first night there for dinner, it was difficult to not just return here every evening. The Slow Food philosophy behind chef Marco Baglieri's approach to his menu means that everything is rigorously local and seasonal. Great wine list focusing on wines from Sicily, especially interesting selections from Etna.

I Banchi
Via Orfanotrofio 39
Ragusa
+39.0932.655000
➢ Ciccio Sultano has been the ranking high-end chef in Sicily since he first opened his Michelin-starred restaurant Il Duomo over fifteen years ago. He continues to reign supreme, but has recently branched out to open a bistro where not only can you experience the same level of attention to detail and creativity in a more casual atmosphere, but you can also do a bit of shopping. I Banchi has a full menu but also a counter (the meaning of the word *banchi*) where you can buy bread, and other delicious baked goods as well as a few pantry items.

Radici
Via Grimaldi 41
Modica
+39.0932.941689
➢ Street food in Sicily is an art. Big *arancini* (rice balls), *sfincione* (focaccia), *pane cunzato* (open-faced sandwiches)

are served all over the island. In Modica, Michelin-starred chef Accursio Craparo has also opened a more casual bistro, this one focusing on these types of street food, brought up a notch.

Caffé del Teatro Modica

Corso Umberto I, 109
Modica
+39.333.728.2145
➤ This bar on the main street of Modica prepares some of the best granite in the region. While their fruit flavors are rigorously seasonal and organic (and if Stefano, the owner, can't find the best fruit he won't bother with the granita) one thing you can be sure of finding is the chocolate granita. This dark frosty treat is intense, and Stefano insisted that I try it in its purest form, with no whipped cream but instead topped with chunks of more chocolate.

Antica Dolceria Bonajuto

Corso Umberto I, 159
Modica
+39.0932.941.1225
➤ See above for a full description.

Where to Stay

Airbnb's abound, especially in Noto, Ragusa, and Modica.

Antico Convento

Giardino Ibleo
Viale Margherita 41
97100 Ragusa Ibla
+39.0932.686.750
anticoconventoibla.com
➤ Antico Convento is a converted monastery whose cells have been transformed into hotel rooms. Located within a park at the edge of town, the setting takes in the valley below and feels more rural than urban.

Casa Talla

Via Exaudinos 1/9
97015 Modica
www.casatalia.it
+39.0932.752075
➤ Casa Talia was one of the most magical places I stayed in Sicily. The B&B is actually a series of restored stone houses, set within a rambling garden, at the upper edges of the old city of Modica. Each room has its own terrace or garden and overlooks the ravine of the city below, and faces the dramatic facade of the main church opposite.

Biancomangiare

Serves 6 to 8

For me this old-fashioned dessert sums up a lot of what I think of when I think of Sicily. It's a mixture of influences, just like Sicily, and the technique of thickening milk with some sort of starch most likely came from the Arabs. The most typically Sicilian form of this dessert, especially around Noto and Modica, is with almond milk, and is, of course, one of the first things I order at Caffè Sicilia.

While you can make your own almond milk, I make my pudding with unsweetened almond milk I buy already prepared.

> 4 cups (1 liter) almond milk
>
> 4½ ounces (120 grams) cornstarch
>
> ½ cup granulated sugar
>
> ¼ teaspoon ground cinnamon, plus more for dusting (optional)
>
> ¼ cup chopped pistachios, for garnish
>
> 8 small molds

Pour 1 cup of the almond milk into a small bowl, add the cornstarch and stir to dissolve.

Pour the remaining 3 cups of almond milk into a small saucepan, add the sugar and cinnamon, and stir to dissolve over low heat. Once the sugar has dissolved, pour in the almond milk–cornstarch mixture, pouring it through a sieve. Continue to stir with a wooden spoon, over low heat, until it begins to thicken.

Remove the pudding from the heat and pour into small molds, which you have slightly wet first, dividing it equally among the molds. You can get fancy with the molds, or just use muffin tins. Let the puddings cool to room temperature, then transfer to the refrigerator to set and cool completely.

Unmold the puddings on individual plates; they should release quite easily from the molds. Sprinkle with the chopped pistachios and, if you like, a slight dusting of cinnamon.

Rustic Pear Cake with Chocolate from Modica

Make one 8-inch square cake; serves 8

This is a version of a cake I make based on a recipe from *Essentials of Italian Cooking* by Marcella Hazan. Although I usually make it with apples, when I find myself with some especially good chocolate, I make this version. It's not a Sicilian recipe by any means, but is how I make use of chocolate from Modica at home.

> Butter (about ½ stick), for greasing the pan and dotting the cake
>
> ½ cup bread crumbs
>
> 2 large eggs
>
> ¼ cup whole milk
>
> 1 cup granulated sugar
>
> Pinch of salt
>
> 2 teaspoons ground cinnamon
>
> 1½ cups all-purpose flour
>
> 2 pounds (1 kilo) pears
>
> 1 cup cinnamon chocolate from Modica, broken up roughly into bits

Preheat the oven to 375°F (180°C). Grease an 8-inch square cake pan with butter and sprinkle lightly with bread crumbs, shaking to coat the pan and then pouring out the excess.

Whisk the eggs and milk together in a bowl. Add the sugar, salt, and cinnamon, and beat until fluffy. Add the flour and mix to incorporate.

Peel, core, and thinly slice the pears. Add to the batter, mixing gently but well. It will seem like it is mostly pears, which it is. Gently fold in half the chocolate.

Pour the batter into the prepared pan, leveling it off with the back of a spoon. Dot with bits of butter, pushing them into the batter with your finger (about 3 tablespoons total).

Do the same with the rest of the chocolate bits, distributing them evenly.

Bake the cake for about 45 minutes, or until the top is lightly browned. Remove from the oven and let cool completely before serving.

Cut into squares and serve topped with freshly grated cinnamon chocolate.

CHAPTER TWENTY

Caper Capers in Pantelleria

D o you have a jar of capers in your refrigerator? Are you now thinking, imaging the inside of your fridge? Because I bet you take these little green fruits (yes, they are a fruit) so much for granted that you may have had a jar of capers hanging out at the back of your fridge for YEARS and not even know it.

Me? I've been a caper convert since I was a teen. I can remember distinctly the first time I took capers seriously. We were on vacation in Spain and a friend of my father's (a visiting artist) had come back home from having done some grocery shopping for the house we were renting. Besides necessities like toilet paper, milk, and bread, he also pulled out a little glass jar. According to Bryan, there came a time every day when he just needed the taste jolt that a caper delivered. I'd always thought my father's friends were kind of strange, but this was taking things to a whole new level.

Intrigued, I popped open the jar and began munching, and was hooked. I was already a pickle and olive devotee, but this was completely different. Behind the obvious taste of vinegar in which they were packed, there was an earthy but green taste of salt, the sea, and almost a meatiness that was explosive.

Over the ensuing years, I've certainly eaten my weight in capers. Not only can I tell you that I do, in fact, have a jar or six of them in my refrigerator and cupboard, but I can also wax poetic about the distinctive qualities that define a Spanish caper from a Greek caper. I've eaten caper leaves preserved in salt, brined in vinegar, and fresh off the plant.

Because I was so immersed in caper love, the possibility of visiting Pantelleria was kind of like the holy grail of any caper groupie. If you've heard of Pantelleria already, it probably has less to do with capers and more to do with *People* magazine. This dot of an island located halfway between Sicily and Africa has become (due to its rugged beauty paired with extreme isolation) the playground of the rich and sometimes famous, but certainly publicity shy.

Another reason you've never heard of this island is because, unlike most of Italy's islands, this one has no beach—at all. The island was formed when a huge volcano blew up about 600,000 years ago, sending lava flows into the water where they remain, hard and razor sharp. So what

it does have is dramatic windswept vistas and almost no tourists. Also? Capers.

Pantelleria is "caper" central in Italy. Although capers can work their roots into almost any hostile environment, Pantelleria is the only place that has the IGP (Protected Geographic Denomination) certification in Italy and the capers from this tiny, windswept volcanic island are generally considered to be the best.

Although capers have been grown on Pantelleria for as long as anyone can remember, the 1980s were the real boom years, with exports making their way around the world. Unfortunately in the following decades, cheaper capers from Africa began to flood the market and so many of the local farmers ripped up their caper fields and began growing what they thought would be more profitable: grapes.

But times are changing once again, and with the unique quality of the capers from Pantelleria finally recognized by chefs all over the world, farmers have begun planting fields of the plants again. What makes the capers from Pantelleria so different is (not surprisingly) the soil they grow in. Since Pantelleria is a volcanic island, the chemical and mineral balance of the soil results in higher levels of *glucose caperina* (I didn't make that up). What that really means is a tastier, and slightly sweeter, variety of caper.

And when I said fields of capers, I really meant fields of capers. Although I've seen capers grown all over the place, I am more used to seeing them stretch their long roots in between the cracks of walls. In Rome, for instance, if you look up, you can see them growing almost everywhere: in the gutters of Roman Palazzi, amid stones of the Roman Forum. They also do grow all over the island, in the nooks and crannies of the ancient stone walls that form the cultivated terraces up and down the hills. But fields of capers were a new thing for me.

In Pantelleria they plant them in rows, in fields, in the ground, in the dirt. While this makes them marginally easier to harvest (at least they are within reach), it's still backbreaking work. The plants stretch out their runners along the red earth and begin to bud in May and continue to do so until the end of August and first weeks of September. The capers that are harvested are actually the buds of flowers, so the plants are continuously harvested, every ten days or so, with the little buds nipped off by hand, before a flower has a chance to burst out. As long as the buds are picked, the plant continues to produce. The runners continue to stretch across the ground, reaching up to 2 meters.

Did I mention how backbreaking and slow this process is? There is no way to mechanize it, and since the runners stretch

right along the ground, pickers must bend over at the waist, picking just a few pea-size capers from each tendril. Over and over, while the season lasts, which, since it's the summer, is blazingly hot.

If the bud is left on the plant, it turns into an incredibly beautiful flower, which, if allowed to fruit, turns into the much larger caper berry. These have become very trendy lately, but evidently it's very hard to persuade the local farmers to let their plants produce them. In Pantelleria if your caper plant has flowers, your reputation suffers. In other words, only a bad, lazy farmer would let his caper plant flower in full season, thus halting the production of capers.

Once picked, the raw, bright green capers are immediately placed under salt (sea salt from nearby Trapani). They are turned regularly and mixed for ten days after which more salt is added, and then left for another fifteen days. But the amounts and times can change, depending on the actual

capers. It's the master *salatore*, salter, who makes that decision. During this time the caper loses about 40 percent of its weight.

The salting at this point is not to preserve, but to cure. The process leaches out the liquid, forming a sort of brine, that allows lactic fermentation to take place, making the capers edible and, frankly, delicious. Specifically, it's an enzymatic reaction that takes place when glucocapparin, the mustard oil that gives capers their specific taste, is released.

The capers are constantly monitored during this time, stirred and adjusted for salt so that the fermentation is just right. This is either done by the farmer himself, or else taken to a local *capperificio* (caper salting plant) to be salted, processed, and stored.

Once cured, the capers are sorted into various sizes. At Bonomo & Giglio, one of the larger capperifici on the island, they even have a special machine that automatically sorts the capers into small, medium, and large. Small ones are the most prized, since they retain their firmness. The small ones are the buds that have not yet begun to open, on their way to becoming a flower. They are the ones that get added to dishes at the very last second to provide that caper zing, as well as a bit of crunch. The bigger capers are softer, since they have begun the process of turning into a flower. They are jarred as well, but cost less and often get put into various sauces or pureed into pâtés. The capers are then salted once again, but this time the salt is meant to preserve them, not to cure them.

Salt or Vinegar?

It's most likely that the only caper you have ever eaten has come from a jar full of vinegar. And while you can still taste the briny, unique flavor of the caper, it is overwhelmed by the vinegar, which preserves it. To get the full, floral, and complex taste that is truly capricious, salted capers are the only way to go.

To consume a caper that is preserved in salt does take a bit more time, but is worth the effort. The capers must first be rinsed off in cool water, to remove the visible salt. Then, depending on how you will be using your capers, you may want to desalt them a bit more and soak them in water for up to an hour, then rinse again, which removes much of the salt. Some people even leave them to soak overnight. When I was in Salina, an island off the northern coast of Sicily with their own well-known caper production, locals sometimes even blanched them for 15 seconds in boiling water.

While ideally you should desalt your capers as you use them, on Pantelleria they also use another method. After rinsing and soaking, they pat the capers completely dry. Then they are put in a jar and covered with olive oil. This way they are ready to use when you need them.

Buying and Storing Capers

- If you can find them, use capers that are packed in salt.

- When it comes to capers, the smaller the better.

- Capers, whether salted or in vinegar, do not need to be refrigerated.

- If you can't remember where or when you bought that jar of capers at the back of your fridge or cupboard, it's probably time to invest in some new capers.

- If you see capers the size of big olives, then these are probably caper berries, which are very good as a snack. Much less intense than smaller capers, they pair perfectly with cocktails or even in cocktails like a martini.

Getting to Pantelleria

In season, flights leave from Palermo and ferries leave from Trapani. But be forewarned: One of the charms of Pantelleria is its isolation. This means that if the weather is rocky, both flights and ferries can be delayed—for days.

When to Go

The high season, and high prices for villas and hotels, is August. So there is no reason to go then. Better to head during the low season, in May or September. Although there are several hotels, most people tend to rent villas, called *dammusi*.

Restaurants in Pantelleria change quite a bit, so it's difficult to recommend places. That said, I had wonderful meals when there at the following restaurants:

Le Cale
Contrada Cala Tramontana, Pantelleria
+39.0923.915.451
➤ Location is right on the water, facing a rocky bay.

La Nicchia
Contrada Scauri Basso, Pantelleria
+39.0923.916.342
➤ Located up in the hills, this restaurant is owned by a family that produces excellent capers and other products that are exported using local capers.

Trattoria La Favarotta
Contrada Khamma Fuori SNC, Pantelleria
+39.0923.915.446
➤ This cozy restaurant is located up in the hills.

At some point make sure you indulge in the local pastry: *bacio di Pantelleria*. The crispy fried dough sandwich with a light-as-a feather ricotta cream filling can be found in almost every restaurant on the island.

Wine

Pantelleria is known for its sweet *Passito di Pantelleria,* made from the local zibibbo grapes. There are several wineries where you can visit including:

Donna Fugata Winery
Contrada Khamma, 91017
+39.0923.917205

Basile Winery
Contrada Bukkuram S. Michele, 91017

Insalata Pantesca

Serves 4 to 5

I had this salad almost every single day when I was in Pantelleria. I know I should have probably gotten sick of it, but I didn't. It's basically their version of potato salad. After finding out that almost all of their vegetables are imported from the mainland, I can see why they depend on potatoes so much. At first I thought they must be local, and some people did tell me they were. But as much else on Pantelleria, it's hard to get a straight answer. But wherever the actual potatoes came from, the salad was delicious.

3 tablespoons capers

3 potatoes (waxy if possible)

5 ripe red tomatoes

1 red onion, sliced

10 olives, pitted (although on Pantelleria they just left the pits in)

¼ cup extra-virgin olive oil

1½ teaspoons dried oregano

Salt

Rinse the salt off the capers, and put them to soak for 20 minutes. Drain and blot dry with paper towels.

Rinse the potatoes and boil then in their skins in slightly salted water. Boil until cooked, but don't let them fall apart; a medium potato should take 15 to 20 minutes. Drain and let cool completely. Peel and cut into 1-inch chunks. Scatter the cooled potatoes on a serving platter in one layer.

Rinse the tomatoes, core and slice into wedges, and scatter on top of the potatoes.

Top with the sliced onions, capers, and olives. Season with the oregano and salt, and dress with olive oil. In Pantelleria the salad was never tossed before coming to the table, which made it especially pretty.

Warm Caponata

Serves 4 to 5

During my week in Pantelleria, I think I ate my weight in caponata. It was the dish that showed up at every single meal I ate. While I'd had caponata in Sicily many times over, the version that appears in Pantelleria is different in a few respects. First of all, it is eaten warm (most other Sicilian versions are eaten at room temperature). It is also topped with toasted chopped almonds, which sounds like a small difference, but, in fact, lends not only a crunchy texture to an otherwise kind of mushy dish but also a warm, earthy balance to the vinegary bite. And finally, since we are in Pantelleria, the dish is chock-full of capers.

- 4 medium eggplants
- Salt
- 3 tablespoons capers
- ¼ cup olive oil
- 1 onion, chopped
- 3 celery stalks, cut into ½-inch pieces
- 2 tablespoons green olives, pitted
- 3 tablespoons granulated sugar
- 3 tablespoons crushed tomato sauce
- Olive oil, for frying
- 2 tablespoons red wine vinegar
- 2 tablespoons toasted, chopped almonds

Peel the eggplant and cut it into cubes. Lightly salt and let drain for an hour. Pat dry.

If you are using salted capers, make sure you rinse off all of the salt and soak them for at least 20 minutes before using. Drain and pat dry before using.

Warm the olive oil in a frying pan and add the celery and onion. Cook over low heat, until tender, adding water to avoid browning as needed. Add the capers, olives, sugar, and tomato sauce and simmer for 15 minutes, adding more water as necessary.

In a separate pan, heat about an inch of olive oil. Fry the eggplant cubes in the oil until golden. Using a slotted spoon, transfer to a paper towels to drain for a few minutes,

Add the drained eggplant to the pan with the onions and let simmer 5 to 10 minutes to blend the flavors. Add the vinegar and sugar. After it simmers for a few more minutes, taste and adjust the seasoning.

Serve topped with toasted almonds.

Note: If you want to get fancy, you can use chopped pistachios instead of almonds.

Caper Pesto

Makes enough pesto for
1 pound (½ kilo) of pasta

Pesto comes in an infinite number of varieties in Italy. This extremely intense version is a far cry from the Ligurian basil-based one you are probably used to. Although it can be used to top pasta, I also like to use it to spread on crostini as an antipasto.

¼ cup capers
¼ cup sun-dried tomatoes, packed in olive oil
10 big green olives, pitted
6 anchovies
1 garlic clove, chopped
3 teaspoons dried oregano
1 cup packed fresh flat-leaf parsley
¾ cup extra-virgin olive oil

If you are using salted capers, make sure you rinse off all the salt and let them soak for at least 20 minutes before using. Drain and pat dry.

Place all the ingredients, except the olive oil, in the bowl of a food processor. Pulse, processing the mixture until it is chopped into a uniform consistency. With the motor running, drizzle in the olive oil. Like other versions of pesto, store in a container either covering the surface with olive oil or pressing plastic wrap into it to keep it fresh.

CHAPTER TWENTY-ONE

Home to Rome...
and an Escape to Paradise

When people ask me when is the best time to come to Rome, I always tell them that I love the winter. First of all, it's blissfully empty. Even though there will always be tourists in Rome, during January and February there are few of the larger tour groups that make getting around the center a bit of a challenge. But I also love the weather. Rome is a city made for walking, and the brisk temperatures these months bring, means that you are never flagging like you would under the unforgiving summer sun.

Yet, even though it's cool, and definitely wintery, there are still days when the sun is shining and the sky is so blue it can make you cry. And it is on days like this, when, as much as I love being in Rome, I also start longing for an escape. And often, during the months of May and September, when Romans are already back to work, the beaches are blissfully empty, but still warm enough for a swim.

A lot of people don't realize how close Rome is to the water. It's really only a 40-minute drive away, whether you want lake or sea. Actually, lake escapes should be the topic of my next book, so overlooked are they in central Italy. Here are three of my favorite wet escapes, which, of course, are mostly about the food.

Paradise Beach

I actually cannot take credit for my discovery of just how nice the beach near Rome is in winter. It was my friend Gillian who first introduced me to Paradise Beach. At first, frankly, I thought she had made up the name. As in "We are going to Paradise, want to come?" Gillian has been going to the beach near Rome regularly since she first moved here twelve years ago. So, when she referred to it as paradise I just thought she was being descriptive. Because if she has to choose between city and beach, Gillian will pick beach every time. Actually? She is such a beach bum that I think she would pick beach over just about anything.

But as it turned out Paradise Beach is actually a name of a *stabilimento* in Fregene. There are two words you probably didn't catch in that last sentence. Fregene is a beach community 20 miles due west of Rome. And *stabilimento* is the Italian word for beach club, but it's a particular type of beach club that exists in Italy. They are

usually set up only in the summer, where you can park, rent a beach chair and umbrella for the day, and use their showers and bathrooms. It's all extremely civilized and stylish in a completely Italian kind of way.

Since Italians are creatures of habit, they usually not only have a stabilimento that they have been going to for years, but that their mother and grandmother went to as well. And although Gillian is a relative newcomer to Italy, she fully embraced the whole loyalty-to-your-beach-club thing and has been faithfully going to Paradise Beach for twelve summers. And also twelve winters.

Because Paradise Beach is one of those rare stabilimenti that stays open through the winter, they are not only in the business of renting beach chairs, but are also a restaurant year-long.

The winter routine is simple: Arrive in time for an hour-long walk on the empty beach. Then we make our way to Gillian's regular table, set up outside to enjoy the winter sun, but within a wind barrier so that we don't get chilled. (Italians believe in fresh air, but god forbid you should sit in a direct draft—certain death.)

We pretty much order the same thing each time. In fact, if we are with Gillian (and we are always with Gillian), there isn't even any need to order. The food just magically appears at the table. I'm not 100 percent sure they even have a menu, since I've never seen one. First up is *spaghetti alle vongole*, full of massive amounts of garlicky

vongole verace (tender local clams). Then a mixture of fried calamari and totani, crispy and piping hot. Our main course is always the catch of the day, usually a perfectly grilled *spigola* or *orate*, which makes you remember that when it comes to fish, fresh and simple make all the difference.

By the time we are on our second bottle of chilled white Pecorino, nibbling on whatever rustic cake they've made that day, we are just about ready for one more walk along the deserted beach before heading back to Rome.

A Fishy Outing: Santa Marinella

It's very odd, but eating fish in Rome is not that easy. Or rather, I should say it's easy, but it's very expensive. For some reason all the restaurants that do feature good fish are on the fancy/expensive end of the spectrum. Although some trattorie do have fish, the simpler places will usually just have *baccalà* on Fridays, and maybe *spaghetti alle vongole.*

While a lot of my friends head to the coast, to Ostia, to eat fish, Domenico and I often go a bit farther to Santa Marinella. Santa Marinella is one of the string of little seaside towns that dot the coast just north of Fiumicino, before you get to the large port of Civitavecchia. The town was very chic and popular in the '50s and '60s, with people like Rossellini and Ingrid Bergman buying houses there. These days it's a cute, quiet little town, and easily reached by a local train or a short car ride.

While it's a perfect place to spend a beach day during the summer (midweek is the best way to beat the crowds), in the winter the population shrinks down to just the locals. The nice thing about Santa Marinella is that there is a permanent community during the rest of the year to support several restaurants year-round. I'm not talking about picture-perfect restaurants by the sea, with umbrellas above and the waves at your feet. But the places where the locals go, on the main road, that look like nothing but have some of the freshest best seafood, right off the boat.

There are two restaurants that I love there, and while both feature fish, they couldn't be more different from each other.

L'Acqua Marina

L'Acqua Marina is located right in the center of town, but with a view of the water from the terrace and only a short walk to the main beach. Even in the dead of winter, if there is sun, you can often sit outside on the terrace.

Lunch? Fish of course. The tables are about 100 meters from where the fishing boats come in and everything on the menu is almost still swimming. Or crawling, as the case may be. One of Marina's, the owner, signature dishes is an incredible pasta with a huge local lobster. They have been farming a variety of lobster in this area for a while now. And to emphasize the freshness? Marina brings it to the table, so you can wave *arrivederci* before it makes its way back to the table as *sugo* atop a tangle of linguine.

I often just satisfy myself with endless antipasti. Breaded, stuffed *cozze* (mussels), are big, fat, and just crispy enough on top. A plateful of lightly fried balls of fried whitebait, which is hard to find unless you are almost sitting in the sea. Various types of seafood salad, some with octopus, some with squid, fresh and crunchy with celery, olives, and potatoes. And almost always fried sardines. But my favorite may be the tiny bruschetta topped with teeny stewed octopus.

We usually skip real dessert, and content ourselves with a basket of homemade *ciambelline*, still hot from the oven and crispy. These sugary cookies are perfect for dipping in whatever wine we have left at the bottom of our glasses.

Tavola Azzura 2

Tavola Azzura 2 is my favorite restaurant in Santa Marinella, but I hesitate to recommend it to everyone. First of all, you really do need a car to get to it, since it's about a kilometer outside of town along a very busy road. Secondly, even if you do have a car, it kind of looks like the type of dive you'd not only pass up, but probably not even notice: a rusty sign out front, cars almost driving through the dining room, and architec-

ture that is reminiscent of an illegally built addition to an illegally built strip mall. I first heard of it through my friend Doug, who lives in Santa Marinella year-round, who described it like "eating in someone's garage." Great. But he also assured me that they had the freshest, and most affordable, fish in Santa Marinella.

Once we sat down in what has got to be the most jerry-rigged restaurant I've ever seen, the food started to arrive. Directly from the sea, with the all-important stop in the Sardinian cook's kitchen. Because while this place—a simple *tavola calda*—has rotated through a succession of owners over the years, the current proprietors hail from Sardinia and are now preparing and serving what everyone agrees is the best seafood in town.

First up: antipasti. Small plates alternate between fish and land. And by land, I mean vegetables. It is so extremely rare to find wonderfully cooked, fresh vegetables brought to the table with so much pride and care. Usually relegated to sad *contorno* status, these veggies shine as a main event. Zucchini tossed with mint; lemony bean and red onion salad; and a plateful of paper-thin *finocchio* with big chunks of orange tossed in olive oil. We all agreed that the house-marinated olives—with fennel seeds and red pepper—were the best any of us had ever had.

The small plates continued, but in a fishy manner. Slowly stewed cuttlefish; snails bathed in tomatoes; raw squid "cooked" in

lemon juice and olive oil; tiny, crispy fried anchovies; the best seafood salad, full of crunch celery and carrots, ever; crayfish that held on to the tender morsels of sweet flesh for dear life. And since the owners were from Sardinia, there were also brittle sheets of *pane carasau* drizzled with oil, to make sure we pushed every last bite onto our forks.

While I would usually content myself with this array, since we are usually there with a big group and it's usually Sunday, we forge ahead. One of my favorite pastas speaks Sardo in a big way: *mezzemaniche* tossed with plump mussels and strong pecorino from Sardinia. Another is more local, but just as good: a tangle of spaghetti and every kind of bivalve imaginable and just a few smashed cherry tomatoes for good measure.

One of my favorite dishes that I order, but only if I've foregone the antipasto and pasta courses, is their take on lobster (remember, it's local). Fresh lobster, steamed just enough, piled dramatically atop a salad of potatoes, winter tomatoes, and crunchy celery. But I'm warning you: It's a scary massive plate of food. (When is the last time you heard those adjectives in conjunction with lobster in Italy?)

What Tavola Azzura lacks in ambiance, it makes up for in skill. I know you can go to other restaurants and get similar-looking dishes. But believe me when I say, someone really knows what they are doing in this kitchen. Every single dish was perfectly prepared, using not only the freshest fish (which isn't hard in this part of the world) but combining them with just the right seasonal vegetables (which is harder than you think and takes way more effort and skill).

We usually go in the dead of winter and eat in the wood-paneled architectural folly they call their addition. I guess in the summer you can nab one of the outside tables. No. You won't have a seaside view. And yes. It may feel like you'll be hit by one of the cars speeding by on the Aurelia. Or eat in the main dining room, which makes no claims to be anything other than the fluorescent-lit tavola calda it is.

But when you realize that you are paying about 25 euros per person for a more-than-you-can-eat fresh seafood lunch, wine included, I don't think you're going to care that much about the setting. And if you do want a walk along the sea, it's just across the street. Watch out for the speeding cars.

Lago di Bracciano

Lago di Bracciano is so close to Rome that many people actually live there and commute into town. Yet still, spending the day there always feels like a mini holiday. When we don't have the time to get away for a full weekend, a day spent here is so relaxing, gorgeous, and delicious that it feels like a full-fledged vacation.

Lago di Bracciano, is only about a

50-minute drive north. It's a volcanic lake, and the waters are deep, clear, and surrounded by dark, pebbly stones. My friend Jane went there for years. And Domenico even lived in the main town of Bracciano for a while.

It is my friend Jane, who got the whole day-trip-to-the-lake-thing down to a science. A quick drive up the Cassia Bis, we head straight to Trevignano, the smallest of the towns on the lake. There are several stabilimenti along the shore, but we just head to "Jane's' place," Casina Bianca. We park in the back "parking lot" (really just a field with trees), walk past the restaurant's jungle-like vegetable garden, through the restaurant, across the street to the narrow beach.

Since the first time I went, I always follow Jane's advice: "Swim now, before lunch, because after lunch the waves really pick up." Waves? For real? On this lake? The waters in the morning are so becalmed that you can see yourself in their reflection. But, since I usually blindly follow Jane's advice, I spend most of the 2 hours before lunch swimming all the way out to the buoys and back in the surprisingly warm water, alternating with getting in as much sun as I could on the near empty beach.

I remember the first time we went. Jane had reserved a primo table for us at lunch, right at the edge of the vine-covered pergola, with a view out toward the far shore. As we sat down, sure enough, the wind started to pick up. "I told you so," said Jane.

Actually, she didn't say it. But she gave me that look. And indeed, gazing out at the view I could see the now choppy waters lapping at our beach chairs.

Lunch is always simple, delicious, and shockingly affordable. When is the last time you've seen primi that cost 6 euros? They even offered half portions for 4 euros. Nothing fancy, mind you. But we were all soon happily tucking into big plates full of *spaghetti al pomodoro, fettuccine con funghi porcini,* and *pasta e fagioli.* The main dishes were mostly variations of simple lake fish: *coregone, persico,* and *luccio.* Fried or *alla piastra.* Simple, straightforward, and—at 9 euro—the most extravagant items on the menu. The side dishes, including roasted peppers—which came straight from the garden out back—were my favorite.

The rest of the afternoon was spent soaking up the last rays of summery sun, cooled by the lake breezes, doing absolutely nothing. Mini vacation 101.

Getting there

Paradise Beach
Via Monti dell'Ara 425 Maccarese
+39.06.6671451
➤ Sorry, but the only way to get here is by car. It's a short ride from Rome (about 40 minutes) and renting a car for the day can be surprisingly affordable. To arrive here it's best to plug in the exact address into your GPS. And also best to call ahead, to

reserve at the restaurant, and—if it's the weekend in summer—sun beds and a parking space.

Santa Marinella

➤ Trains leave about every hour, from the Termini train station in Rome, as well as the smaller (and much more pleasant) stations of San Pietro, Trastevere, and Ostiense. The Santa Marinella train station is a 10 minute walk to L'Acqua Marina and a 5-minute walk to the beach. If you have your heart set on Tavola Azzurra it's a half-hour walk along rather busy road. Better to arrive by car.

Tavola Azzurra 2
Via Aurelia 111/B
Santa Marinella
+39.0766.510.632
+39.389.973.9256
Open daily. Closed Monday during winter.

L'Acqua Marina
Piazza Trieste 8
Santa Marinella
In winter closed Monday evenings and Tuesday.
+39.0766.511715

Lago di Bracciano

➤ Lago di Bracciano is located about 50 kilometers north of Rome and trains leave from both the Tiburtina and Ostiense stations. Unfortunately they only go as far as Anguillara, the southernmost town on the lake. There are a few beaches within walking distance. La Casina Bianca is on the opposite side of the lake, a further 20-minute drive.

La Casina Bianca
Via della Rena 78
Trevignano Romano
+39.06.999.7231
To drive from Rome head up the Cassia Bis and get out in Trevignano Romano. Head in to town and take the road along the lake. La Casina Bianca is about 5 minutes out of town. The parking lot is reached by the little road right after the restaurant, on the right, and reserved for guests of the restaurant. Umbrellas and beds are 4 euros each for the day. Parking is free for guests of the beach club and restaurant. Call ahead to reserve both a table as well as beach chairs.

RECIPES

Spaghetti alle Vongole

I always try to use *vongole verace* (true clams), which are available in Rome. They are more expensive, but more flavorful and usually free of sand since they are self-cleaning. If you use regular clams, you should probably soak them first, to make sure they open and get rid of any sand inside. And even though I've titled this recipe "spaghetti" alle vongole, we actually use linguine, which I tend to prefer. But any long pasta will do. Just not short (like penne or rigatoni) please. Why? Just not done.

¼ cup extra-virgin olive oil

3 garlic cloves

½ cup chopped fresh flat-leaf parsley

3 pounds (1½ kilos) small clams (vongole verace, if you can find them)

¼ teaspoon crushed red pepper flakes (optional)

1 pound (½ kilo) good-quality spaghetti or linguine

1 cup white wine

Finely grated zest of 1 lemon (optional) (see Note)

Bring a large pot of water to boil.

While the water is heating up, pour the olive oil into a wide pan, large enough to hold all the clams and cooked pasta. Place over medium heat and add the garlic. When garlic becomes fragrant (about 2 minutes), add half of the parsley, all of the clams, and the red pepper flakes, if using. Put a lid on pan and let the clams steam open (this should only take about 5 minutes).

In the meantime, add the pasta to the boiling water, which you've lightly salted (not as much as usual, since the clams are salty).

Once the clams have opened, take off the lid and add the wine. Let the wine bubble away. Then turn off the heat while the pasta finishes cooking; there should be quite a bit of liquid left in the pan, from the wine and the clam juices.

When the pasta is still VERY al dente, about 4 minutes away from being done, drain it.

Turn on the heat under the clam sauce and add the drained pasta and the remaining parsley. Stir gently, or shake the pan, coating the pasta with the sauce, then let the pasta finish cooking in the pan juices. Serve immediately.

Note: When you add the parsley at the end, you can, if you wish, also add lemon zest, which is not traditional, but very nice.

Insalata di Mare

Seafood salad is a standard at almost any seafood restaurant in Italy. There are as many recipes as there are restaurants. This is one I make at home, and is as simple as you can get. Rather than get fussy preparing various types of seafood (shrimp, clams, squid, etc.), I just stick with easy-to-cook octopus. And, taking my cue from Tavola Azzura 2, I use tons of fresh vegetables—in this case celery— and not much else.

1 pound (½ kilo) octopus, cooked
   as for Octopus in Its Own Water
   page 207
6 to 7 tender celery heart stalks,
   leaves still attached
¼ cup, plus 2 to 3 tablespoons extra-
   virgin olive oil
10 fresh basil leaves
3 tablespoons freshly squeezed lemon
   juice
10 black olives
Grated zest of 1 untreated lemon
Salt
Freshly ground black pepper

Cut the room-temperature octopus into bite-size pieces.

Thinly slice the celery on the diagonal. Tear the celery leaves into bite-size pieces.

Place the octopus, celery, and leaves in a bowl.

Add the olive oil, basil leaves, lemon juice, olives, and zest. Toss and season with salt and freshly ground pepper to taste.

Let sit for an hour, at room temperature, so that the flavors can marry.

CHAPTER TWENTY-TWO

The Next Trip

When I first thought of this book, one of my greatest worries was how on earth could I fit everything I had learned over the last couple of decades into one slim volume. There was just so much that I wanted to share. And, of course, I couldn't fit it all in one book. Instead, I managed to choose those stories that I felt would best give you a good taste of what the roads less traveled look, smell, and taste like.

But a funny thing happened along this road. The more I wrote—and the more I edited down my tales—the more I realized that my stories really had no ending.

The one thing that came home to me, as I came back home myself and was sitting at my desk, was that there is so much more to discover. For every piece of cheese, slice of prosciutto, or glass of prosecco, I realized that there were hundreds more like it left to discover. Just when I thought I'd hit the end of one road, I would find, literally and figuratively, that there were at least another hundred smaller paths to follow.

So there really is no conclusion to this book, just as there is no conclusion to my travels through Italy. I will keep on following my appetite wherever it takes me. My greatest hope is that you'll follow my example, discovering your own hidden gems whether on a boat off the coast of Sardinia, amid a vineyard in the hills of Friuli, or on a deserted alleyway in Torino. Who knows? Maybe we'll run into each other.

Resources

Over the past few decades living in Italy, I have learned the importance of ingredients. When discussing food with any Italian words like pasta, olive oil, flour, or capers are always loaded topics. Throughout my career in writing about food I've always emphasized the importance of using specific ingredients, not only from specific places but made by specific producers. That said, I realize that not everyone can tag along with me to my local market. But I am happy to say that over the last twenty years it's become much easier to source some of the best Italian ingredients outside of Italy.

Here follow a list of some of the places in the United States that carry many of the products that I know, use, and cook with.

Zingerman's
www.zingermans.com

Gustiamo
www.gustiamo.com

Manicaretti (wholesale only)
www.manicaretti.com

Market Hall Foods
www.markethallfoods.com
➢ They carry many of the products imported by Manicaretti.

Formaggio Kitchen
www.formaggiokitchen.com

Eataly
www.eataly.com

iGourmet
www.igourmet.com

Going to the Source

One of the great joys of living in Italy is the opportunity to share my discoveries. I obviously do this through my books, but I also share places to eat and shop all over Italy in my app, *Eat Italy* (available for both iTunes and Android).

But my favorite way to share my discoveries is in person. Along with my daughter Sophie we lead culinary tours. Our tours explore the markets in Rome, as well as day trips to nearby places like Umbria and Naples. And our Week in Italy tours let us take you on an in-depth, 6-day, fun- and food-filled exploration of Rome, Umbria, Puglia, and an ever growing list of other regions and cities.

For more information
elizabeth@elizabethminchilli.com
www.elizabethminchilli.com

Index